artistic photography

artistic photography
Methods and Techniques

Harald Krauth

AMPHOTO
American Photographic Book Publishing Co., Inc.
Garden City, New York 11530

Library of Congress Catalog Card No.: 75-42771

ISBN: 0-8174-2402-4

Manufactured in the United States of America.

CONTENTS

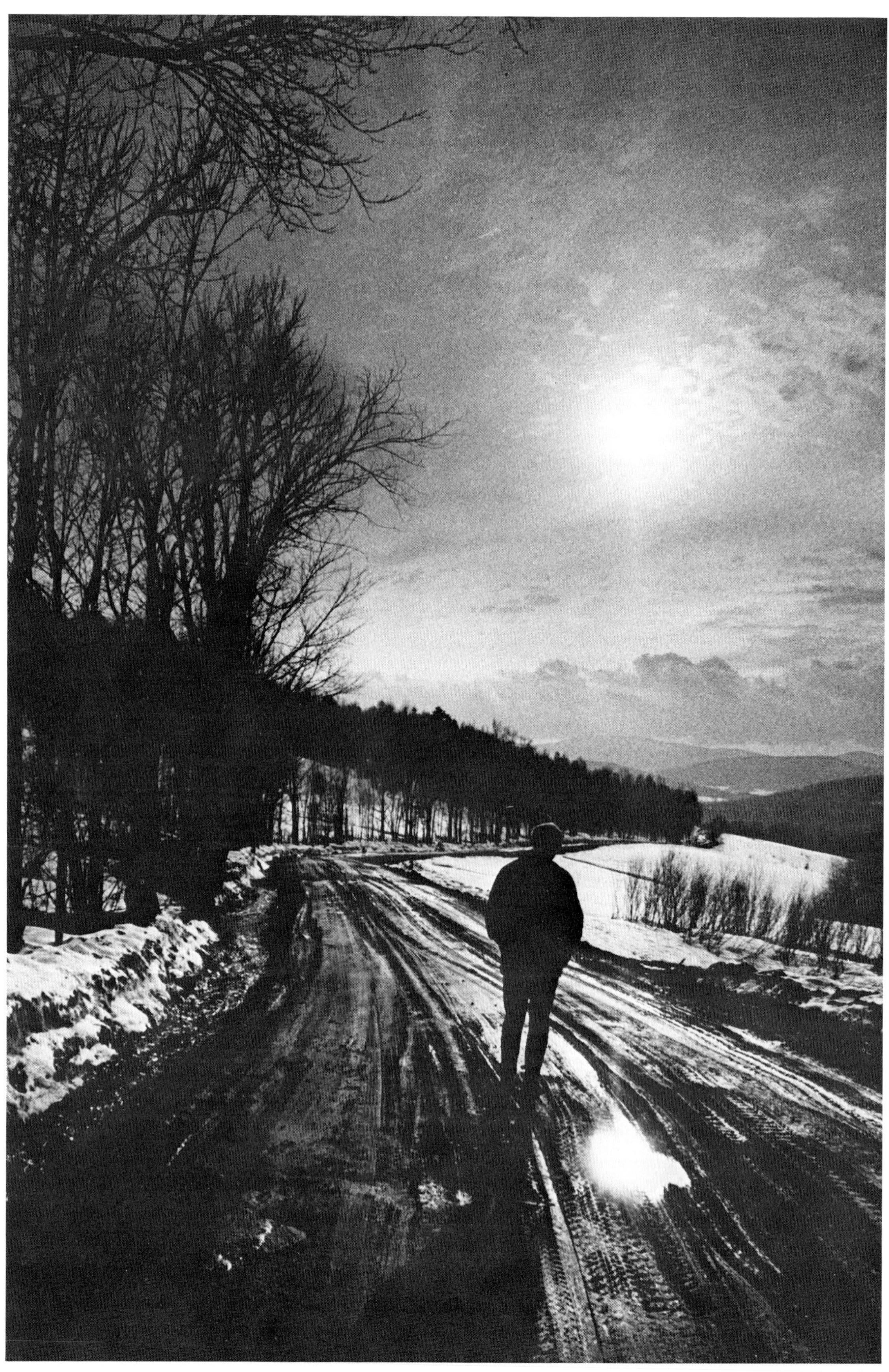

INTRODUCTION

A great number of books on photography have already been written. Why, then, should there be another? In my own experience in teaching a photographic college course for several years, I have observed that most textbooks are more or less either simple "how-to-do" books or works of such technical nature as to be unsuited for a student interested in exploring photography as a means of artistic expression. And so a book that makes the technical as well as the artistic part of teaching photography easier seemed to me to be appropriate.

Just as a painter needs a solid knowledge of grounds, pigments, and mediums for his art, so to the student of photography should be given a solid technical foundation in his craft. The photographer must achieve mastery of the technical side of photography to the point where it does not interfere with his creative processes. The training of a fine-arts painter or sculptor is a very complex undertaking, involving the study and mastery of visual forces such as balance, shape, form, space, light, and color. Such visual training should also be essential in the making of a good photographer, because learning to **see** is the most necessary phase of training for the future photographer who wants to make more than records of objects. For this reason, the content of this book concentrates on the **visual** part of artistic photography.

It is not very satisfying for a teacher to turn out a student who can make a living only as a phototechnician but who is never taught to think of photography as an art. But incredible as it sounds, in photography, a background in visual education is rarely provided.

Art cannot be taught. But training and exposure to art can certainly help to cultivate visual perception and visual awareness, thus preparing the student to find his own creative potential.

Painters, photographers, and designers are all concerned with visual communication. Those most likely to survive are the sophisticated ones with a good knowledge of painting, photography, sculpture, and architecture.

Right: The rigging of a square rigger constructs a picture triangle. Nikon FTN, 35mm Nikkor, 1/250 sec. at *f*/11 on Tri-X.

Below: Packing a hot-air balloon after a winter flight. Nikon F2, 20mm Nikkor, 1/60 sec. at *f*/8 on Kodak Tri-X.

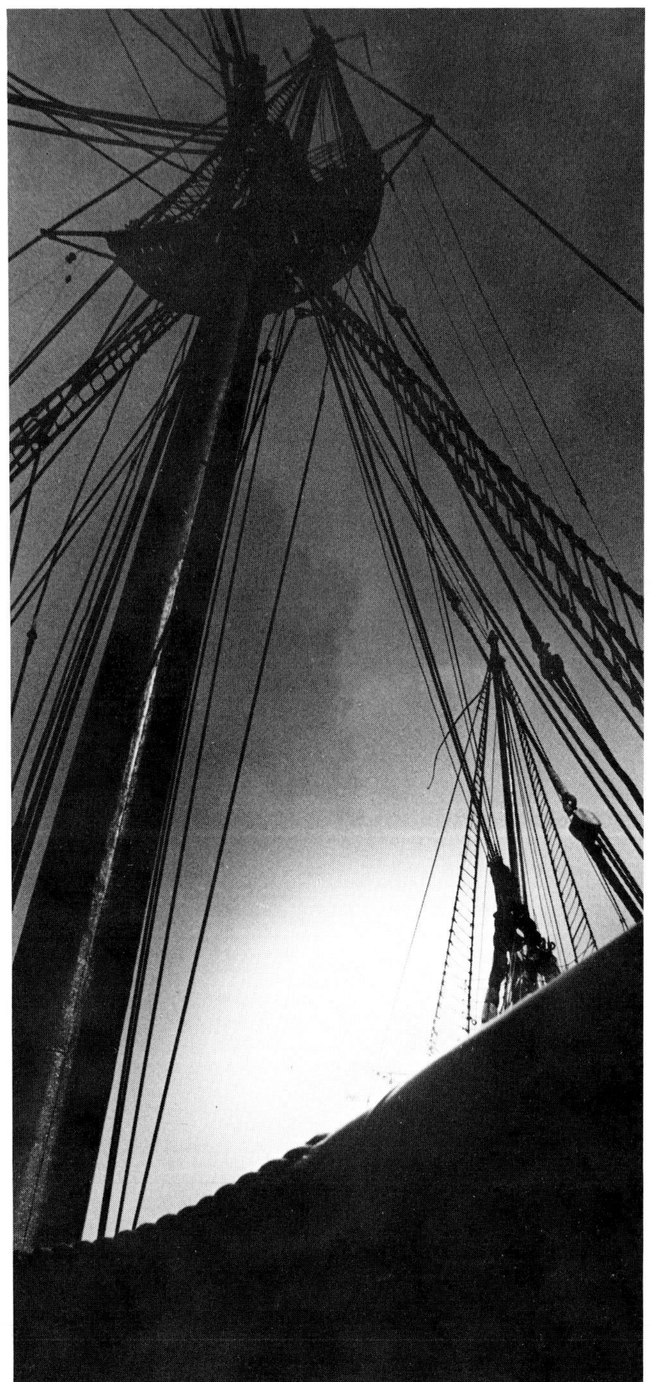

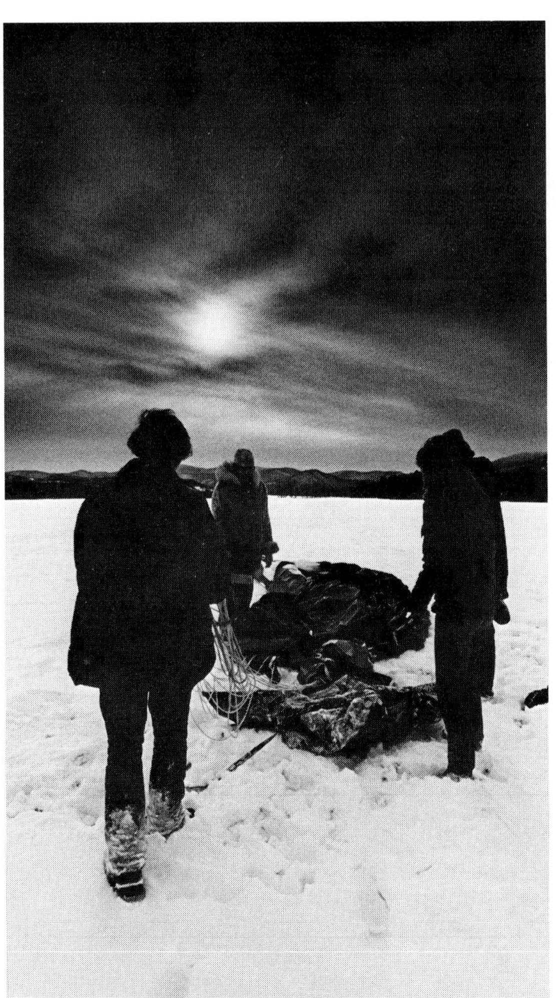

1

BALANCE

Visual perception seems to have a need for balance and symmetry. For example, if we find a picture not hanging straight, we have a compulsion to straighten it. This occurs also when we make a photographic print: We arrange the visual elements on the work surface so that they will balance.

There are many visual elements that must be structured in order to communicate: shape, form, balance, space, light, and color. There are no set formulas that could be applied mechanically in the structuring of these elements, but the artist's sensitivity dictates the final decision. Two painters in the same landscape setting will produce different pictures, each reflecting the artist's personality. This personal "handwriting" of a visually structured and organized painting makes the style of a work of art. But regardless of the medium of expression—abstract or representational—balance is part of a good composition.

Assume you had to photograph a ship's rigging to show it silhouetted against a white sky. Your main concern would be the balance of compositional forces within the boundaries of a given two-dimensional space. By showing such a common subject in a new way—an angle strange to the accepted way of seeing it—it may become a new visual experience with artistic value. This necessitates constant search to find new ways of seeing that result in original forms of expression.

For a photograph to be a really good picture, it must have universal interest; only then will it communicate ideas and evoke feelings. It is well known that a well-painted bunch of asparagus can be a greater work of art than a poorly painted madonna.

The following method can be employed to discuss balance and point out the hidden structural forces in any visual field.

Take a white board, almost the size of an 8″ × 10″ sheet of photographic paper, surrounded by a black border. Cut various circles and squares from black cardboard. Using any number of these pieces, arrange them in such a way that the finished product appears to be a balanced arrangement.

It will become apparent that a single piece placed in the center will convey a position of rest (Figure 1A) and, moved along the diagonals of the given space, will be experienced as well balanced. This also holds

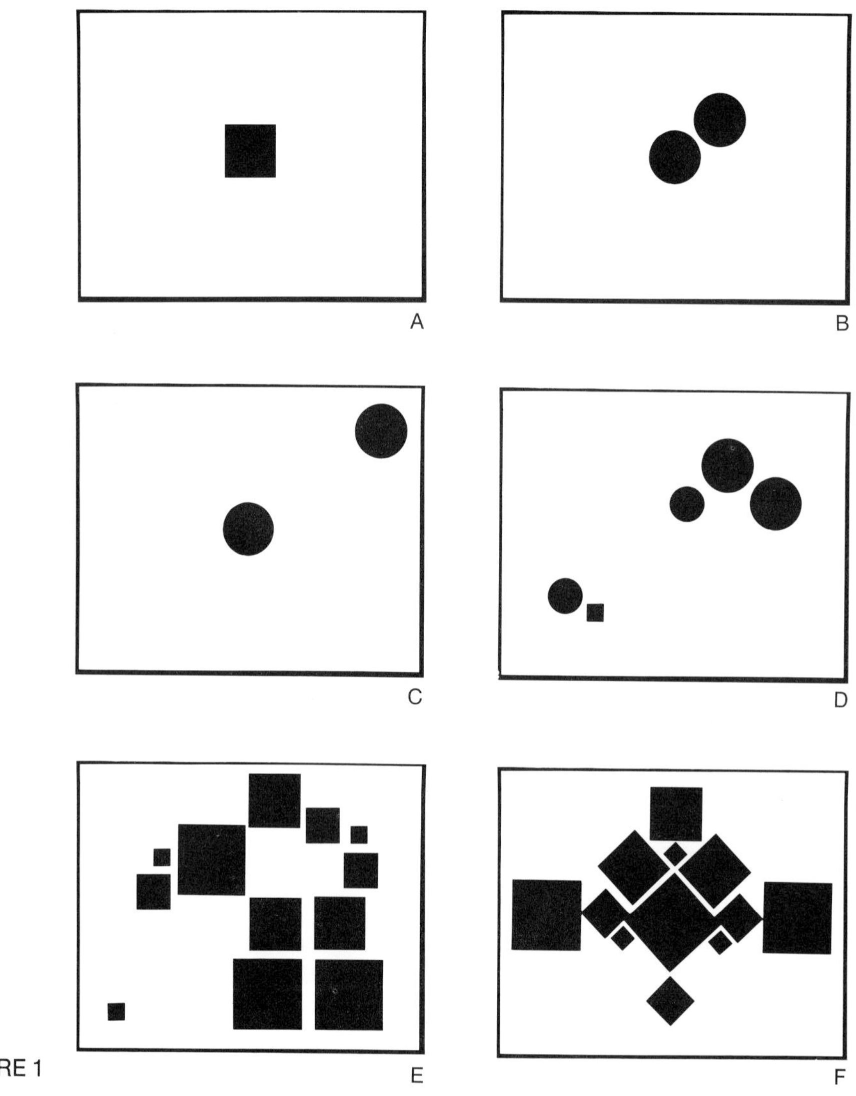

FIGURE 1

true for movements along the central, horizontal, and vertical lines. Balance problems increase with the number of pieces trying to occupy a space.

One interesting phenomenon should be pointed out. The simple addition of one more piece to a centrally placed one illustrates the principles of attraction and repulsion. If you place this new piece on one of the previously described axes, you will perceive it as being attracted to the central one (Figure 1B). If you move this piece farther out, there will be balance, but placed still farther, you suddenly get the feeling that the two pieces seem to repel each other (Figure 1C).

Very complex patterns can be created in this way. Usually, more weight is carried on the left side of a composition. The reason is probably the fact that people generally read from left to right and that they therefore "read" pictures in the same way. A pleasing balancing effect can also be achieved by arranging two seemingly different patterns on opposite sides and having them balance each other in such a way that the total area on the right has more weight (Figure 1D). In this case, the pattern on the right has been moved to the upper boundaries of the visual space.

Applying all that has been said about balance may cause you to wonder at some old master prints. Would not some of them look better if they were reversed? The fact is, engravings were done on plates the artist could view during the process; and although knowledgeable about balance, he generally forgot that in printing his composition, it would appear reversed.

Look at Figures 1A through 1F again. Figure 1A shows a square occupying a central position in a visual field, thereby looking solidly at rest. In Figure 1B, two disks are introduced into the field; they are close together, actually attracting each other. In Figure 1C, the second disk has been placed beyond the critical distance. The disk is perceived as flying away, and attraction is converted into repulsion. In Figure 1D, disks of various sizes and a small square are balanced. With great economy, a pleasing balance is achieved. An eighteen-year-old girl tried Figure 1E, using a greater number of squares. Figure 1F, done by a twelve-year-old boy, is balanced in an absolute geometric way.

THE GOLDEN SECTION

No discussion about balance and composition is complete without the "Golden Section," or the "Golden Cut." Throughout the ages, artists in the various disciplines have searched for a key, a mathematical formula, to unlock the mysteries of composition. The golden section, or the proportion ϕ (pronounced phi), served often to compose the great masterpieces of the Renaissance.

This proportion was already known to the pharaonic Egyptians, who incorporated it in constructing their pyramids. The relation there is found in the triangle of height, half base, and apothem. In our times, these proportions are still used and valid. The great French architect Le Corbusier (1887–1965) developed an architectural system based on the golden section and on the ϕ relation in the human body. He called this system "modular," and he was able to relate architectural scale in proportions not only to human inhabitants, but also to interior furnishings. The

GOLDEN SECTION

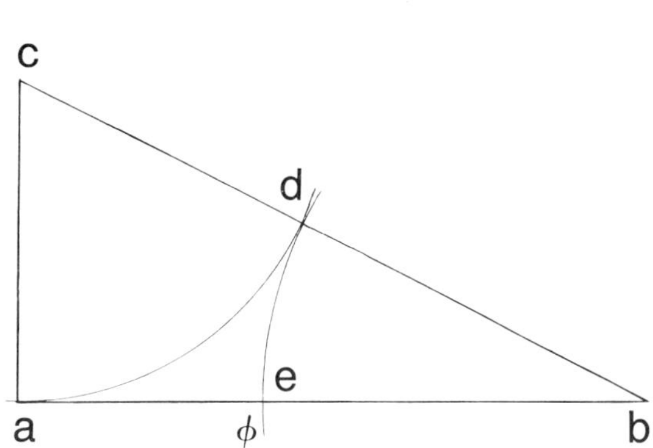

FIGURE 2 A

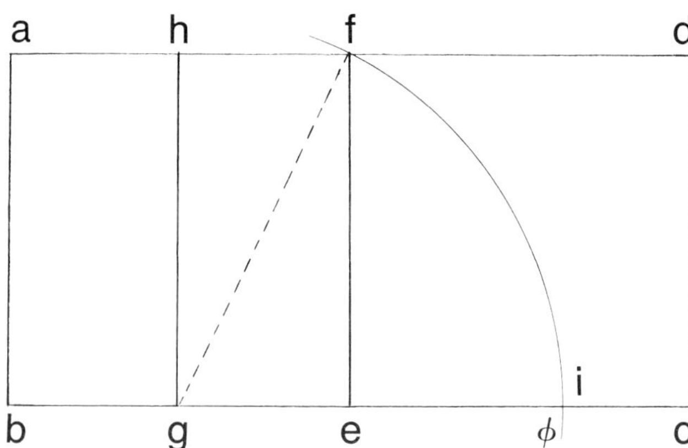

FIGURE 2 B

United Nations Building in New York City is a good example of this kind of construction.

ϕ is a constant proportion and equals 1.618. It is the division of a line or space ab into two parts, whereby the relationship of the larger portion eb to the smaller one ae is the same as the entire length to the larger. This means that:

$$ab:eb = eb:ae = 1.618 = \phi$$

(see Figure 2A).

In order to divide line ab into a ϕ proportion, it is best to construct a 90° triangle whose base is double the length of its side ca. With a compass, bring ca to intersect the hypotenuse at point d. Now use bd to intersect ab at e. This divides the base ab into a ϕ proportion. The same result can be obtained by halving a square with line hg (Figure 2B). Swing the diagonal gf down to intersect the baseline of the second square at i. The point where the diagonal intersects the base is ϕ, or 1.618, in relation to the side of square, which is 1.

The mathematical fact that $\phi + 1 = \phi^2$ and that $1 + 1/\phi = \phi$ leads to the so-called "Fibonacci" series (after the great Italian mathematician of the Middle Ages), where each new number is the sum of the two previous ones. For example: 13–21–34–55–89, and so on. The larger the numbers grow, the closer their ratio becomes ϕ (89:55 = 1.6).

Almost all outstanding architecture, sculpture, or painting can be overlaid with geometric grids to make the student aware of the endless use of intricate ϕ proportions. Such proportions are very pleasing to the human eye. A simplified golden section may be thought of as a ratio of 8:5.

I always make it a point to show my students the many ϕ relationships around them. Insert the first part of your index finger—from tip to first joint—into the next section, joint to joint. This is a length relationship of 1:1.6. You can continue by inserting this section into the third finger section, joint to knuckle, or this into the section of wrist joint

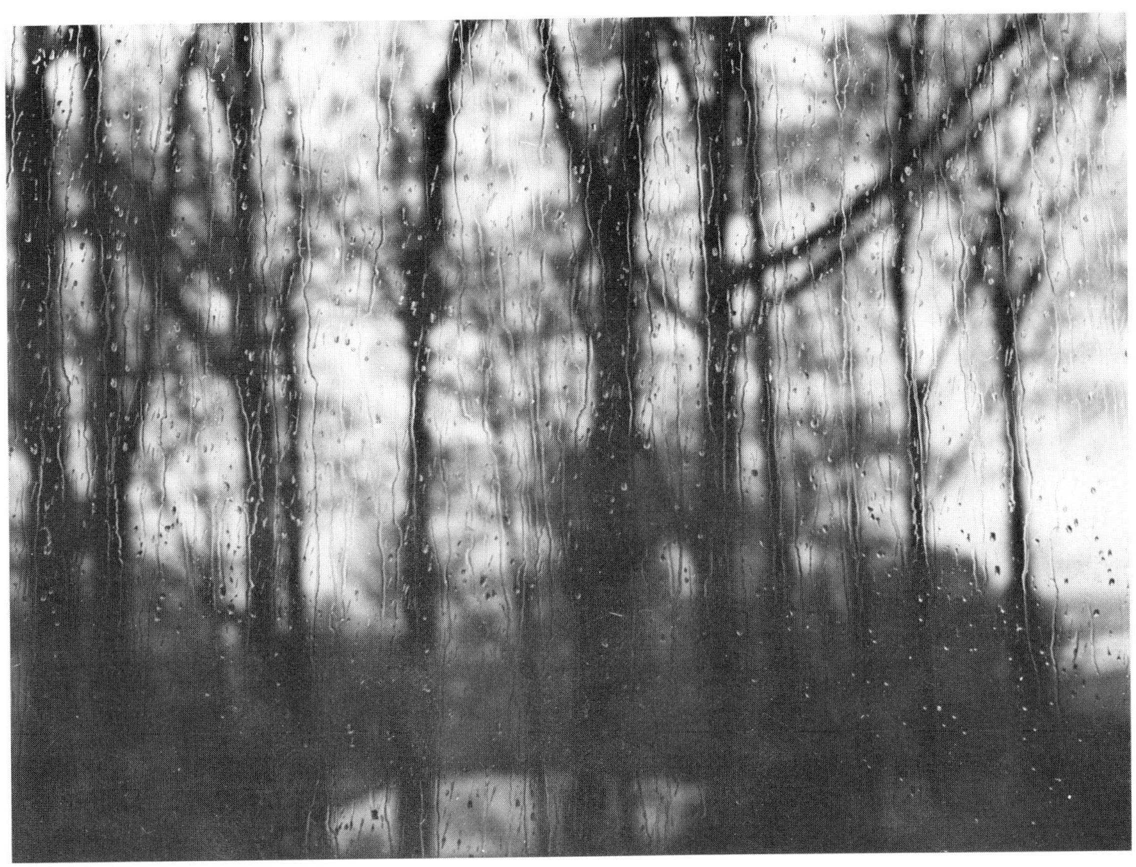

Above: Rain on a windowpane. Shot from inside with 35mm Nikkor, 1/60 sec. at *f*/11. Below: Foggy morning on the lake at 6 a.m. 50mm Nikkor with medium yellow filter, 1/500 sec. at *f*/16 on Tri-X.

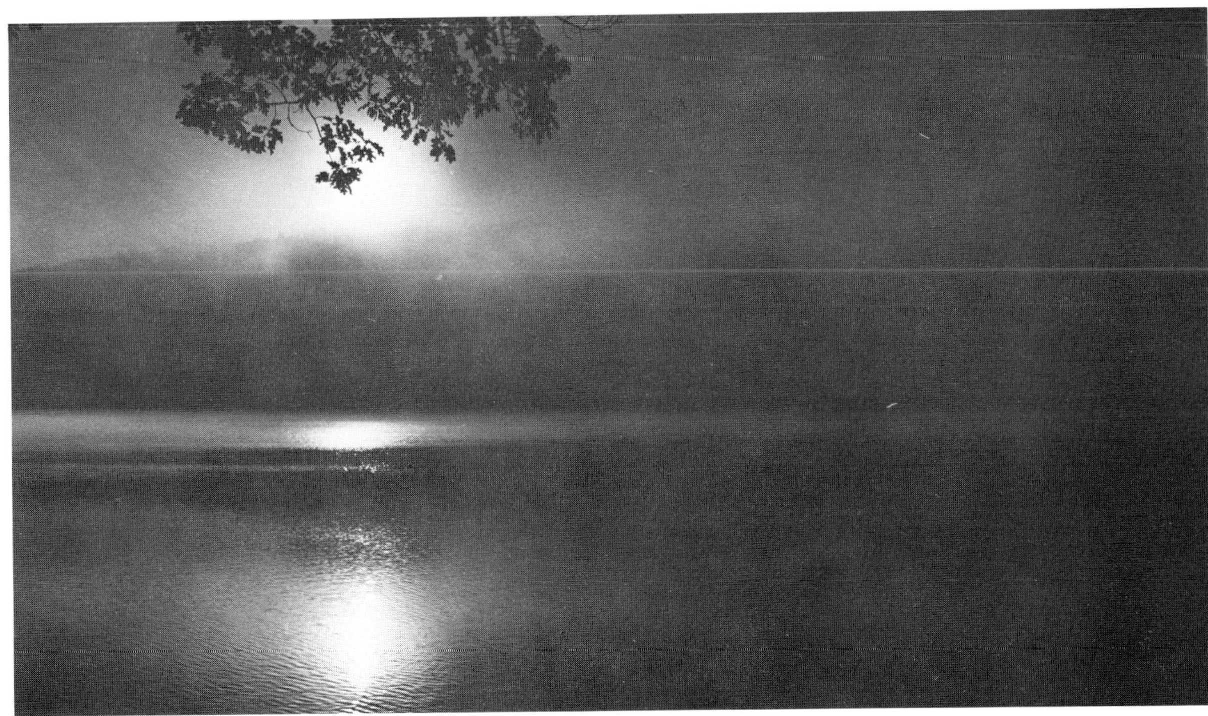

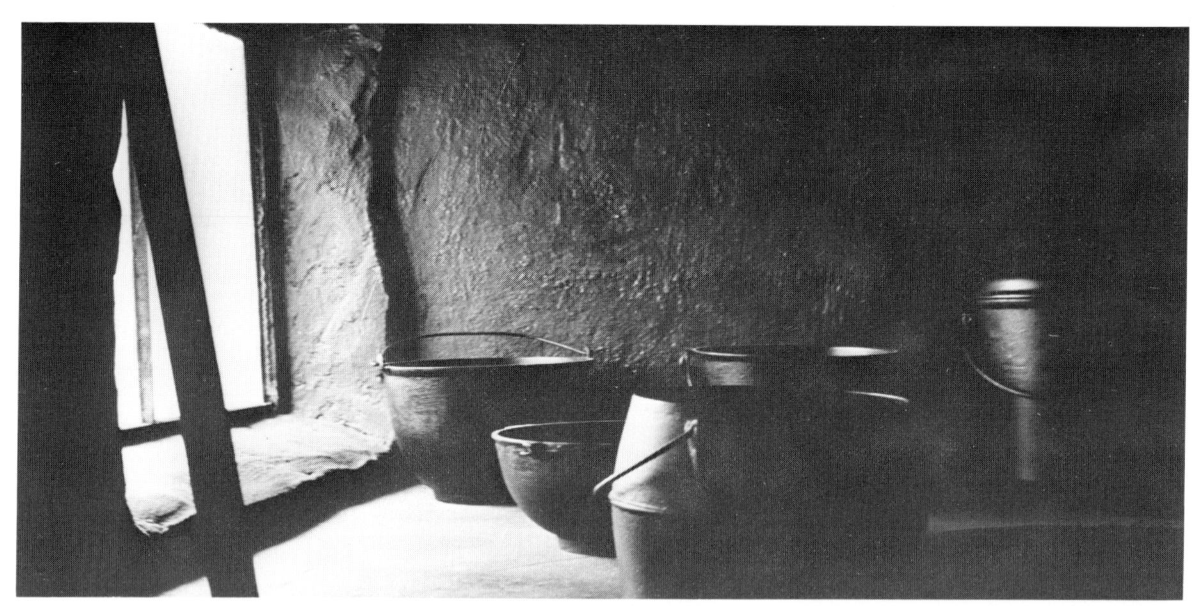

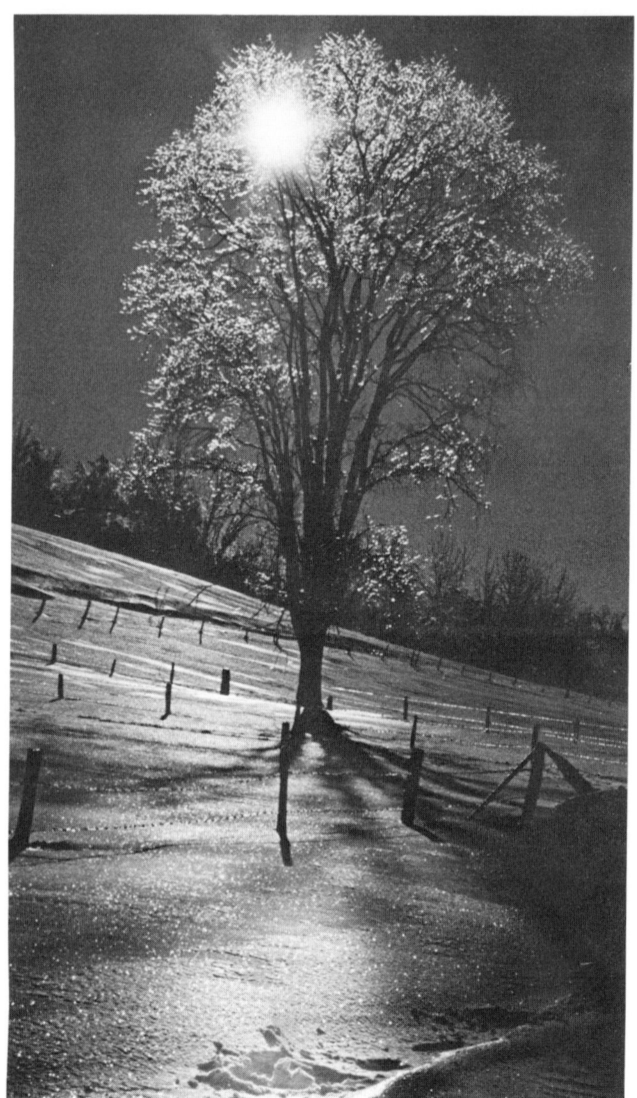

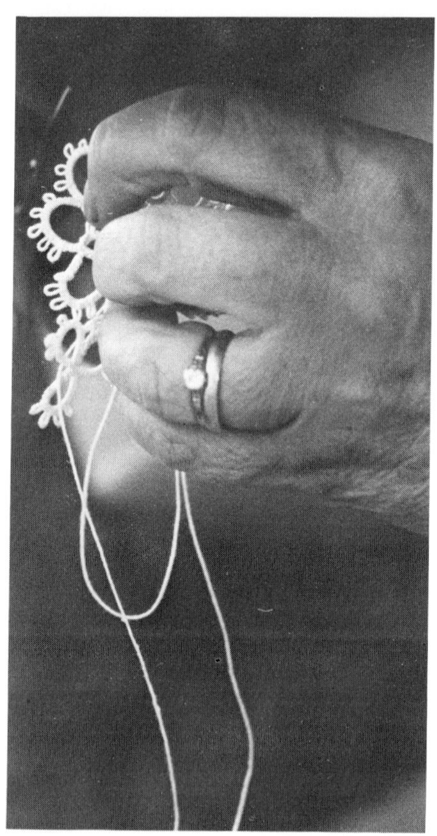

Opposite page: Left: Amish country. Windowlight, Nikon FTN, 50mm Nikkor, 1/30 sec. at *f*/5.6 on Tri-X. Bottom left: Ice storm in Vermont. Nikon F, 135mm Nikkor, 1/1000 sec. at *f*/22 on Tri-X. Bottom right: Lace work. Nikon FTN, 135mm Nikkor, 1/60 sec. at *f*/8 on Tri-X.

to knuckle. Again, the same relationships. Equal relationships exist in the measurement of sole to navel and navel to the top of the head.

Artists in the Renaissance had golden section compasses that, when opened to any length, also showed the golden proportion for this particular section. Leonardo da Vinci (1452–1519) wrote a whole book on the golden section, and it was this hermetic structure which allowed him to compose great masterpieces.

It is usually very helpful to have the student divide a certain length into two parts that exhibit such a relationship. This can easily be accomplished by constructing a triangle whose base is twice the length of its height and then proceeding with a compass in the manner described above. This exercise helps to develop a "feel" for these relationships.

LAW OF THIRDS

In the quest to establish guidelines for balance in composition, the "law of thirds" should also be mentioned. It concerns a super simplification for balance. With this system, a visual field is seen as divided with lines into equal thirds. At any intersection of these lines, a *focal point* of interest is achieved. These points attract the eyes and can carry the main weight of a balanced composition.

DIRECTION

Direction has already been shown in the sample of the placement of circles. The location of these will either attract or repel and thus impose direction upon them. Elongated forms and the shape of objects in general create directed forces. Any deviation from the horizontal or vertical carries weight and introduces some "pull" in that direction. For example, a triangular shape with a broad base on a horizontal line will thrust your eyes upward. Moreover, geometric forms seem more powerful than objects with organic outlines.

ACHIEVING BALANCE

It has been shown that balance must be achieved by ratios of parts, and that certain proportions are perceived as more pleasant than others. Balance problems also exist in the ratios of light and dark, large and small areas, quantities and color. To the student of photography, this chapter is a guideline, not a rigid rule. Most of all, you should remember that one cannot achieve harmonic balance without a dominant picture content. A work of art may incorporate many different forms in balance and minute counterbalance so as to create a total balance through complexities. This is what contributes to our perception of dynamics and liveliness.

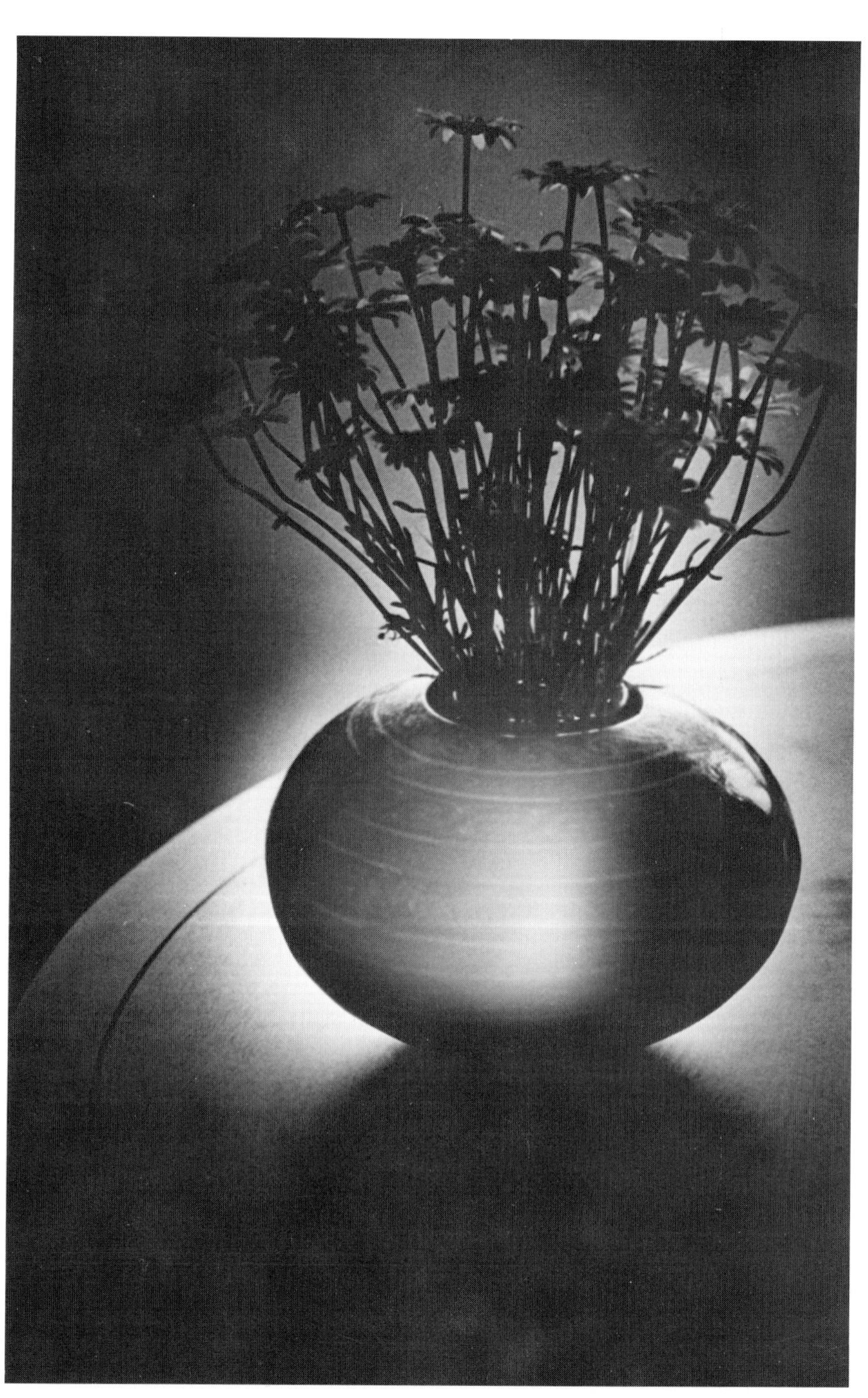

In this photograph, note the repetition of round forms as design element. Nikon F2, 105mm Nikkor, 1/125 sec. at *f*/5.6 on Tri-X.

2

SHAPE

It is the nature of artistic expression that it should carry meaning, although complex meaning and simple form may represent ends so opposite that no solution is possible. Simplicity in the visual arts requires good organization to reveal meaning in a presented pattern. Gestalt psychologists refer to the phenomenon as isomorphism, a hypothetical identity of psychological manifestation and brain processes.

Certain conditions must be met under the laws of simplicity, which state that we always perceive out of ambiguous patterns those things which are easiest to perceive. The stimulus from which we perceive must be simple just as the meaning conveyed by the percept must be simple. The frame of mind and the ratio between meaning and percept must be equal. The perceptual result is always a combination of interaction of (simple) structure and the preconditioning of the brain field to perceive the most elementary shape. It is well known, for example, that persons who have been told to expect a circle on a screen will see a circle even when a square is projected with low light intensity.

SHAPE, FORM, AND MASS

Shape refers to the spatial aspects of objects. It concerns boundaries: A three dimensional object is bound by two dimensional surfaces or can be thought of as a projection of its shape outline on a two-dimensional surface.

Since shape, form, and mass are sometimes rather loosely used terms and in some discussions often interchanged, many students are confused. The use of the word "shape" in connection with sculpture, architecture, relief art (showing depression and elevation), and the like is of course correct. But here when reference is made to three-dimensional objects, the word "form" would seem more appropriate.

The word "shape" is often used in reference to molding processes and means, in this instance, the opposite of an undifferentiated mass. But since the discussion concerns mainly the visual aspects in painting or photography, such as the two-dimensional surface of a painting ground, the film plane, and printing paper, shape should be understood in a strictly geometric sense. Shape then becomes spatial shape, which is

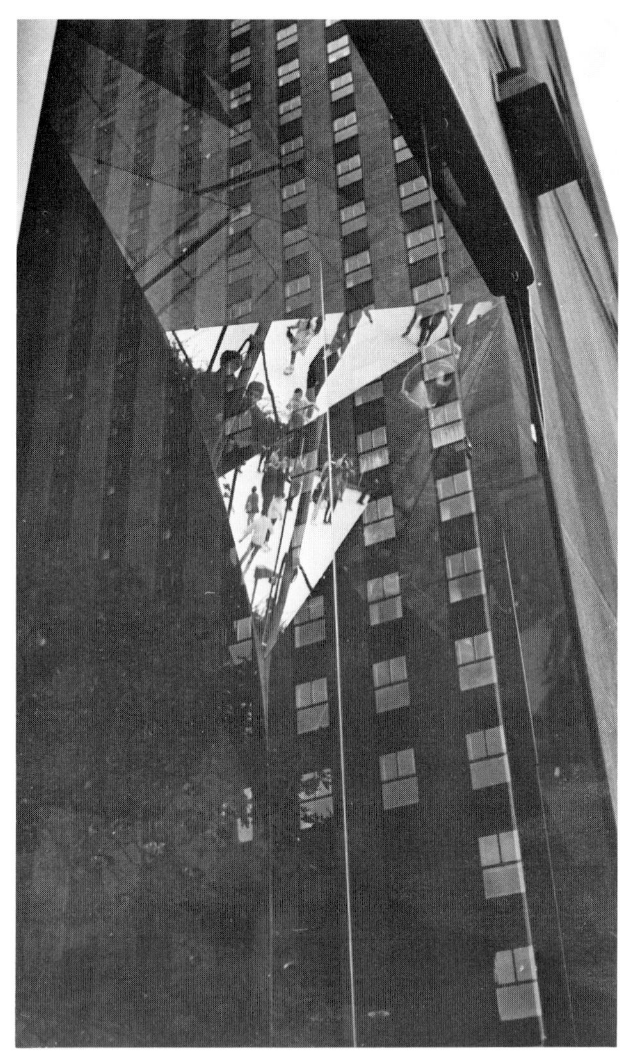

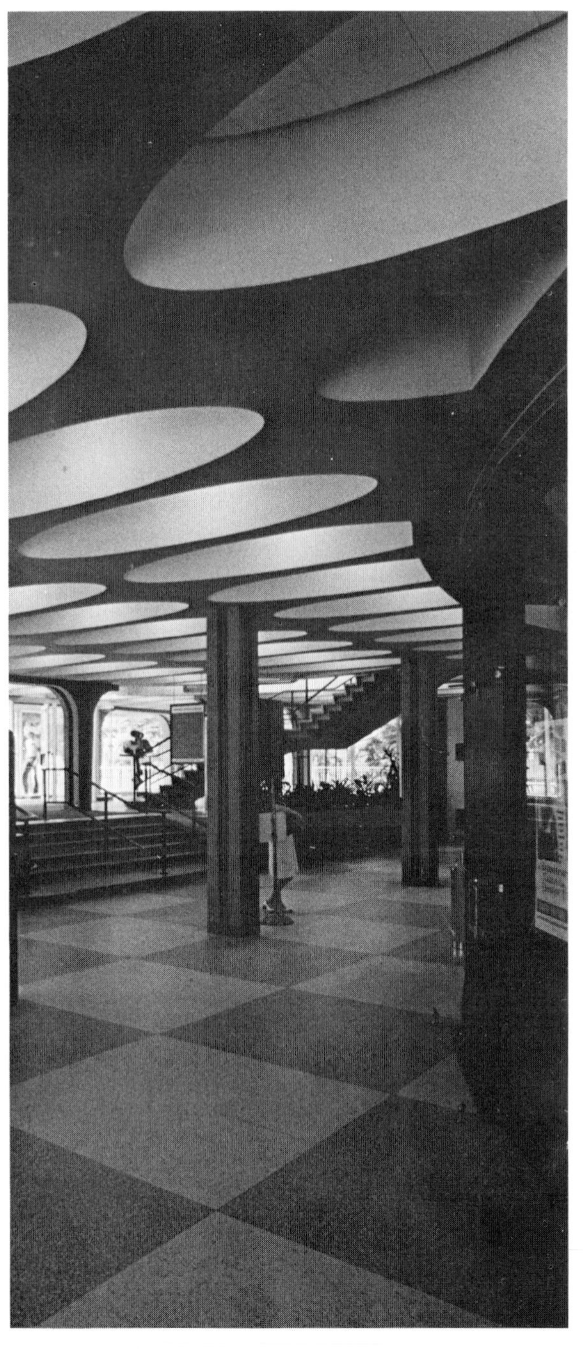

Above: Rockefeller Center, New York, shot from low angle into upper corner of shop window. Triangles are the basic design element in this scene. Nikon F, 35mm Nikkor, 1/250 sec. at *f*/11 on Tri-X.

Left: Hopkins Center, Dartmouth College. Again note the repetition of geometric forms as design element. Nikon F2, 20mm Nikkor, 1/60 sec. at *f*/8 on Tri-X.

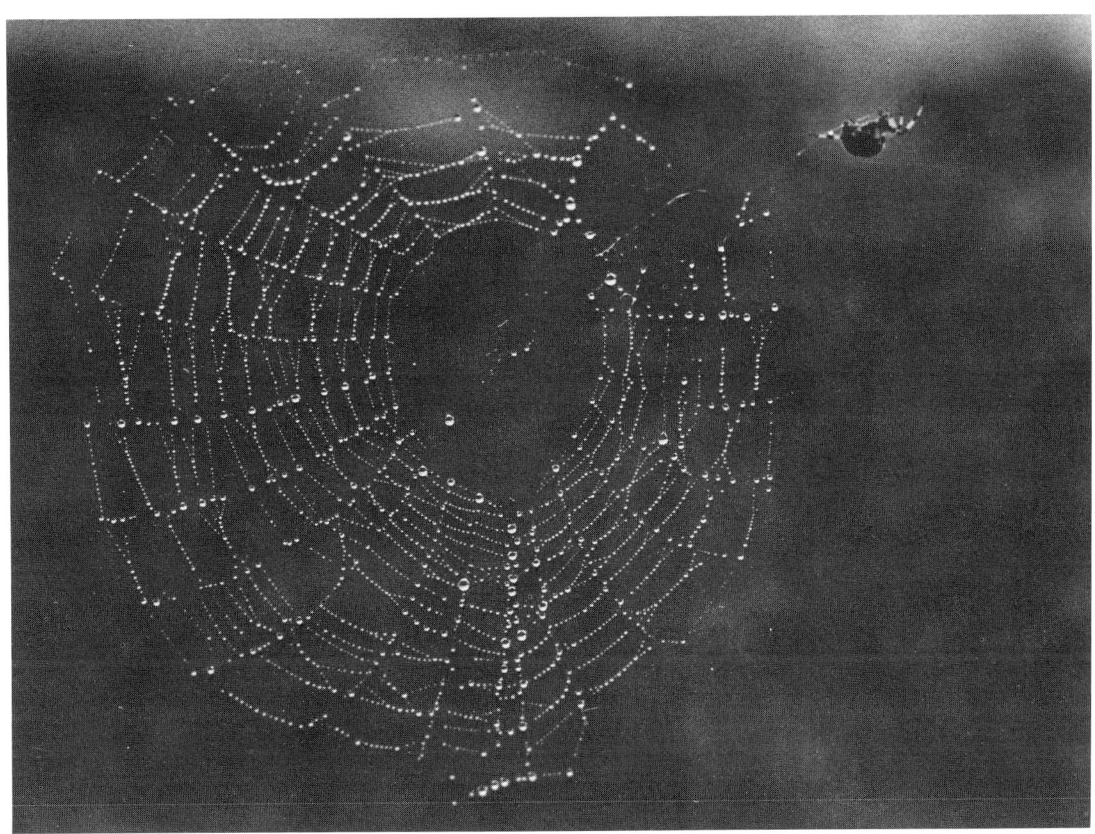

Spiderweb in early morning dew. Nikon F2, 135mm Nikkor, 1/500 sec. at *f*/2.8 on Tri-X.

fixed in relatively spatial relations to the boundaries of a surface. If later in this chapter reference is made to landscapes or buildings, which are three-dimensional forms, you should perceive or understand them as projections onto a two-dimensional surface.

Shape needs balance; shape sets up forces such as direction and weight. Shape can be the confinement of space by line or of one shade or color by another.

Since nature itself tends to search out the most simple solution to any specific task, we may safely say that also in art, simplicity must be a goal. Some biological forms show characteristic features involving such basic shapes as triangles, squares, and circles—basic shape-units of repetition—and in small and simple organisms (few-celled), this seems to be even more pronounced. There are parallels to modern modular construction because their building blocks consist of almost identical shape-units. Through this observation, we find instantly a link between nature, technology, and all art.

Below: Waterlillies. Nikon FTN, 35mm Nikkor with orange filter, 1/125 sec. at *f*/8 on Tri-X. Bottom: Meadow. Nikon FTN, 35mm Nikkor with dark yellow filter, 1/500 sec. at *f*/8 on Tri-X.

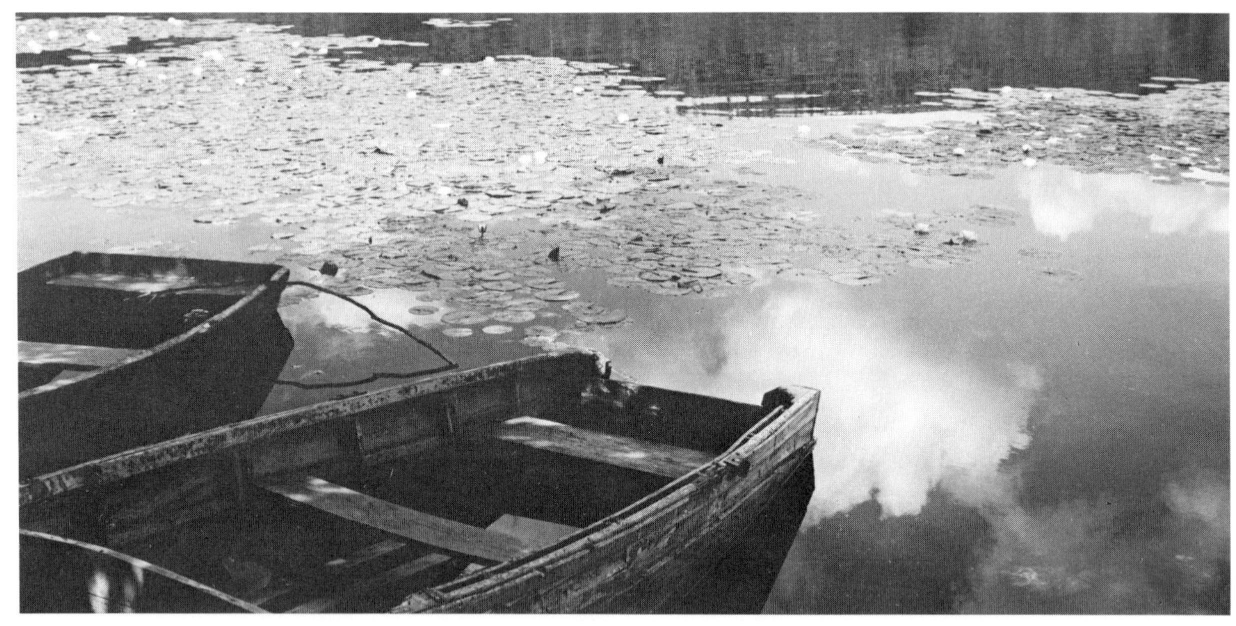

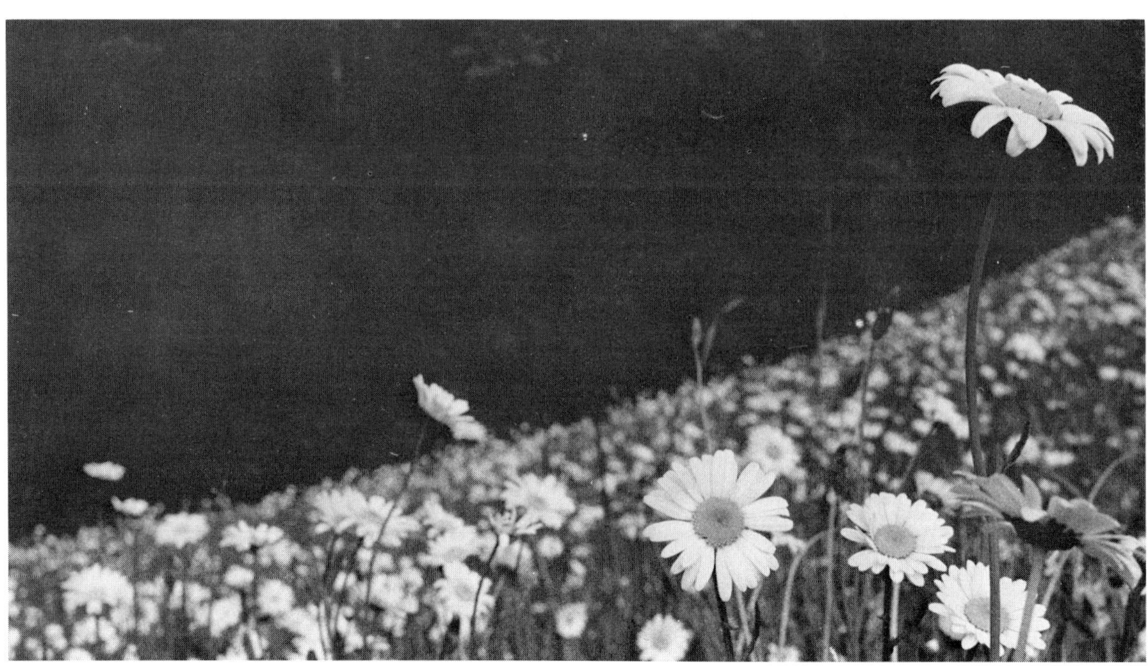

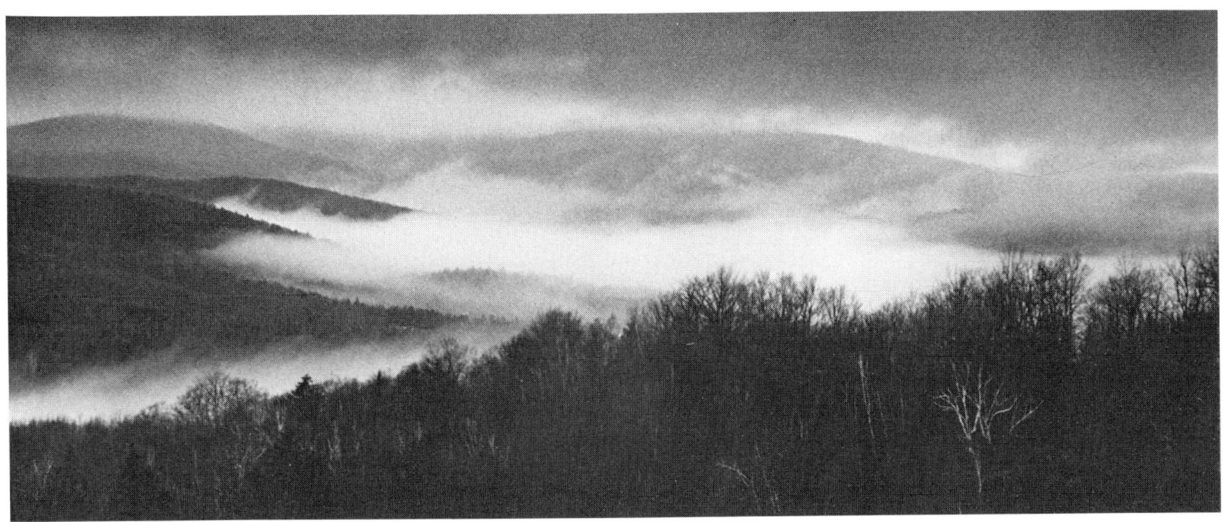

Early morning from the author's living-room window. Nikon F2, 50mm Nikkor, 1/60 sec. at *f*/8 on Tri-X.

If you look at certain photographs made with electron microscopes, you can observe how order, simplicity, and repetition of basic shapes have been carried by nature to absolute perfection. These particle modules, like the tiles of mosaics or the groupings of shapes in art, occur in families or sets of continuity. There is order in biological and submolecular worlds, never a conglomeration of unrelated parts. Any shape modification is embraced as alteration within a general system; this is always a gradual change of shape and could be referred to as the "growth gradient." In biological and visual patterns, it can be called the recognizable relationship of neighboring parts.

VISUAL ORGANIZATION

In dynamic visual patterns, you need rhythm, sameness, and change simultaneously. The overall product here requires a pattern of identity where parts of the whole introduce just enough variety to give change and direction. This is an important point in any visual organization where shapes fill our canvas or paper as representation of isolated and bounded areas. When these things become clear in your mind, a whole new world of seeing opens up to you. Looking at a landscape, for instance, you may suddenly become aware of basic shapes—trees forming triangles or circles, rolling hills forming waves, fields forming patterns of rectangles and squares, even banks of clouds that remind you of shapes already present in the landscape. Everywhere you look, you may now find such basic building stones of similar shape that have proportional ratios between them.

If you try visually to organize the world around you, you have to amplify or simplify, to reduce or strengthen, to be selective in applying the basic elements of shape and form in your environment. This is not an easy task, but rather one that requires decision. You can achieve full-scale variety with a single concept if it is presented in a diverse way. In architecture, for example, entire building facades are made up of modules of similar shape. Whether you look at the recurrence of geometric shapes such as arches, whether rounded or pointed, the proportional ratios between them, or the continuity of squares on modern glass buildings, they all form intricate systems of rhythm of sheer visual pleasure.

Among the visual elements, shape is probably the most powerful component. It not only determines forces, but implies their direction, weight, and balance. Anything you wish to photograph or paint appears as shape on the two-dimensional surface of pictures, there again creating outlines to form shapes outside the first boundaries.

Shape offers very powerful suggestions. Regardless of the outlines, a main axis can always be found. This main axis gives direction to shape, whether it favors the horizontal or vertical concept. If the horizontal is emphasized or further amplified by inclusion of more horizontal parallels, the psychological reaction of the veiwer will be one of subdued feelings or quiet. His state of mind may be reduced to calm, peace, and tranquillity. If the vertical is predominant in a composition, feelings of being alive, of restlessness, and of activity might be the subconscious result.

In the previous chapter on balance and here, you begin to realize how important the organization of visual space is, and how important it is to balance and harmonize shape.

TRANSFORMING SHAPE

The photographer faces different problems from those of the painter. The latter can willfully transform reality to make it conform to his ideas. Whatever exists in reality as random shape outlines can be reduced or transformed for a well-structured, more expressive visual presentation as the painter perceives it. The photographer, on the other hand, has less freedom. Only up to a certain point can he alter shapes. However, if the photographer learns to see shape as an element of visual construction, he is on his way to building himself a visual vocabulary of expressive values.

To be creative, the photographer must preselect and extract from nature shapes and patterns that best represent his own vision. In photography, we speak of the "decisive moment," where shape, form, light, and color of a fleeting instant are just right. To capture this moment requires the most concentrated alertness of perception on the part of the photographer. Thus, in comparing the photographer with the painter, you can say that after the photographer pushes the button, his decision is final, whereas the painter can always change his work during the process of its creation. Of course, the photographer also makes some changes from his original conception, but only in cropping his picture or changing its tonal values. The visual statement he intended to make was decided the instant he pushed the camera button.

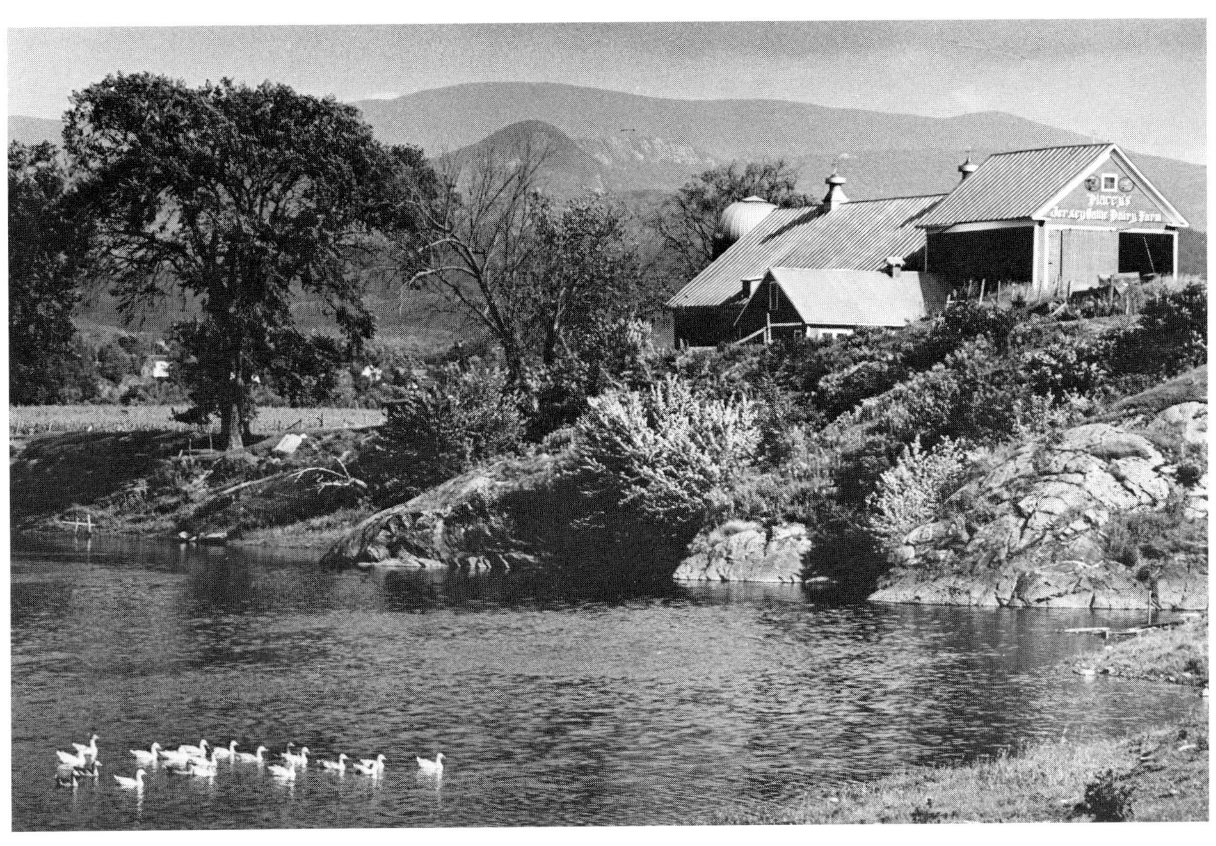

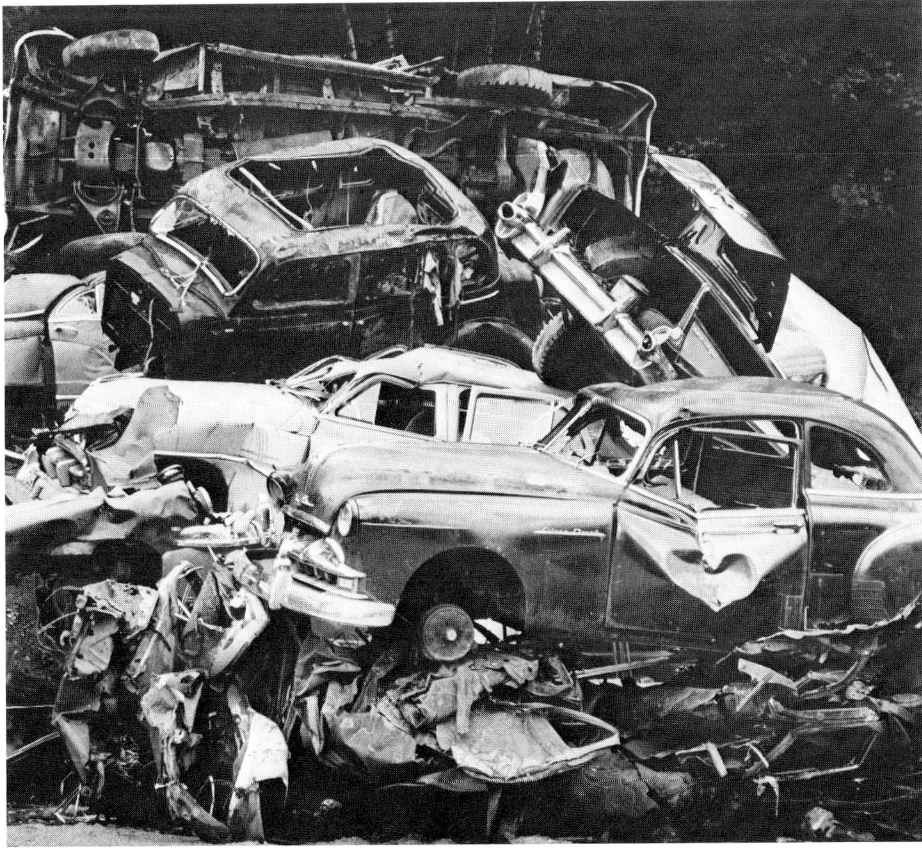

Above: Vermont farm scene. Nikon FTN, 135mm Nikkor, 1/250 sec. at *f*/11 on Tri-X.

Left: Junkyard. Nikon FTN, 135mm Nikkor, 1/500 sec. at *f*/16 on Tri-X.

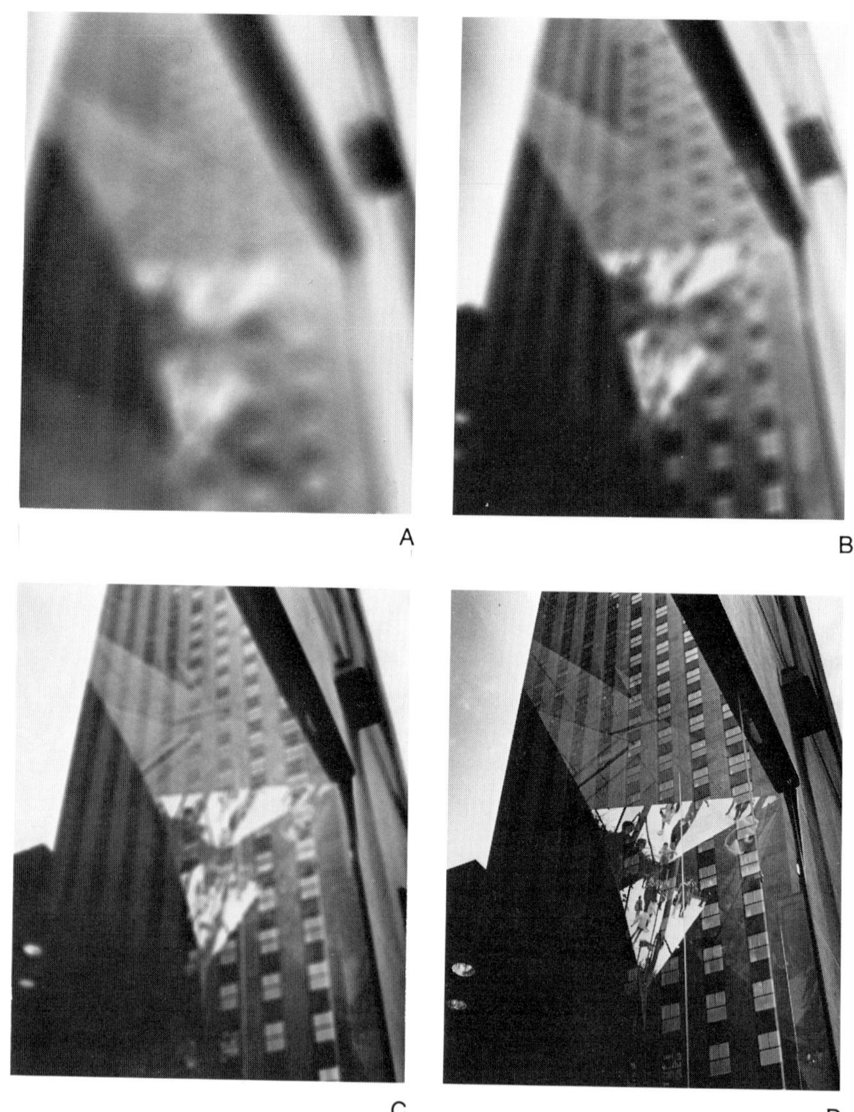
A B C D

FIGURE 3

Figures 3A through 3D. Figure 3D is a photograph of a store window and its reflections, shot against the outside of the building with the camera position near the sidewalk. Figures 3A, B, and C represent the same scene in progressing stages of sharpness. With increasing blur, the overall pattern becomes simpler (C, B, A), but the stimulus input diminishes. In addition, the overall shape and weight distribution become more evident. The pictures carry a theme of simple triangular shapes, and the darker shapes force the eye to the triangular center of interest, which reflects an ice-skating scene. The composition carries more weight on the left side but is balanced on the right by the light triangle. There is an all-over emphasis on vertical lines. Observe how these pictures serve to illustrate all the principles discussed thus far. Basic shapes organize the visual field presented. They not only relate to each other because of their basic triangular shape, but they also carry subtle ratios of light and dark, large and small areas, and certain quantities of repetition. All this, however, is only a means of communicating the dominance: the picture content. Most viewers will grasp the meaning instantly; that between all the steel, cement, and glass, man has still reserved himself a small area for fun.

3

FORM AND SPACE

Form is a combination of various components in a visual work of art, such as line, shape, color, texture, and volume. Form can be defined as the three-dimensional aspect of an object apart from its two-dimensional aspect of shape. Since pictorial space in painting and photography is presented on a plane surface, three-dimensionality must be translated into a two-dimensional concept. A true visual concept of form seems possible only in sculpture and architecture. Pictures on plane surfaces can be either flat (like children's drawings) or can simulate depth.

The normal human eye constantly focuses back and forth to perceive depth. Depth perception is greatly aided by the fact that human vision is binocular and stereoscopic. The camera in most cases is monocular and can produce images in any degree of unsharpness, but it can be selectively prefocused to yield sharpness in a shallow zone of depth. Our eyes and most photographic lenses convey the feeling of space through rectilinear perspective. Other lenses will, however, produce different perspectives that are spherical or cylindrical. To simulate depth on a plane surface, you can employ certain cues to aid and guide the eyes. The direction from which light is received, the way shadows are cast, and the way in which near objects usually overlap forms of objects toward the horizon are some of these cues.

MONOCULAR DEPTH CUES

In the sixteenth century, Leonardo da Vinci wrote about spatial representation. He made suggestions to other artists about his findings on "monocular depth cues" and reported his observations on vision. These findings on how to portray three-dimensional space on flat surfaces are still valid today. A list of these depth cues would read as follows:

1. *Interposition.* Some forms are positioned in such a way as to interrupt the outlines of others more distant.

2. *Linear perspective.* Parallel lines in nature must be presented by converging lines on a picture plane. Square areas on the ground in nature must become trapezoids on a picture plane.

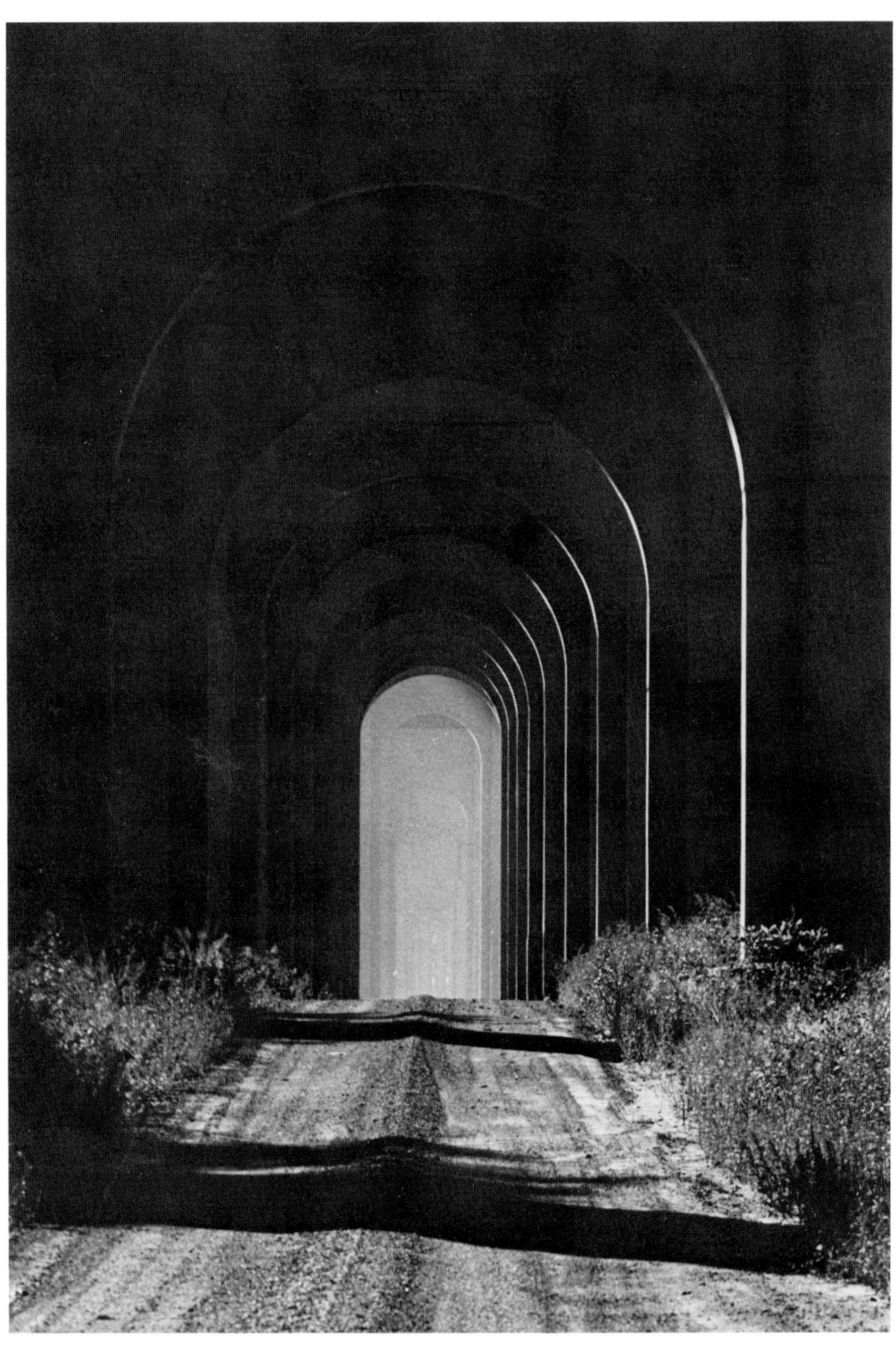

Under a highway bridge. Nikon F, 200mm Nikkor, 1/60 sec. at *f*/16 on Tri-X.

3. *Size perspective and familiar size.* When same-size objects are pictured, ones that appear smaller must be more distant. The reverse is also true. You know, for example, that a grown man is taller than a child. If both are of equal height in a picture, then the man must be more distant.

4. *Direction of illumination.* The distribution of shadows and illumination is a very powerful cue in the perception of volume and form. It gives the direction and the way in which objects occupy space. There are four ways of illumination in nature: overcast sky, frontlighting, sidelighting, and backlighting.

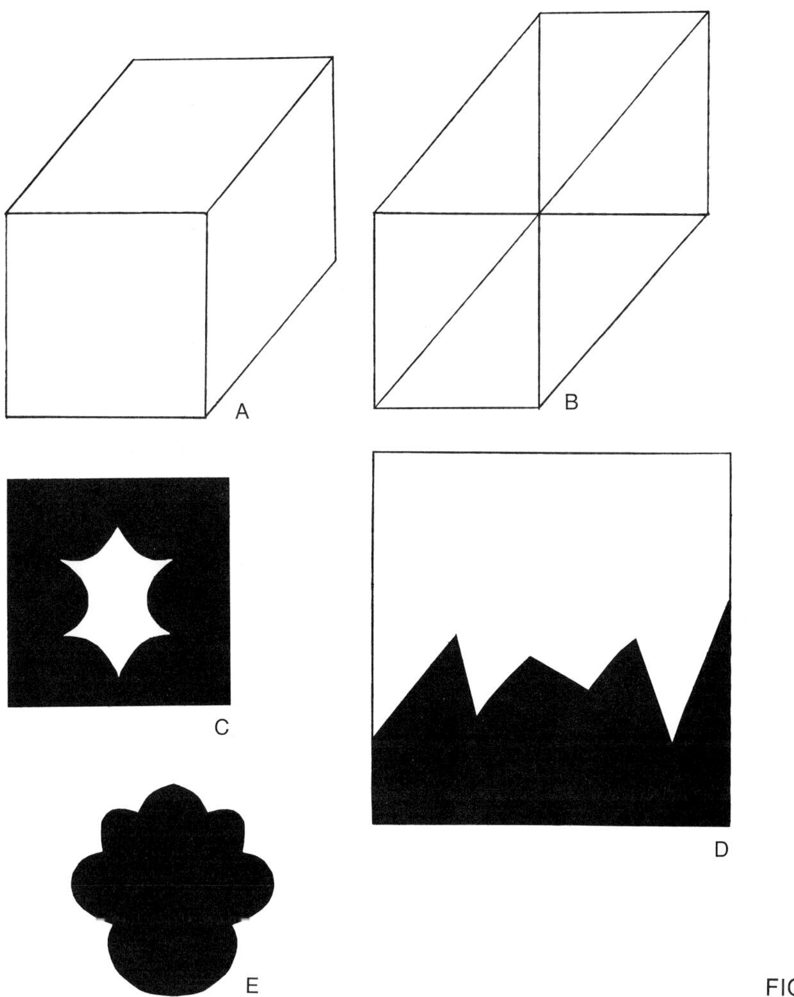

FIGURE 4

Figure 4A is seen as a cube in three dimensions. The perspective is isometric, the frontal plane is not oblique, and the sides are three even parallels. In central perspective, all lines would converge toward a vanishing point. Figure 4B is seen as a two-dimensional shape, although at first glance it might look like a folded napkin. It is rather difficult to read Figure 4B as a transparent cube. Figure 4D shows the figure-ground phenomenon. The lower half of a picture is generally seen as lying in front. This illustration might suggest mountains against a clear sky. Visually, there is depth between mountains and sky. Turning the page upside down, the same phenomenon occurs. You can now see snow-covered mountains against a dark sky. If you concentrate on the concavity (Convexity is always seen as figure; concavity is always seen as ground.) of the white pattern in Figure 4C, the figure seems to shrink. The black square takes on this function of a figure and lets you see ground as through a window. Figure 4E seems to grow and lies solidly on top of the ground.

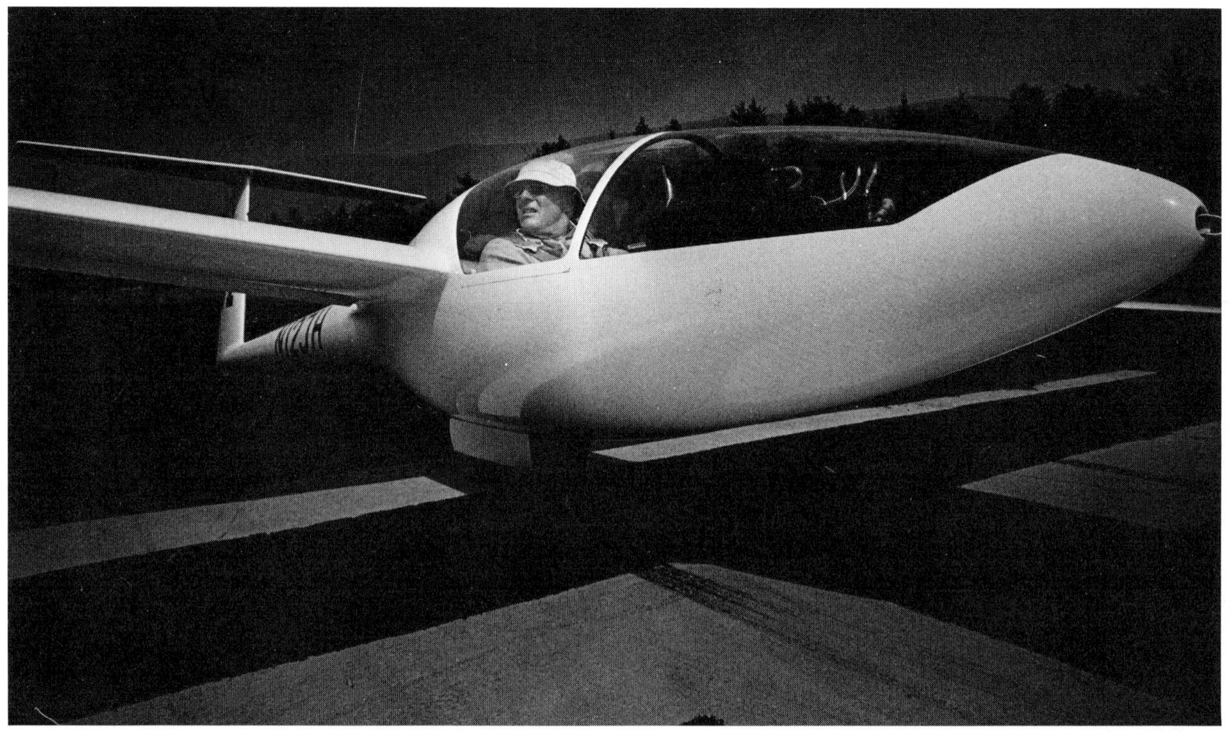

Ready for takeoff. Nikon F2, 20mm Nikkor with red filter, 1/125 sec. at *f*/8 on Tri-X.

An overcast sky diffuses light. Under such lighting, the eyes can find no specific point on which to focus, and all things are seen in a multitude of detailed little pieces. In frontlighting (with the sun at the photographer's back), the illusion of space is diminished. With sidelighting, objects begin to reveal their form; they take on a certain plasticity, and space becomes visible. This effect is very much heightened in lighting situations where light comes toward you. Shadows then give strong cues to the spatial aspects of objects. With backlighting, an object is silhouetted and its total shape is outlined. (See Figure 5 opposite.)

BINOCULAR VISION

The four cues listed above are monocular depth cues. Human vision, however, is binocular. Your eyes view your surroundings constantly from different points; the images received therefore have some disparity. By taking two pictures of a scene, so as to simulate the distance your eyes are set apart (65mm), and then viewing these pictures through a stereoscope, you can produce a spatial sensation.

Modern theories claim that there are other cues aiding space perception, citing as example the fact that people who have the use of only one eye have some spatial judgment. There are numerous theories on vision and space perception. According to Gestalt theories, perception falls under the laws of simplicity, which stipulate that we always perceive out of ambiguous patterns those which are easiest to perceive. The reader is referred to the book *Perception* by Hochberg, published by Prentice-Hall.

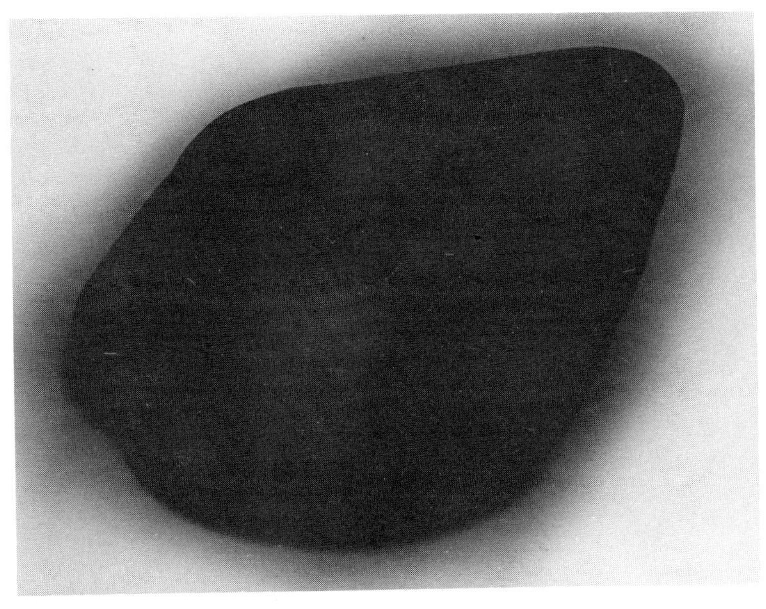

SHAPE

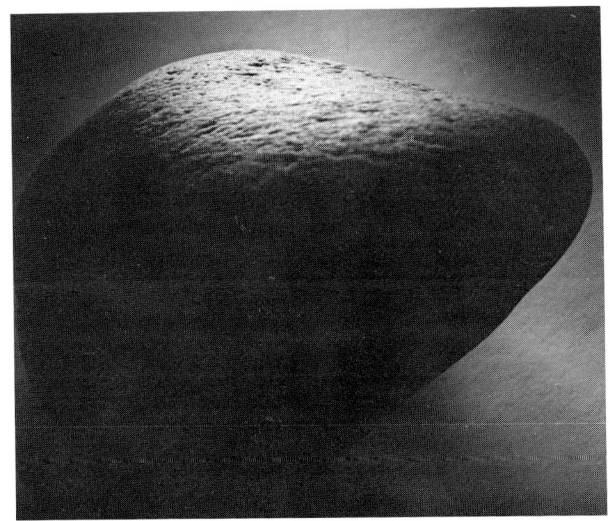

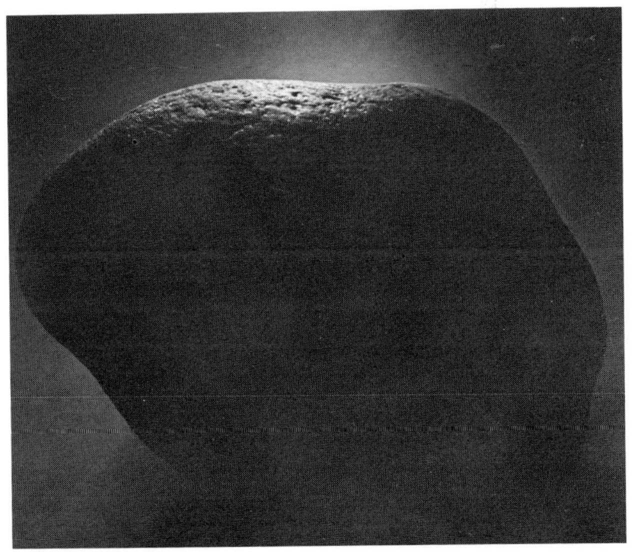

INTO FORM

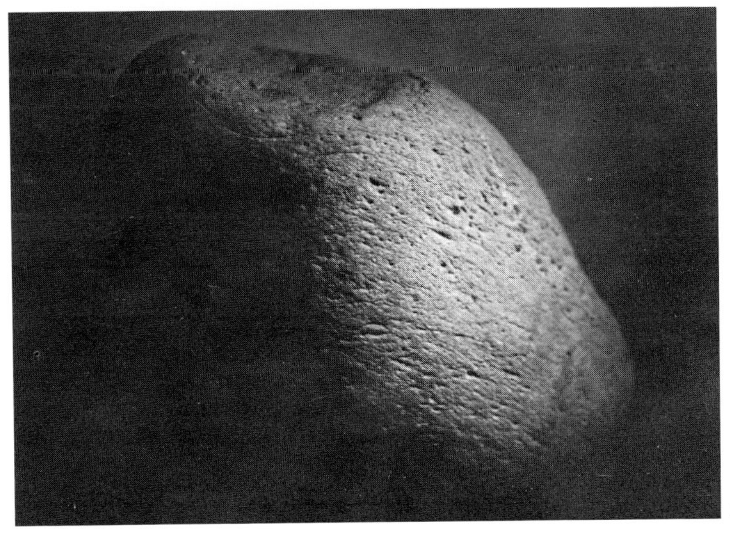

FIGURE 5

Opposite: This composition of a bread baker implies movement. Nikon F, 50mm Nikkor, 1/125 sec. at *f*/5.6 on Tri-X.

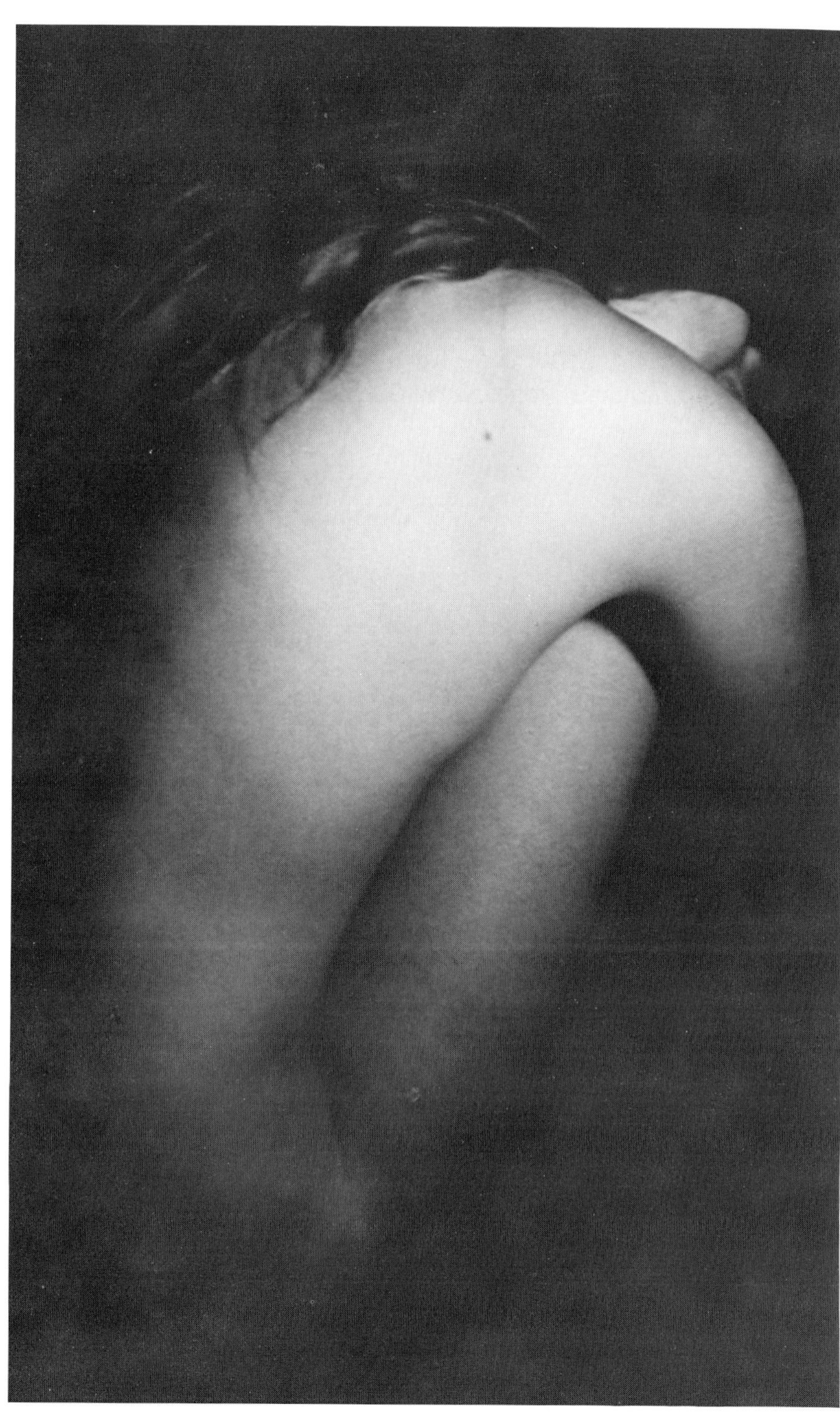

Basic forms of the body have been composed into a strong diagonal, but the figure is almost coiled back into itself. It evokes feelings of an embryonic state. A 60-watt light bulb in a diffused reflector, Nikon FTN, 105mm Nikkor, 1/30 sec. at *f*/4 on Tri-X.

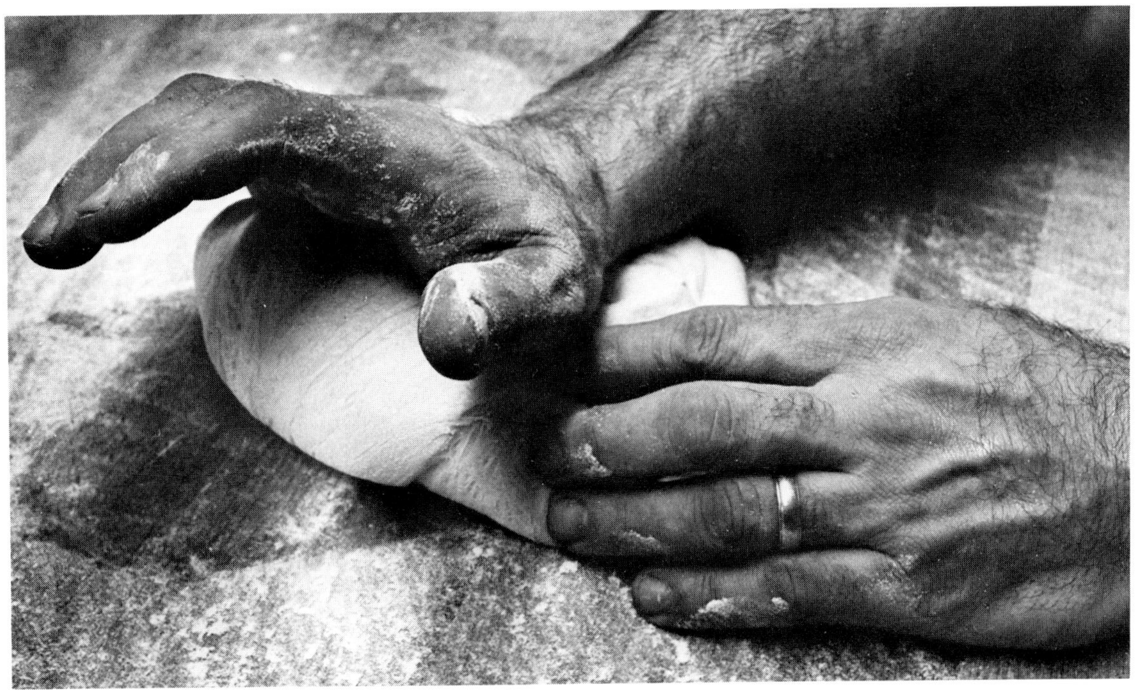

Through perspective overlapping, the artist not only establishes spatial arrangements, he also establishes a hierarchy of important and subordinate elements. In order to convey the essential elements of an object, you have to show its form in a clearly unambiguous figure-ground relationship and in its spatial aspects and lighting. If you can photograph a rock or a tree in such a way as to extract some inherent abstract pattern, you will enhance its aesthetic quality, and it will be more meaningful than an exact copy of reality.

GRADIENTS

There are other perceptional cues to help the illusion of space on a flat surface. These are called *gradients*.

Texture gradients are perceptional cues because there is a decrease in texture as it becomes more distant, and objects in the far distance take on a flatter, two-dimensional character.

Sharpness gradients, or pronouncedness of outline, decrease also in the far distance, helping the perception of space. By focusing a camera on a plane near the first third of a desired field of depth, you can create space extending in two directions. The sharpness gradient diminishes toward the horizon and creates space in the direction of the viewer.

Light and color form a gradient. Color becomes lighter in more distant objects. By creating shadows, light also creates space.

Uninterrupted spatial cues, such as railroad tracks or telephone poles along a roadside, are powerful depth cues. Without such cues, our spatial judgment is greatly impaired. If you look at a landscape through a window, or if you try to judge the altitude of a high-flying airplane, you cannot trust your depth perception because of a lack of cues.

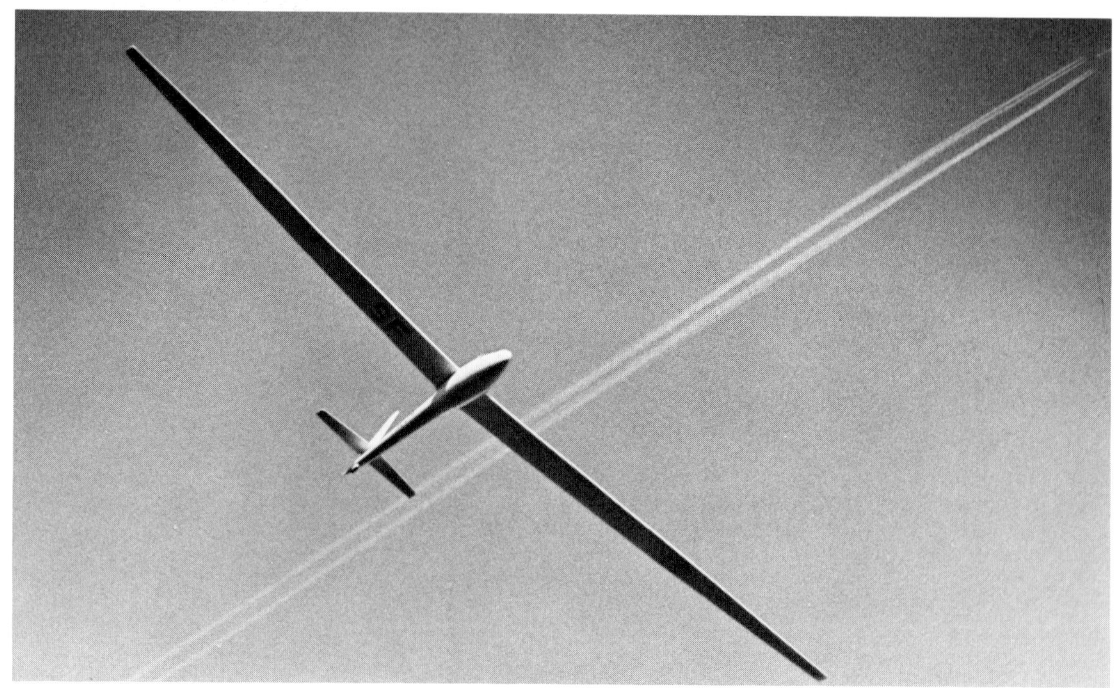

High-performance glider and jet. Nikon F2, 200mm Nikkor with light yellow filter, 1/2000 sec. at *f*/16 on Tri-X.

PICTORIAL SPACE

Throughout the ages, artists have been fascinated with the presentation of space. However, presenting volume in a spatial relationship on a flat surface always presents problems; there is no right or wrong way.

The ancient Egyptians were satisfied with narrow space, permitting the body to be viewed from the front and side. In Oriental art, aerial but not linear perspective was employed. The Greeks and Romans were to some degree concerned with pictorial space but did not understand the mathematical laws involved.

The one-point perspective, an invention of the Renaissance (Brunelleschi, 1377?–1446, Italian sculptor and architect), is a device to bring order to pictorial space. Today's painters utilize these alternatives, so too the photographer who, with new lens designs, is not limited in the choice of his representation. Extreme wide-angle lenses with a field coverage of more than 180° enable the photographer to employ spherical perspective; those with 140° permit cylindrical perspective.

Artists of today sometimes incorporate all these various systems in a single picture to achieve more dynamic results. Regardless of your choice, you may still agree with the great Italian painter Piero della Francesca (1420?–1492) who, in the first treatise ever written on perspective remarked: "The greatest beauty is inherent in those forms which have the clarity of geometric form." And long before him Plato also remarked: "The excellence of beauty in every work of art is due to the observance of measure."

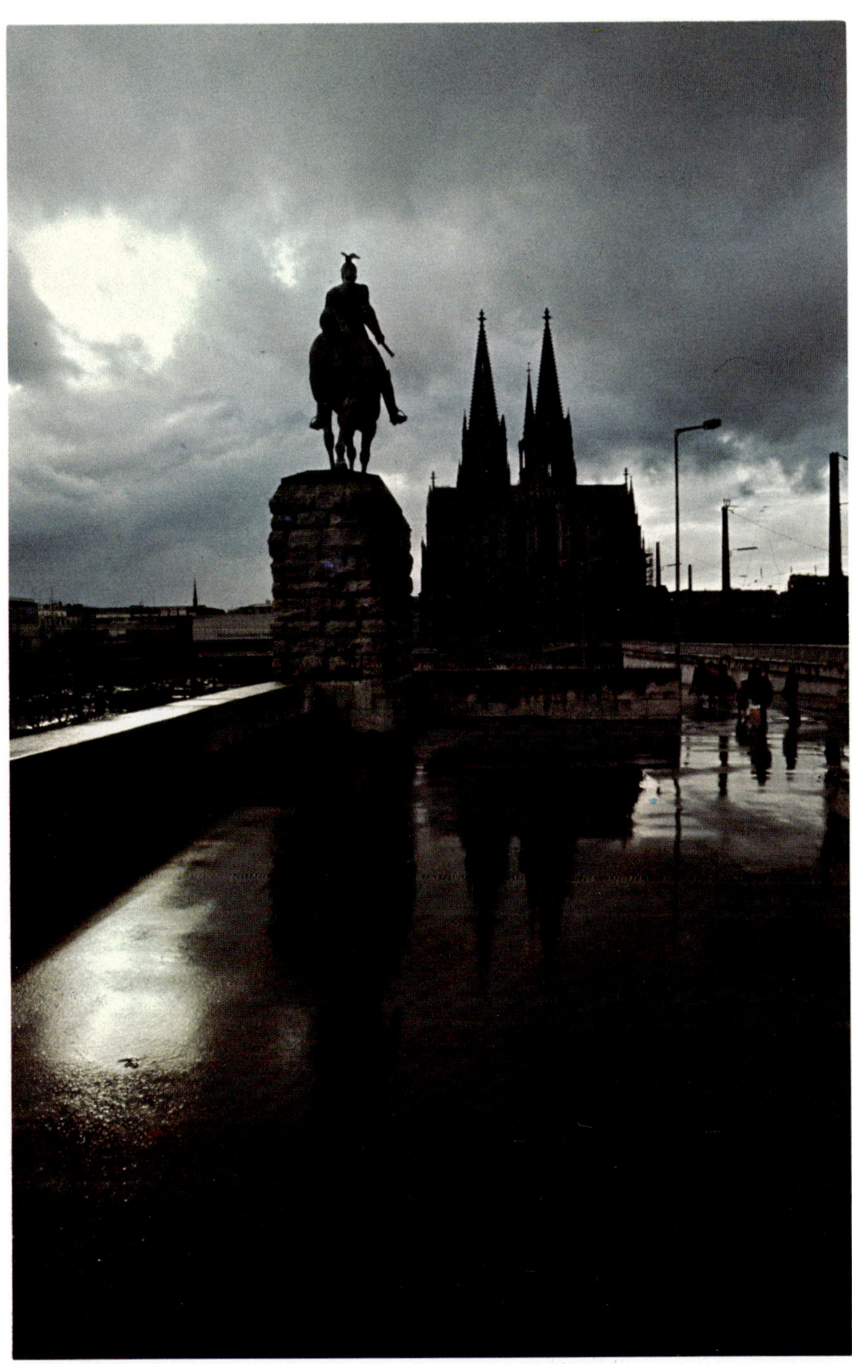

Statue in Cologne, West Germany. Nikon F2, 35mm Nikkor Auto, 1/60 sec. at *f*/8 on Ektachrome.

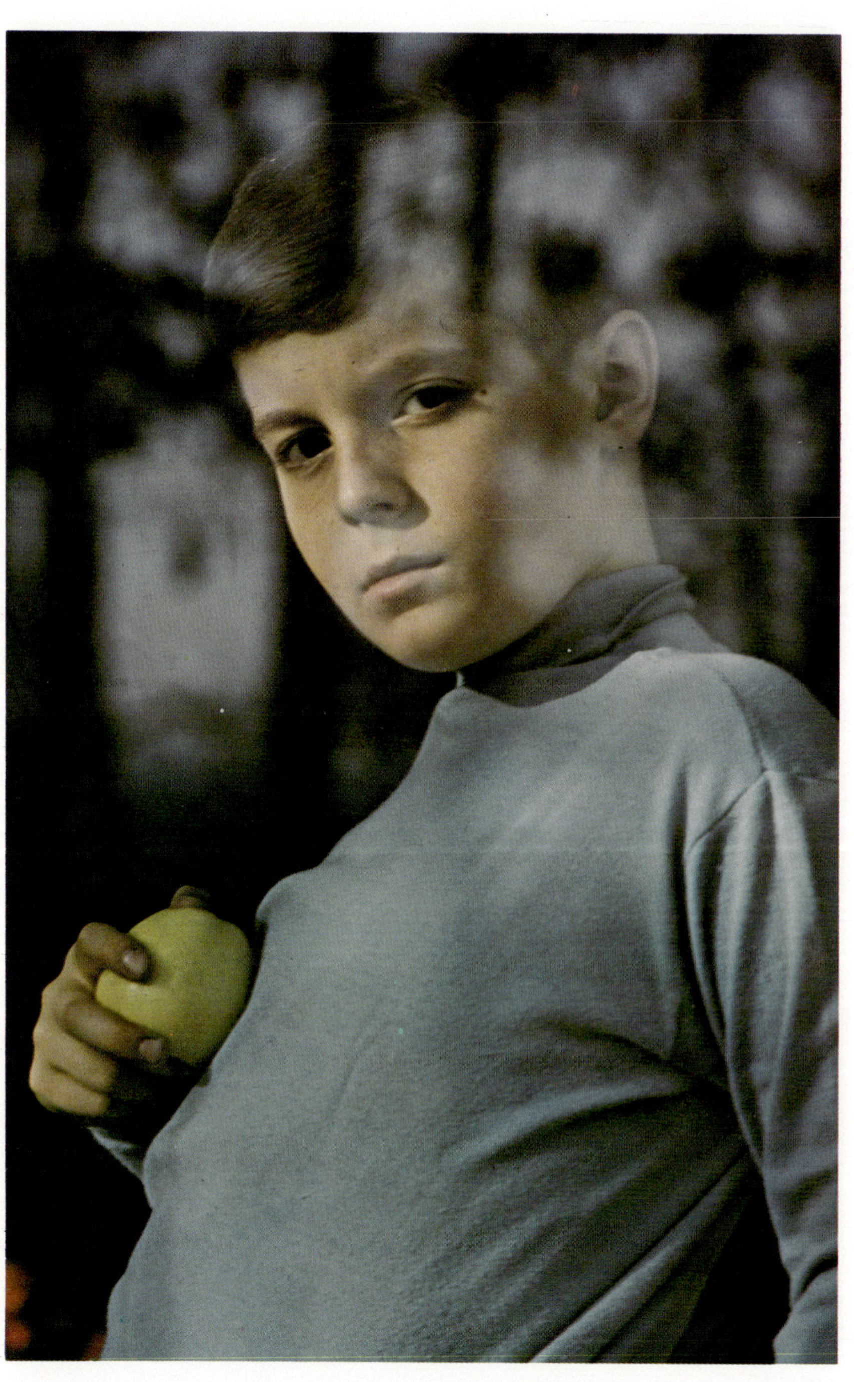

A young boy behind a windowpane. Nikon F, 135mm Nikkor Auto, 1/60 sec. at *f*/5.6 on Kodachrome 25.

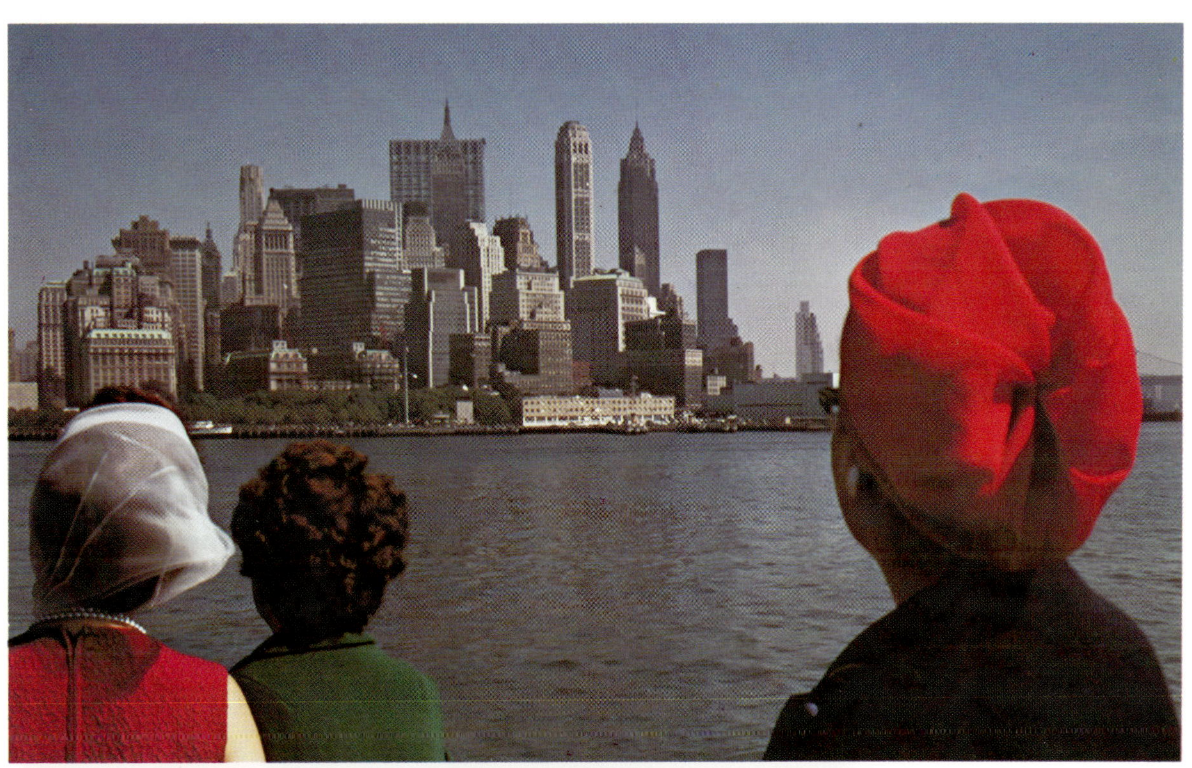

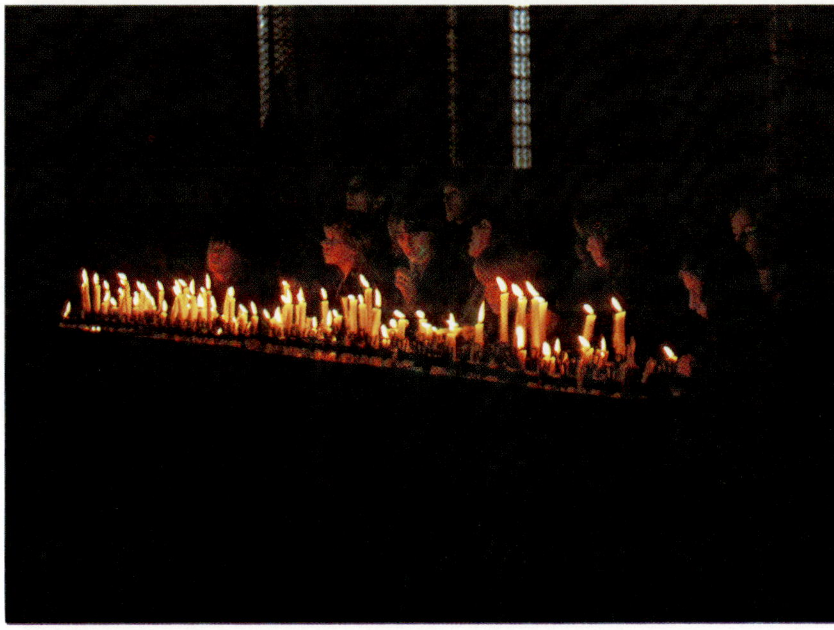

Above: Ferry ride. Nikon F, 50mm Nikkor Auto, 1/125 sec. at *f*/11 on Kodachrome.

Left: Candlelight service in Cologne Cathedral. Taken with Nikon F2, 50mm Nikkor Auto, 1/60 sec. at *f*/11 on Ektachrome.

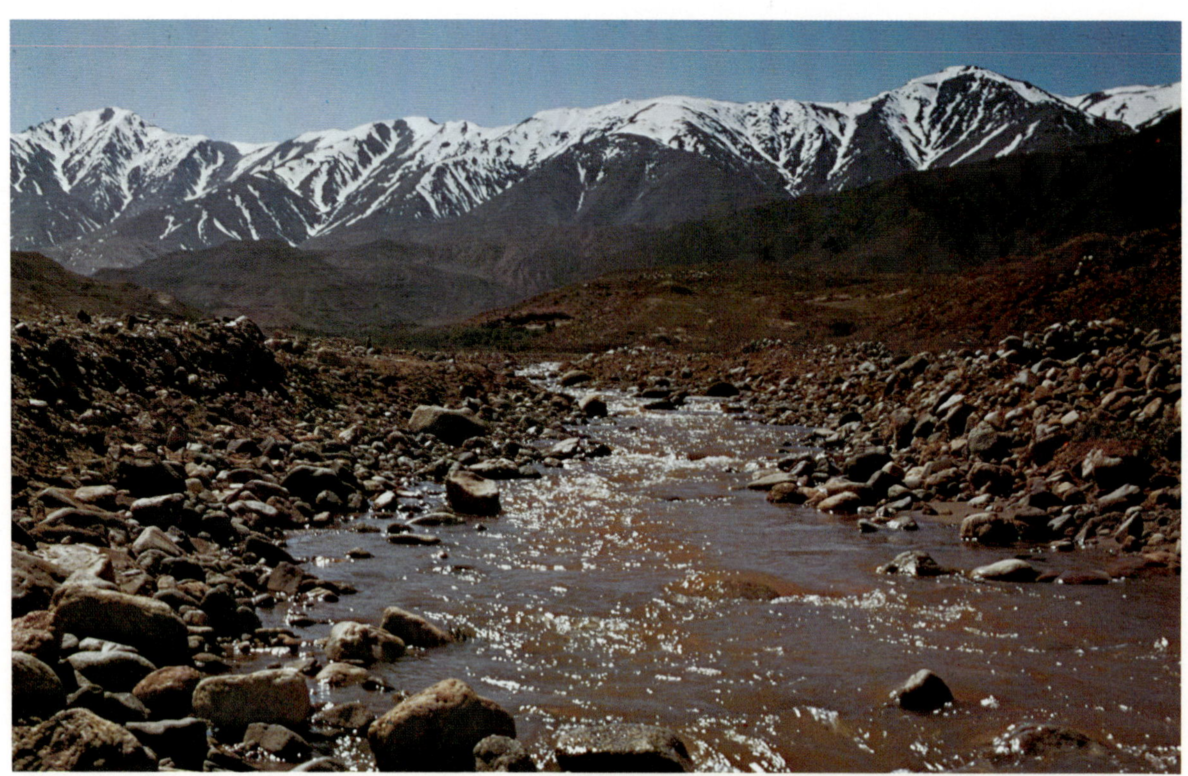

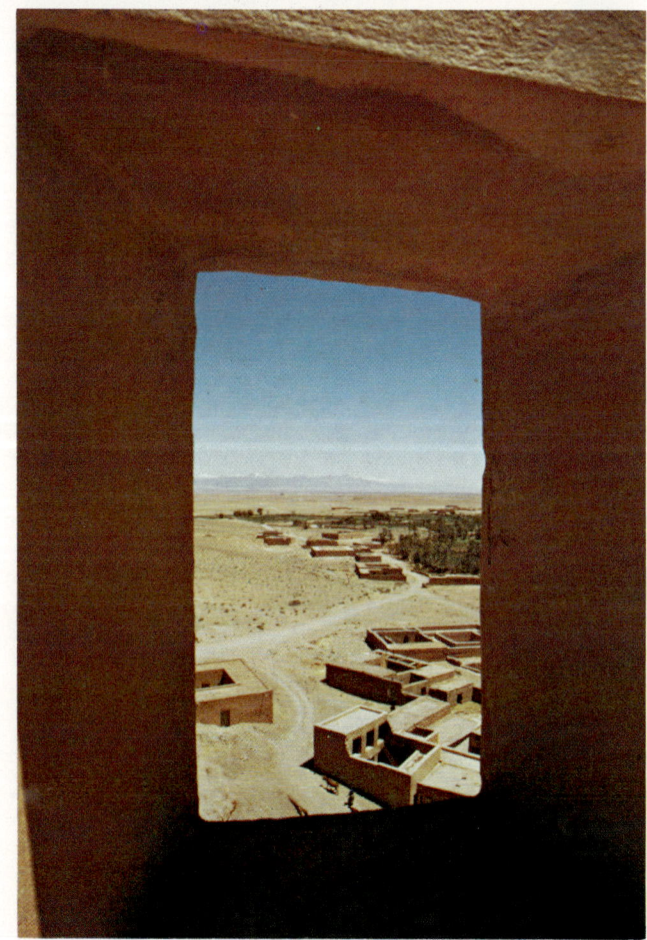

Above: Atlas Mountain Range, Morocco. Nikon F2, 135mm Nikkor Auto, 1/125 sec. at *f*/11 on Kodachrome 25.

Right: Where the Sahara starts. Nikon F2, 50mm Nikkor Auto, 1/500 sec. at *f*/11 on Kodachrome.

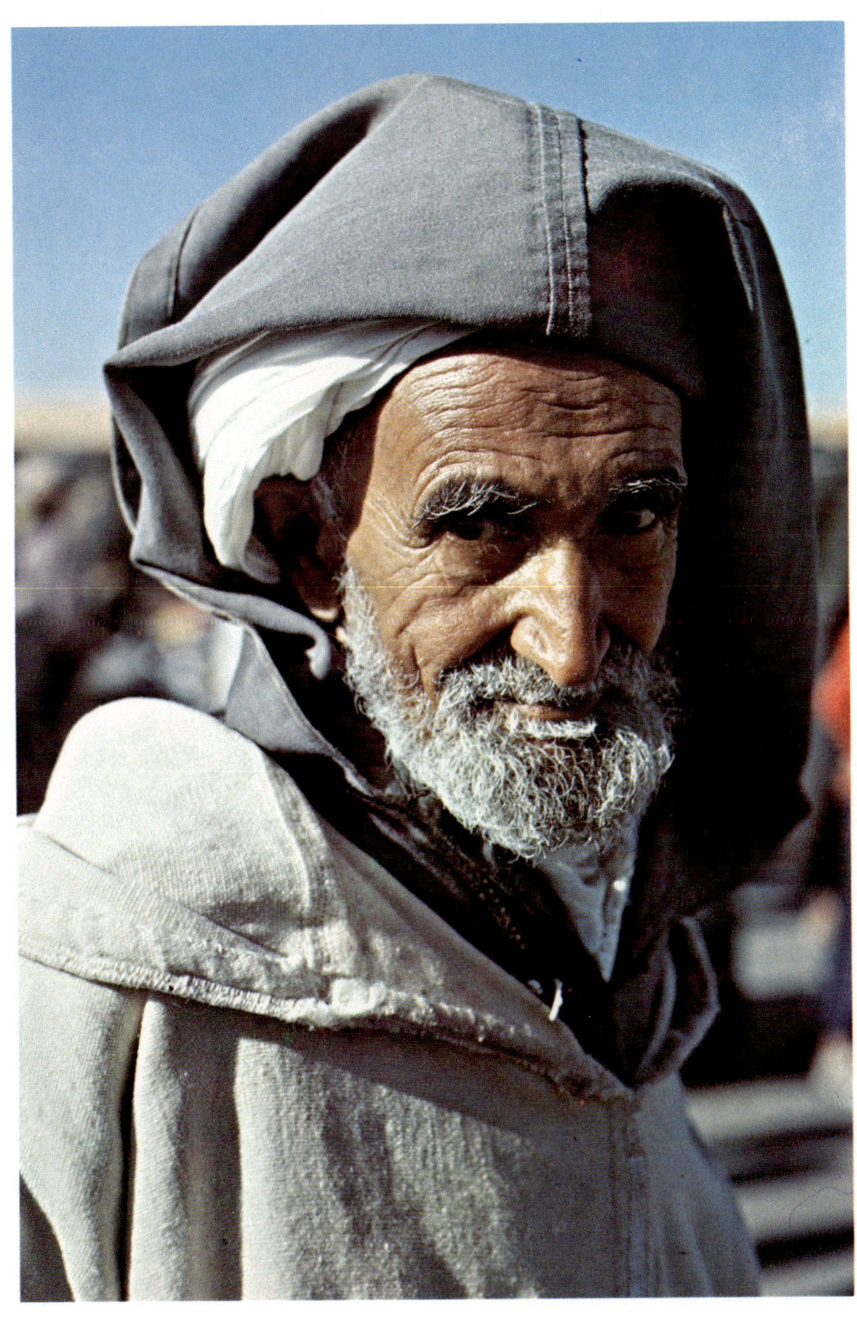

Old man in Marrakech, Morocco. Nikon F2, 135mm Nikkor Auto, 1/125 sec. at *f*/16 on Kodachrome.

Right: Verticals. Nikon FTN, 135mm Nikkor Auto, 1/125 sec. at *f*/11 on Kodachrome 25.

Far right: Signal at a crossing. Nikon FTN, 135mm Nikkor Auto, 1/125 sec. at *f*/16 on Ektachrome.

Bottom: Glider over Vermont countryside. Nikon F2, 135mm Nikkor Auto, 1/125 sec. at *f*/8 on Kodachrome 25.

Vermont farm. Nikon F2, 20mm Nikkor Auto, 1/250 sec. at *f*/8 on Kodachrome 25.

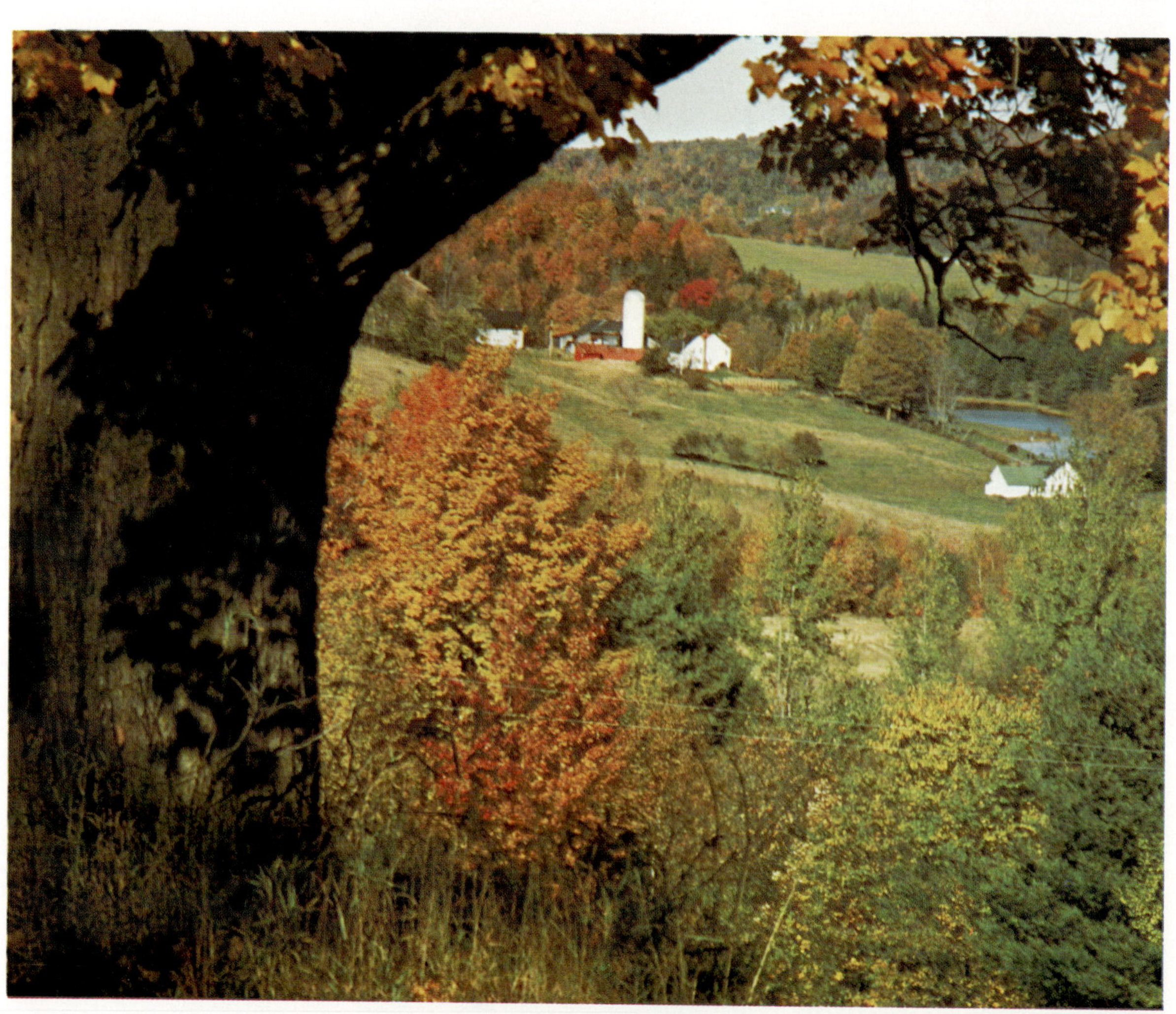

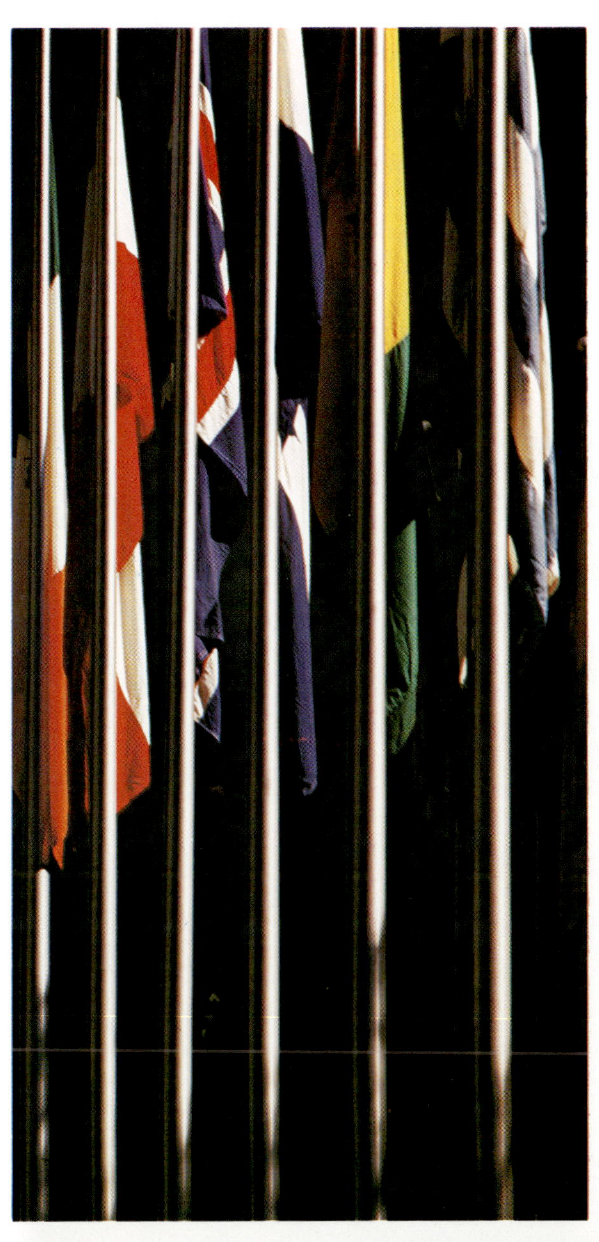
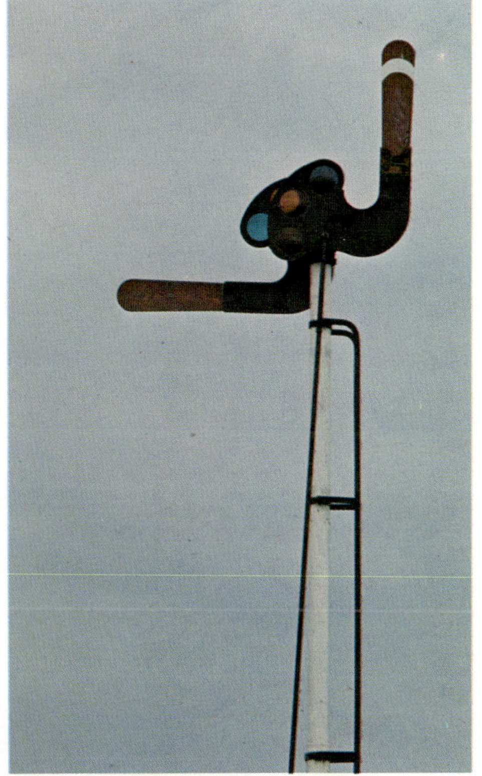
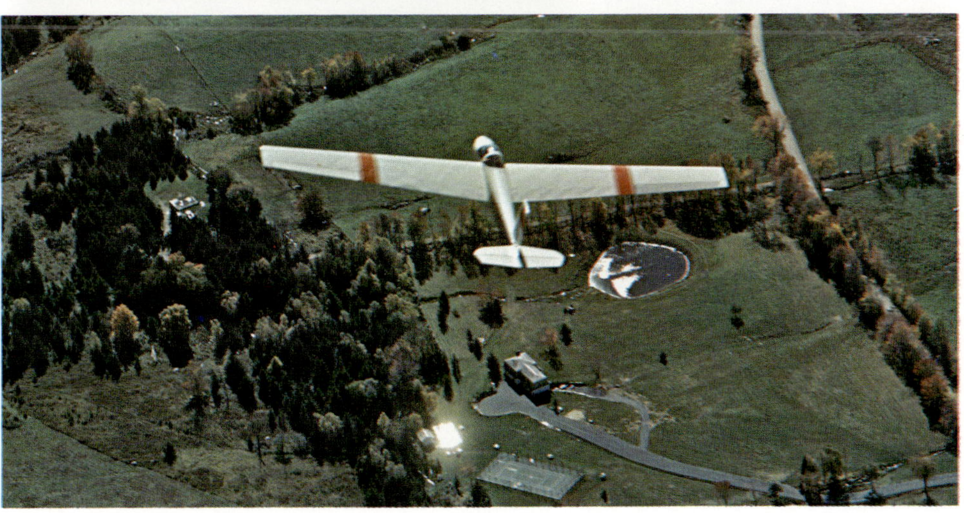

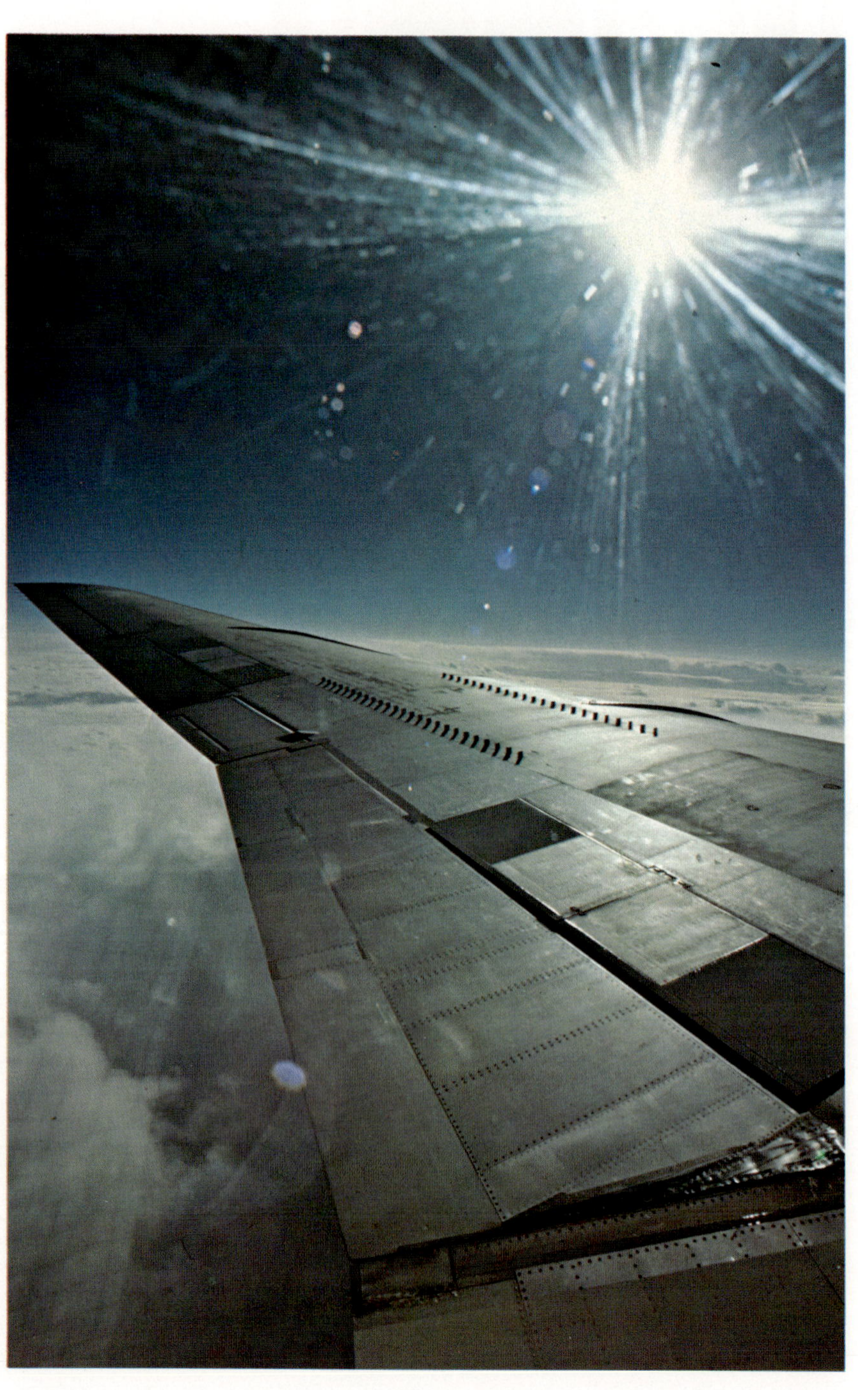

Over the Atlantic. Nikon F2, 20mm Nikkor Auto with UV filter, 1/250 sec. at *f*/8 on Kodachrome II.

4

LIGHT

As you sit back and start to read this page, light reflected from its surface carries letter images to your eyes. This light may be daylight radiated from the sun, or artificial light radiated from an electric light bulb or the flame of a candle. We take light for granted.

LIGHT THEORIES

It was in 1666 that Sir Isaac Newton (1642–1727) demonstrated to his contemporaries that with the aid of a glass prism, a beam of white light could be broken into a colored band resembling a rainbow, and that a second prism combined these colors to produce white light again. Many more experiments with light convinced Newton that white light was made up of tiny particles, and he announced his discovery as the corpuscular theory of light. Another contemporary of Newton's, the Dutch physicist Christian Huygens (1629–1695), observing that objects cast shadows whose edges are not sharp, formulated the wave theory of light. There were bitter arguments among scientists who believed in the corpuscular makeup of light and those who could only accept its wave nature.

By now scientists knew that sound waves needed air in which to travel. Defenders of the wave theory of light argued that the empty spaces between the stars had to be filled with a transparent medium to propagate light waves. They named this theoretical material "ether" and started a frantic search for experimental proof. None could be found.

In 1860, the English physicist James Clerk Maxwell (1831–1879) formulated the electromagnetic theory of light, pointing to an electrical nature of light. The breakthrough, however, came with the theory of light as suggested by the German physicist Max Planck (1858–1947). In 1900, he published his quantum theory, which states: "The amount of energy in a quantum depends on the length of the light wave, or the number of times it vibrates a second. Planck's theory combined those of Newton and Huygens, and today we think of light waves as being corpuscular in makeup but traveling in wave form.

The distance from crest to crest of a light wave is called its wavelength. The number of wave crests passing a fixed point in a given

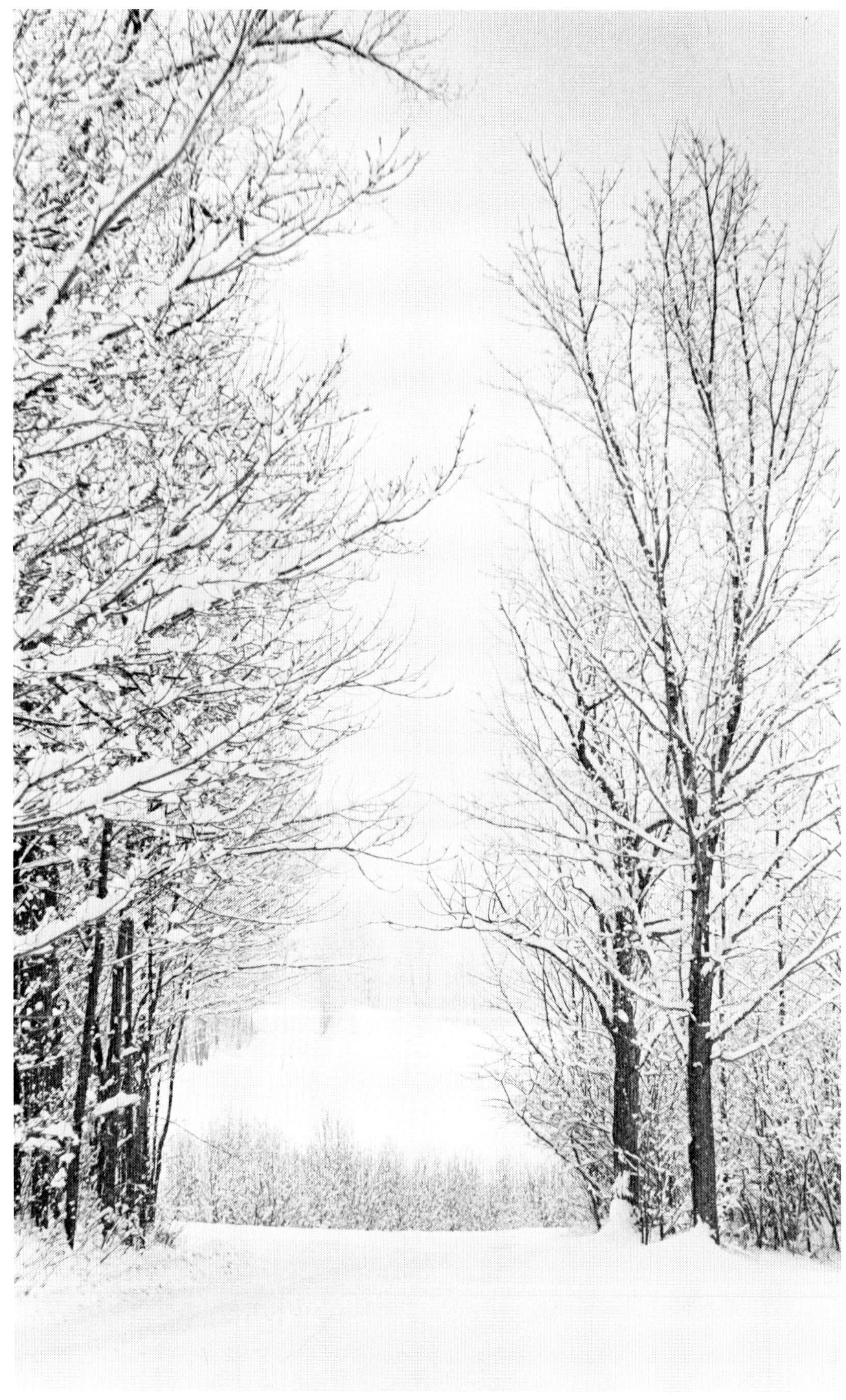

Opposite: This photograph was taken during a snow storm. Soft colors are well presented in black-and-white. Nikon F2, 135mm Nikkor, 1/60 sec. at *f*/11 on Tri-X.

time is the frequency. The light you perceive with your eyes is a very narrow band within the large band of electromagnetic radiation. Each wave band of light creates a different color sensation, but the combined light from 4000 to 7000 Ångström is perceived as white light. The following sentence will help you remember the order of colors in the visible spectrum: "**V**ery **B**ig **G**erman **Y**acht **R**aces." The first letters of these words, going from 4000 to 7000 Å, represent the colors violet, blue, green, yellow, and red.

In photography, we quote wavelength in Ångström units:

1 Ångström unit equals one ten-millionth of a millimeter

LIGHT AND PHOTOGRAPHY

Light, which travels to us at the great speed of 186,282 miles per second, is indispensable to photography and is the raw material of any visual communication. Light sends information from objects to the light-sensitive photographic emulsion, and it is again light that conveys the photographic record to the eyes. With certain photographic emulsions, man can extend the narrow vision of his eyes, and with the aid of modern telescopes, he can photograph deep into space. Where the electromagnetic band is of such wavelength that man cannot perceive it as visible light, a photographic record might still be possible. We can, for example, photograph in infrared, ultraviolet, and we can obtain X-rays.

The word "photography," literally "light drawing," comes from two Greek words (*Photos* = light, and *graphos* = drawing). In photography, you are able to record what you see by using the energy of the electromagnetic spectrum, but you must also be concerned with the matter aspect of light, for it is this property which enables you to create a photochemical effect. If light reacts with photographic emulsions, it is the quantum (also called photon) that strikes a silver-bromide or silver-chloride molecule and causes a latent image to be formed. (This phenomenon is treated separately in Chapter 9: "The Light-Sensitive Emulsion.")

It takes an enormous amount of practice and patience to be able to see in photographic terms, and you must understand that film is sensitive in different ways than the eyes. Film records objectively whereas the visual image created with the eyes is subject to manipulation by the brain. You must also learn to see light not only in quantitative but more importantly in qualitative terms if you are to make the most of its infinite potential.

Another characteristic of light that concerns the photographer, painter, sculptor, and architect alike is that it casts shadows. Through various shadings of light, volume and depth are perceived. Not only is the brightness range from shadow to highlight an important pictorial

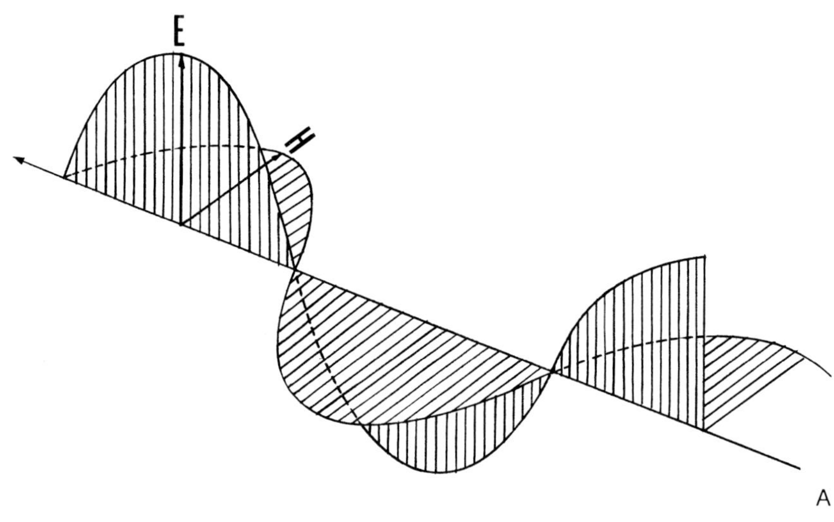

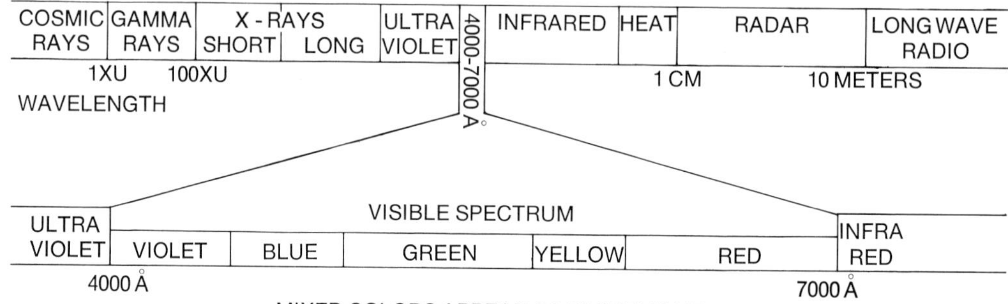

FIGURE 6

Figure 6A shows the characteristics of electromagnetic waves. Waves are transverse and electric and magnetic vectors are perpendicular to the direction of travel. Since the electric and magnetic vectors are mutually perpendicular, they are in phase. Looking in the direction of travel, E to H is clockwise. Figure 6B shows the electromagnetic spectrum. The small band of radiation from 4000 to 7000 Angstroms contains the colors of the visible spectrum. If these colors are mixed and perceived together, the sensation of white light is created.

factor, it is also a cue for the spatial orientation of an object—it can reveal its surface and texture.

Light brings many variations into our daily world. It changes with the time of the day, creating many moods, and it changes in intensity and quality with each season. Light also changes with geographic locations. For instance, the northern European light is very different from the light in the Italian Tuscan plains or the brilliant light of North Africa.

LIGHT VALUES

Light provides value. In the arts, value refers to the amount of light that is apparently reflected from a surface. Apparent value is a subjective experience and you can demonstrate how an area in a visual field is affected by its surrounding areas. Cover with two sheets of paper everything but the center bar of the accompanying illustration to see whether it is of uniform value. It appears darker if the bar borders a light area and lighter where it borders a dark area.

Effect of border value on apparent value. The value of the center bar is constant.

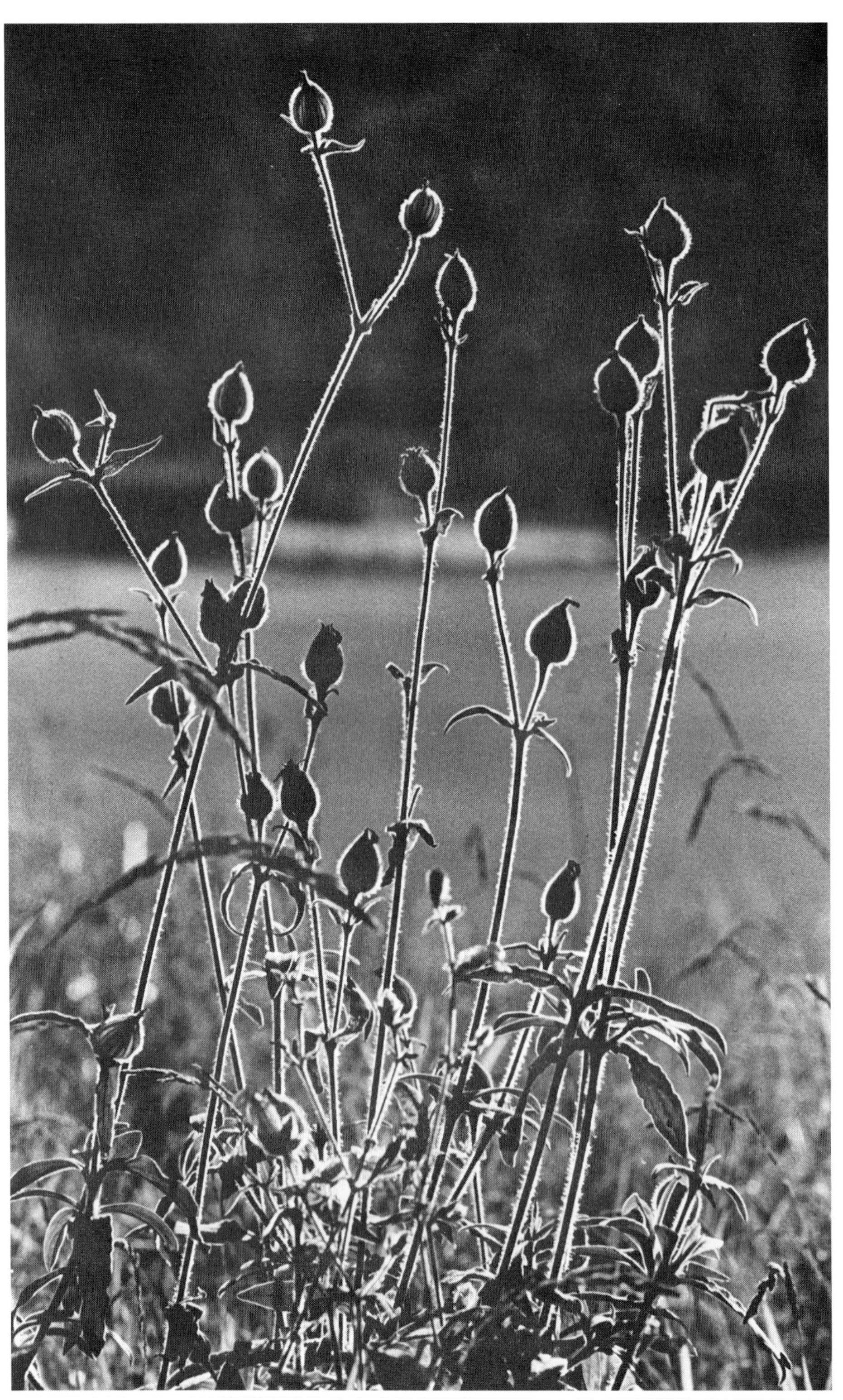

Sunglow. Shot in a meadow directly into the sun. Nikon F2, 135mm Nikkor, 1/1000 sec. at *f*/16 on Tri-X.

LIGHT SOURCES

With artificial lights, the photographer is faced with the organization of various lights into a hierarchy, assigning a dominant role to one light and subordinate roles to all others. If he fails to use this principle, cross-shadows will appear and the scene or portrait will look unnatural.

Available light conditions, indoors or out, can vary greatly. However, there is some degree of control. You can, for example, change your position and thereby change the direction of shadows. You can even wait until another time if lighting conditions are not suitable. If, however, it becomes necessary to photograph under noontime conditions, overhead sunlighting can be controlled through overexposure and later underdevelopment in the darkroom. The results will be lower contrast and open shadows.

In indoor situations, it is sometimes better to neglect all shadow detail. Completely black shadows here can be the compositional backbone, the structure necessary for a scene that concentrates on highlights only. In this case, you should take closeup light measurements. If it becomes necessary to photograph people against a window, a closeup light measurement becomes a must. Such a reading will permit normal exposure for faces. Most built-in camera meters are averaging meters and in such a situation would read the window brightness right, leaving everything else hopelessly underexposed.

OBSERVING LIGHT

From now on, force yourself to observe light and never be without your camera. Learn to see how light affects everything around you, whether you are indoors or out. Observe the small differences and how objects look at different times. Look at as many photographs, magazines, and films as you can and again study the effects of light in them. As you gain experience, try to previsualize the image you intend to capture and how the finished product will look in the darkroom. There is no such thing as bad and good light if you know how to handle it. With such know-how, you can make a picture at four o'clock in the morning or at midnight; you can take pictures in fog, snow, and rain. If you can discipline yourself to such an approach, you have made the first step toward communicating something new and perhaps better.

The experienced photographer has learned to see light almost as a tangible substance. If he works mostly in black-and-white, he has learned to translate the color of objects into a scale of gray tones. He can judge how the tone value of objects in our three-dimensional world will affect neighboring areas on the flat surface of a finished print. He sees

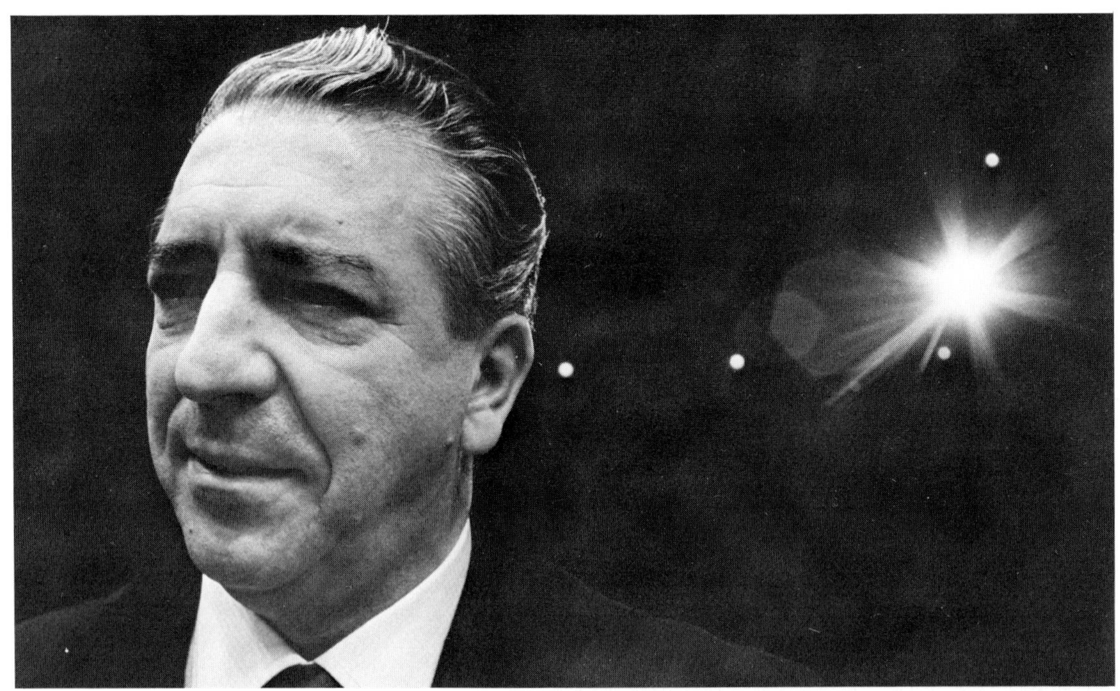

light as a constantly active force. If we marvel at the use of light by such painters as Masaccio (1401–1428) or Leonardo da Vinci (1452–1519), we know that the incredible illusion of space which they achieved was only possible through minute and constant observation of light. They became masters by directing light so that it would sometimes simultaneously reveal parts of a form and conceal others.

As I sit here, one of my pipes is on the desk next to me. When I stand up and move back, its shape reveals its form as a pipe. Its brown color blends with the wood grain of the desk. But as I bend back and forth in my chair, strong sidelighting from my desk lamp flattens or increases its volume and some reflections play over its surface. At one point, I am able to place the main shadow on the pipestem in such a way that I perceive maximum roundness. It also gives me maximum highlights from the side where the main illumination comes. Since my desk is also next to a white wall, I can observe a reflected light along the stem bounded by another minute dark shadow. From this position, the pipe separates itself from the background; it best displays itself. Many of my students show astonishment when I ask them to look at a certain object for several minutes, to walk around it, to even come back to it again. Learning to see in painterly and photographic terms is hard work.

What light reveals for you to see is not really optical fact; you learn from birth to organize what you perceive. Light and dark patches in your visual field are translated into pictures and aided by other senses. Walking toward a beach, for example, you may already see the ocean, but you hear the action of the waves, smell the salt in the air, and associate the sand on your feet with the location. If you make a picture of the same scene, you communicate these feelings with light only. Your statement has to be very strong, so strong in fact that your viewer can experience subconsciously what is now absent.

We take light and seeing so much for granted.

Opposite: Stage lighting. Nikon F, 35mm Nikkor, 1/60 sec. at *f*/5.6 on Tri-X.

Below left: Electronic flash from ten feet. Nikon F2,105mm Nikkor, *f*/22 on Tri-X.

Below right: Windowlight from one side. Nikon FTN, 135mm Nikkor, 1/60 sec. at *f*/11 on Tri-X.

Over: Music room with backlighting. Nikon F2, 20mm Nikkor, 1/60 sec. at *f*/8 on Tri-X.

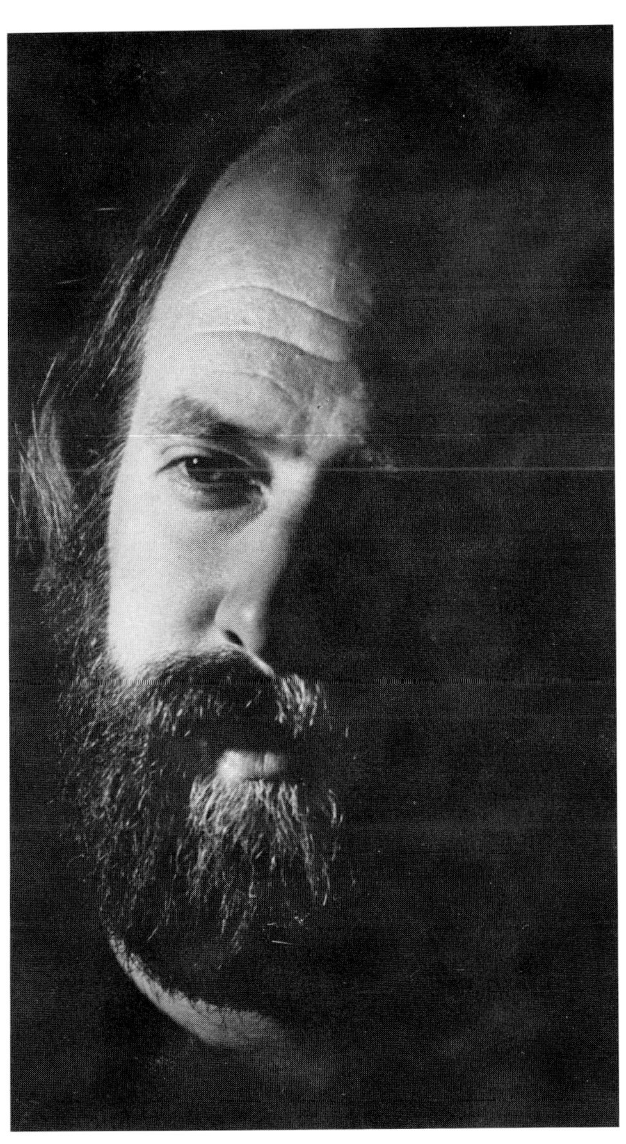

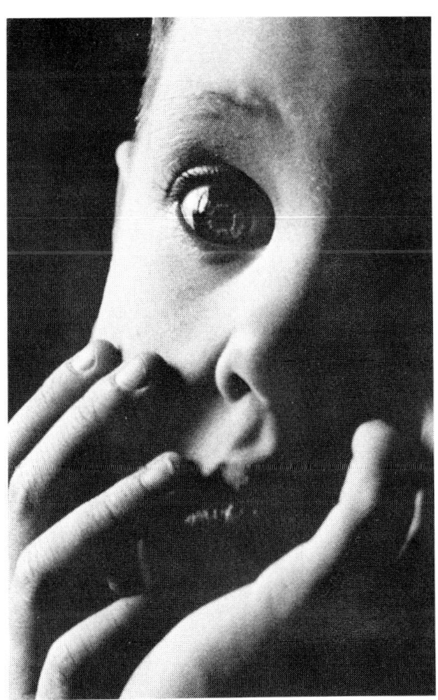

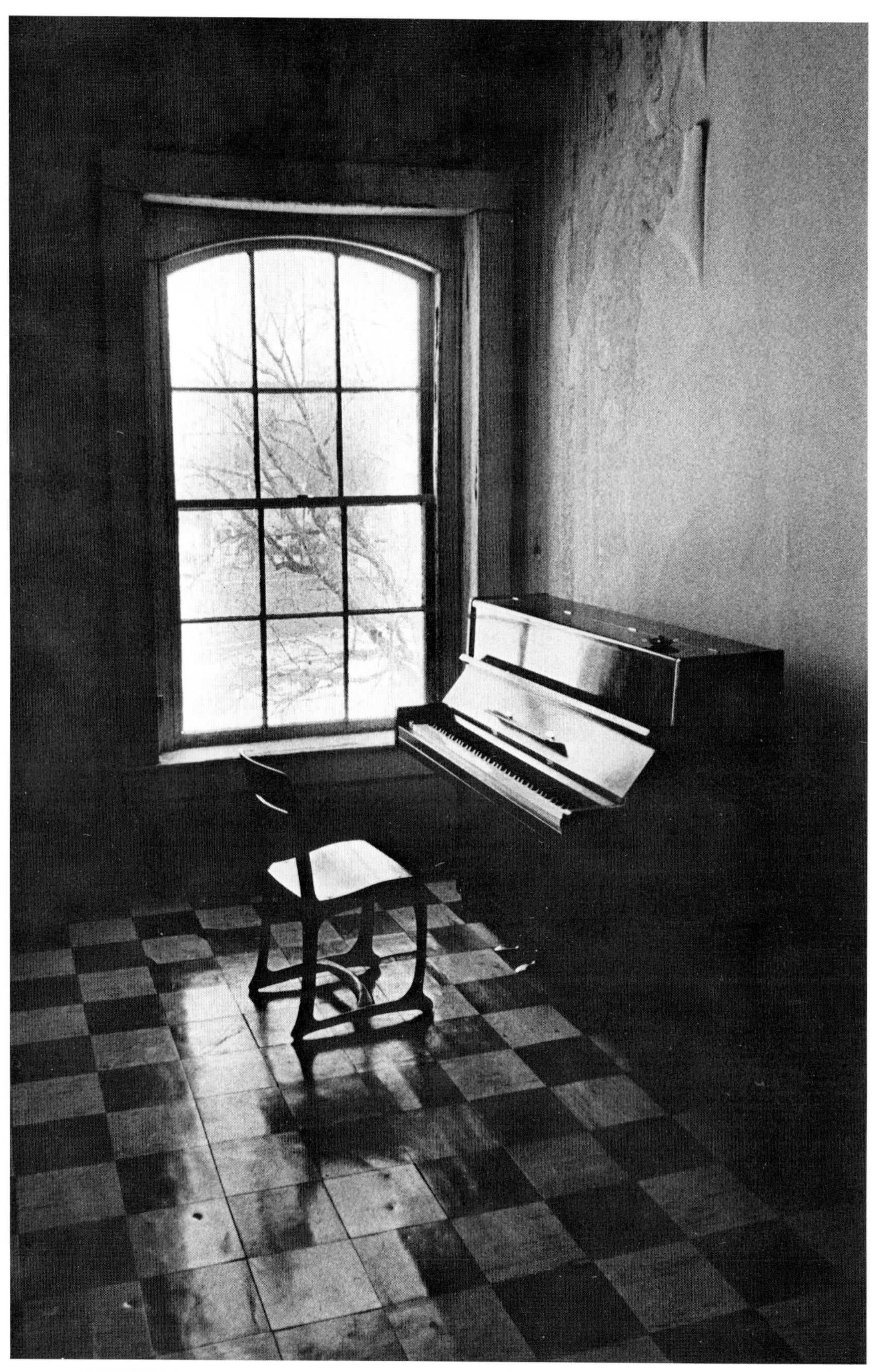

5

COLOR

Color is basic to all visual appearances. For the artist, it is a powerful tool to organize the picture plane. Color can be made to dominate or it can be subordinated to line and shape. With subtle gradation, it reveals form because it is inseparable from light. In art, the picture elements of balance, shape, form, and space call on the active mind in seeing, but color is perceived and interpreted by the passive mind.

To understand the role of color in art, you must be familiar with its three basic properties. These are:

Hue
Value (or lightness) and
Chroma (also called saturation)

HUE

Hue refers to the name of a color. Blue or red is a hue. Yellow, red, and blue are the primary colors of the painter; he can use these to create all others. Please note, I said "for the painter." For the photographer, the primary colors of light are blue, green, and red.

There are many systems for organizing these colors. The color wheel is well known and colors on it are arranged like the numerals on the face of a clock. Colors directly opposite on the color wheel are complementary, or secondary, colors. A primary color and a secondary color complement each other. Complementary colors mixed in equal amount by a painter produce black or at least dark gray. Colors that lie nearly opposite on the color wheel (yellow, red, and violet) are near-complementary, and colors that lie equal distances apart (yellow, red, and blue) form so-called triads. Artists even speak of tertiary colors—those formed by mixing secondary colors with each other. Since in color photography our shapes and forms are filled with hues, an understanding of the color wheel will help with the theories of color harmony.

VALUE

Black and white do not appear on the color wheel, but the amount of black or white present in a hue determines its value, or lightness. The American painter Albert H. Munsell (1858–1918) introduced the Mun-

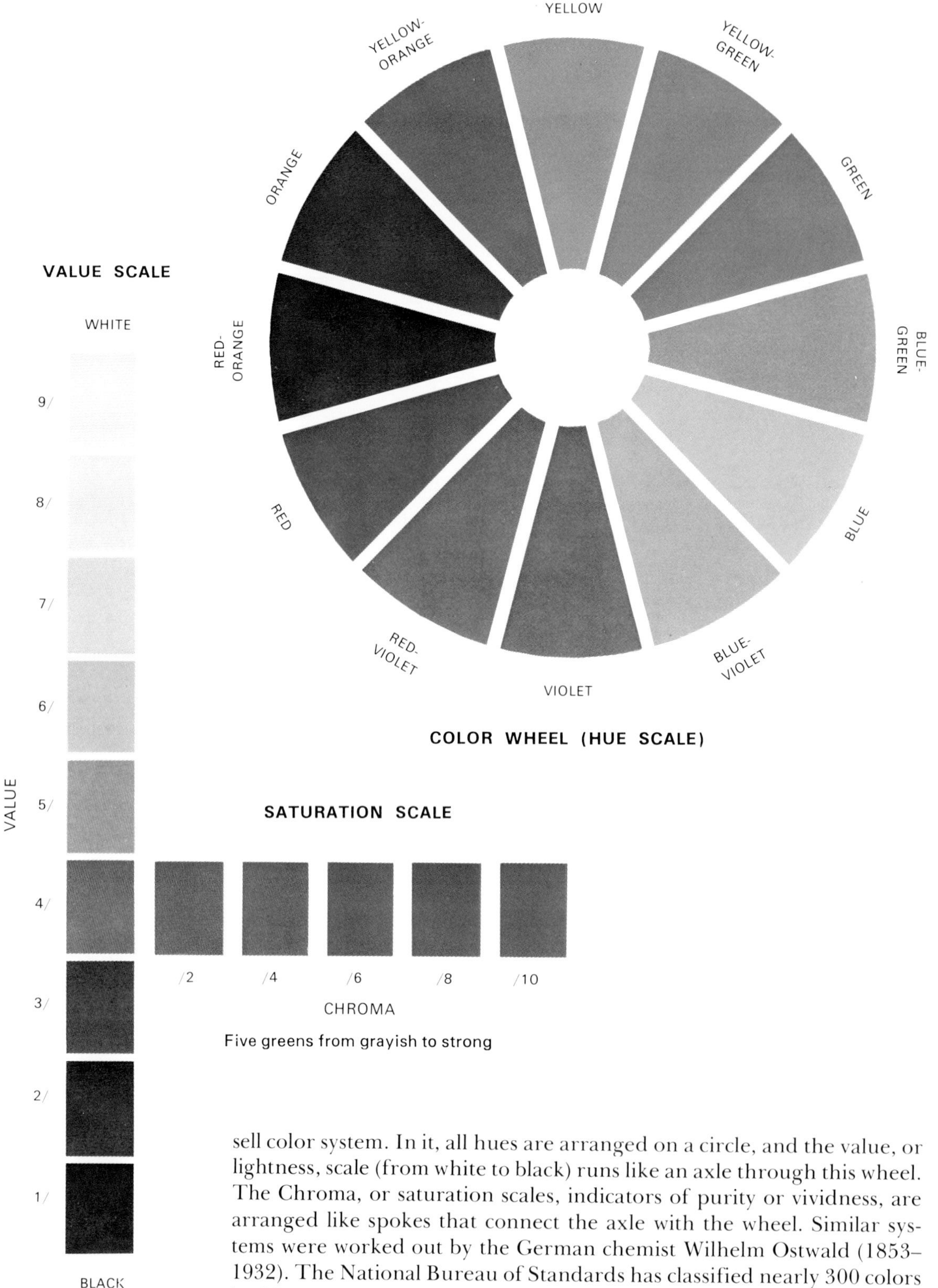

COLOR WHEEL (HUE SCALE)

SATURATION SCALE

Five greens from grayish to strong

sell color system. In it, all hues are arranged on a circle, and the value, or lightness, scale (from white to black) runs like an axle through this wheel. The Chroma, or saturation scales, indicators of purity or vividness, are arranged like spokes that connect the axle with the wheel. Similar systems were worked out by the German chemist Wilhelm Ostwald (1853–1932). The National Bureau of Standards has classified nearly 300 colors in this way.

The International Commission on Illumination, a French organization, uses still a different system. This system of color notation is international. In it, a horseshoe-shaped curve represents colors of the visible spectrum by their x and y coordinates. White, a mixture of all

Opposite: Illustrations from *Art in Context* by Jack A. Hobbs, published by Harcourt, Brace and Jovanovich.

spectral colors, has the chromaticity coordinates x 0.33 and y 0.33. A spectrophotometer can measure the reflectance (in the case of dyes and pigments) or, in the case of a light source, the energy radiated by it versus the wavelength. We can say: The value, or lightness, of a hue is the relative presence or absence of black. Value contrast, like hue contrast, differentiates objects from surrounding areas.

CHROMA

Chroma, also called saturation, refers to the purity of a hue and also to its intensity. It is the amount of hue in a color. There is, for example, a great amount of red in vermilion, but there is only a small amount of red in pink.

COLOR VISION

We take color so much for granted because we live in a world full of color. As soon as light reflected from an object reaches the retina of the eye, receptors are stimulated. Under a microscope, they can be seen to have differing shapes. One group of these cells is called rods, the other cones. The rods are very sensitive to light, and in dim light you see with them. They do not respond to color, and you can prove this to yourself. In a dim-lit room, the brightest red apple will only look gray. The cones, which take over in bright illumination, give you your color vision. If daylight enters a room, or if you provide *suitable artificial illumination,* the same apple will appear red.

I have stressed the phrase "suitable artificial illumination" for a reason. Now place another apple, this time a green one, next to the red, and observe what happens if the room illumination is changed to blue, green, or red light. Under blue illumination, the green apple and the red apple will look black. Under green illumination, the green apple will appear green, but the red one will look black. Under red illumination, the red apple looks red, but now the green apple looks black. You see colors in terms of light reflected from objects, and also in terms of the composition of the illuminating light source.

What you see as white light (daylight) is really a mixture of all the colors present within the narrow band of the electromagnetic spectrum called visible light. An object struck by light absorbs some colors of the spectrum and reflects others. The page of this book, the white paper, reflects all colors of the spectrum back to you and that is why you see it as white. The ink of the letters absorbs all colors and therefore appears black. The red apple seen in white light reflects the red portion of the spectrum and absorbs all other colors. This explains why you see such an object as red.

COLOR PERCEPTION

Psychological reaction to color stimuli is personal and subjective. We cannot produce tables and charts that measure the sensations of an observer. Color depends largely on the attitudes, feelings, and interpretations of an individual; it also depends on the specific color surroundings in which one color is seen in respect to another. For example, a blue on a green background will appear to differ from the same blue seen on a yellow background. Yellow seems to have more of a red content on a green background than the same yellow seen on white. Your eyes tend to become more sensitive to one color when you see its complementary color at the same time.

Other color perception facts cannot be explained readily. As early as 1838, the German psychologist Gustav T. Fechner (1801–1887) demonstrated a spinning white disk with imprinted black lines. Depending on the direction of rotation, the colors blue and red could be made to appear on the outside or on the inside of the disk. Some people are able to dream in color; others, blindfolded, can name colors by placing their fingertips on color samples, leading experts to assume that color perception is the result of the mind rather than the eyes.

Not much is known about the relationship of wavelength and light intensity to the receiving nervous system. Red is the most aggressive and advancing color, blue, the most passive and receding color. Green, the color between these two poles, is neutral and quieting. Whether this is due to association—where red equals heat, violence, and danger; blue equals coldness, ice, and tranquillity—or is a direct color influence on the nervous system is not clear. If red circles and blue circles are projected on a screen under low room illumination, the red circles appear to be nearer and seem to expand, while the blue ones appear farther away and seem to contract.

If you like to experiment seriously with color photography, going beyond the snapshot stage, more visual training is necessary. In the previous chapter, I have shown how important it is to see in terms of light, and earlier chapters discussed the visual elements that call for an active mind in structuring and organizing the picture plane.

Color perception adds an enjoyable aspect for the mind. Trained to see color in a certain way, tomatoes are always red and eggs are always white. However, you have to undergo some retraining because color film will record what is actually there, producing a bluish-looking egg instead of a white one if the light under which the picture was taken was actually bluish rather than white. You have to learn to see in terms of local color. You must become aware of how white cloth will appear bluish in diffused sunlight or in shadow; or how red it will become during sunset; or how yellow by the light of a candle. Color film will record skin tones with a greenish-blue tint if you photograph a person under the green leaves of a tree. Distorted color as a dramatic effect can be pleasing in certain situations and is accepted as normal if the tonal value of the entire scene is changed.

Color harmony is best achieved with a minimum of hues that fit together for a unified whole. Simplicity in a color composition helps the eyes to organize the picture surface more easily. Large numbers of color gradations within a key of only a few dominant hues is usually more successful than a multitude of various hues. Sunrise and sunset pictures might be a good starting point. They can be very dramatic because the lack of great detail is overcome by graphic simplicity.

Color photography can be objective and represent what you see in a given moment; it can also be subjective and picture anything the way your memory tells you it should be. There is no such thing as wrong color. There is only effective color, color that can stir the emotions, and color that symbolizes and sums up past experiences. It is exactly here that creative interpretative color photography has to start. Go out and break some rules. Find out how new effects can be created through careful observation.

USING COLOR

Color is a powerful force of the visual elements. To be able to use color in an artistic way, you must be prepared to study and understand the fundamentals and principles of color. As we have seen, color depends on light; that is, without light there can be no color.

This physical aspect of color can be measured, depending on the spectral composition of one light beam compared to another. Not every light source contains all the colors of white light. The eyes, with their color receptors, and the brain, with its interpretative function, will perceive color information quite different from physical measurement. Here, color is subject to feelings, attitudes, recollections, and associations; even the degree of perceptual variance from one observer to the next might be of importance.

Initial discussions with students about color theory reveal many misconceptions. In painting classes, the student learns that the painter needs three primary colors to mix all others. These are identified as yellow, red, and blue. Mixing these so-called "primaries" yields secondary colors such as orange (mix red and yellow), green (mix yellow and blue), and violet (mix blue and red). By mixing these newly gained colors with his primaries, the painter can go on to produce brown (mix orange with blue), and he can make gray by mixing red and green.

This works fine and is true, but the colors identified in your paint box as primaries were wrong. The blue most certainly was blue-green and should have been called cyan. The very fact that this blue can be mixed with yellow to make green confirms this suspicion. So for photography's sake, let's do some rethinking.

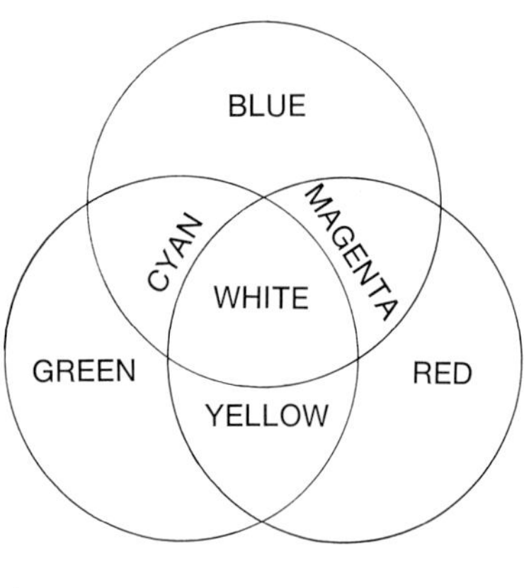

A COLOR BY ADDITION

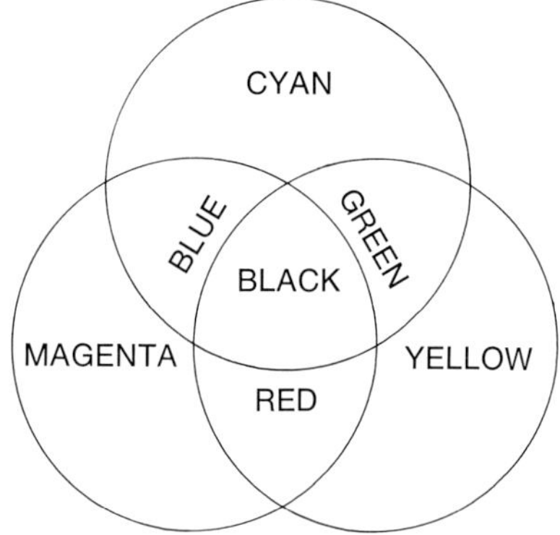

B COLOR BY SUBTRACTION

FIGURE 7

ADDITIVE AND SUBTRACTIVE COLOR

As long as 150 years ago, it was demonstrated that the visual appearance of color could be produced by appropriate mixtures of blue, green, and red light. You can demonstrate this by projecting blue, green, and red light beams onto a projection screen. If you arrange the projectors in such a way that their monochromatic light circles overlap, you can see the following: Where blue and red light beams overlap, the color magenta is created. An overlap of the green and blue beams creates the color cyan. But an overlap of the red and green beams creates the color yellow. In the center where all three light beams overlap, the original spectrum exists in the form of white light. Since you have recombined parts of the spectrum to form colors, such a system is called additive color mixture, or color by addition. This is one of the two basic ways to mix color. (See Figure 7A above.)

The other way involves subtracting parts of the spectrum from white light. Such a process is called subtractive color mixture, or color by subtraction. In the subtractive system, you use filters of cyan, magenta, and yellow dyes to absorb various amounts of red, green, and blue from the full spectrum of white light.

Let me now sum up: The primary colors in light are blue, green, and red, and mixed together they produce white light. Each of these primaries occupies nearly one third of the spectrum. They are not the primaries in your paint box. The blue primary of light is almost without green and the red primary of light is slightly orange. Their complementary colors are cyan, magenta, and yellow. (See Figure 7B above.)

ADDITIVE COLOR PHOTOGRAPHY

Early investigators of color photography pursued the additive route. Color photography was first demonstrated by James Clerk Maxwell (1831–1879). He used three pieces of black-and-white film and exposed one through a blue filter, one through a green filter, and the last piece of film through a red filter. Maxwell then made black-and-white positives from these negatives. These transparencies, each one projected with its original filter, were brought into register upon a screen. Maxwell therefore reconstructed the original spectrum in an additive way to reproduce the original scene in full color.

Later, other systems of additive color photography were introduced under such trade names as Lumière Autochrome, Dufay, and Finlay color. They had one advantage over Maxwell's first demonstration in that only one sheet of film was necessary because a microscopically thin layer of blue, green, and red starch dots took over the function of the three filters. During an exposure, these color patches acted as filters. A positive of such an image was really a mask held toward a light source in contact with its negative; only the color of the unmasked patches could be seen. (See section on "Color Film.")

Color television is an additive process. Turn your set on and, with a magnifying glass, look at an area of white in the picture. You will see tiny spots of blue, green, and red (the primaries of light), which add up in your eyes to give the impression of white. French Pointillist painters (Georges Seurat [1859–1891], the most famous) applied color in tiny spots of utmost purity and intensity so that an optical mix could be perceived by the viewer.

SUBTRACTIVE COLOR PHOTOGRAPHY

The principle of subtractive color mixture, or color by subtraction, forms the basis of all modern-day color photography. Light that is not reflected from a white surface has parts of its spectrum colors removed by absorption. The combination of the remaining light waves is the color you see in an object. In the case of the red apple, the reflected light is not the entire spectrum anymore; all the light waves toward the violet end have been absorbed. If you substitute cans filled with different colored paints, it is the chemical makeup of the paint that is responsible for absorbing certain parts of the spectrum and reflecting others. Color is a function of light; it is not a substance. Without light, there can be no color.

Let's go back to the primary colors of light—blue, green, and red. Any pair of these colors projected to overlap creates the complementary of the remaining primary. Suppose you want to know the complementary color of blue. Simply project the remaining two primaries (green and red) to overlap and produce yellow. Project red and blue to overlap and make magenta, the complementary of green. Project blue and green to overlap and make cyan, the complementary of red.

Some workers refer to these complementary colors as secondary colors, subtractive primaries, and even basic control colors. They all mean the same. But let me take you one step further. If overlapped and projected onto a screen, two complementary colors create a new one. If all three complementary colors are projected to overlap, all wavelengths are subtracted from white light to make black. Projected to overlap, cyan and magenta result in blue. Projected to overlap, magenta and yellow result in red. Projected to overlap, yellow and cyan result in green.

Subtractive color photography works on these principles. The three primary-color images have their silver portions substituted with dyes of yellow, magenta, and cyan. When viewed, these complementary colors of the primaries subtract from white light those parts of the spectrum which let the remaining colors recreate the colors of the original scene. (See section on "Color Film.")

The German chemist Rudolf Fischer (1881–1957) must be credited with the invention of the dye-coupling principle. Because of the difficulty in controlling the rate of dye absorption into the three layers of photographic material, Fischer's proposal to introduce so-called dye couplers in the three emulsion layers along with the sensitive silver opened new avenues for the manufacture of future color films. Great advances have been made since.

COLOR FILM

Color film consists of three layers of emulsion, each layer basically the same as in black-and-white film, but sensitive only to one third of the spectrum (blues, greens, or reds). Thus, when colored light exposes this film, the result is a multilayered black-and-white negative.

To make color transparencies, colored light is recorded as three superimposed black-and-white images in three layers of emulsion, each sensitive to blue, green, or red light. In the exposed film, light of each color produces an invisible latent image on the emulsion layer sensitive to it. Where there is black only, no emulsion is exposed; but where there is white, all three layers are exposed equally. During the first development of the film, each latent image is converted into a metallic silver negative image, and the density of the silver in each indicates the amount of primary color in the image.

Positive color images are created in the exposed film by the reversal process. Here the emulsion is exposed a second time, either by a flash of light or a chemical agent. Silver not previously deposited in the images is now deposited by a second development to form black-and-white positive images in the emulsion. As in the first development, the developer is oxidized as it converts the newly exposed silver to metallic silver. The oxidized developer then combines with chemical couplers to produce dyes, forming three positive color images combined with the metallic silver positive images. In each layer, the dye produced is the complement of the color of the light that was recorded there—yellow dye is formed in the blue-sensitive layer, magenta in the green-sensitive layer, and cyan in the red-sensitive layer.

A color transparency is produced by bleaching out all silver in the emulsion, which leaves only the positive color images in each layer. When a beam of white light is projected through these superimposed color images, each of the colors of the image is reproduced by the subtraction of the other colors from white light. To reproduce the blue in the image, for example, magenta and cyan dye images have been formed, but no yellow; the greens and reds of the beam of white light are subtracted by the magenta and cyan dyes, leaving blue. Varying mixtures of dyes in the transparency produce the whole range of colors of an image. In addition, black is produced where all the colors of white light are subtracted, and white where no color is subtracted by a dye.

The film that is used to make full-color paper prints works in essentially the same way as reversal film but with one important exception: It is processed into a negative rather than a positive of the subject—light areas show as dark areas, and colors appear as their complementary hues.

The negative color results because the dyes are formed during the first, rather than the second, development. During this development, a colored dye is combined with each black-and-white negative image. The dyes are cyan, magenta, and yellow—the complements of red, green, and blue. Once the silver is bleached out, the three layers show the subject in superimposed negative dye images. The color negative has an overall orange color or "mask" to compensate for distortions that would otherwise occur in printing.

After all silver has been bleached away, the negative color image is then printed on paper that has three emulsion layers like those in color film. Where there is a clear area in all negative layers, white light creates a latent image in each layer of the print emulsions. But where the negative has a yellow dye image, for example, only red and green light pass, exposing only the red- and green-sensitive layers in the print emulsion.

The print is developed by a process much like that used for the negative. Each layer of the exposed emulsion develops into a black-and-white silver image—a positive image—corresponding to one third of the spectrum. As the silver is deposited, dyes are formed—for example, magenta and cyan in the layers affected wherever green and red light passed through the negative. The result is three positive images, each consisting of dye plus silver. The silver is then bleached out, leaving the color images.

The colors that appear in a color print are those reflected back to the eye from the white light falling on the print. For example, a blue spot in the subject looks blue in the print because cyan and magenta dyes in the emulsion layers absorb red and green wavelengths from the incident white light, and only blue wavelengths are reflected. The full colors of the print are a product of the colors subtracted from white light by the three superimposed dye images.

CHOOSING COLOR FILM

The color photographer has a tremendous choice of film on today's market. Agfa, Fuji, GAF, and Kodak are the best-known brand names. The resultant color rendition of these materials usually determines the photographer's selection. However, color film must also be chosen for speed (ASA rating) to suit the task at hand. In bright sunlight, a slow film, which yields low grain, would be preferable; under low illumination levels, film with high speed would be the logical choice. Color film can also be pushed to higher ratings. For example, Kodak will process its High Speed Ektachrome, daylight (normally rated at ASA 160), at ASA 400 if a special processing mailer is purchased.

As you gain experience, you will learn to judge which film is best suited for a specific job. If you like snappy colors on a foggy or rainy day, Kodak Ektachrome-X might be best. If extreme sharpness, fine grain, and color rendition as the human eye perceives color are needed, a slow-speed film is best. If you need a more flexible approach and want slides, transparencies, and prints, color negative film is called for. This approach will also give you greater exposure latitude and these materials are generally more tolerant of the quality of illumination. Using color negative film, you can select Type S film for daylight and flash exposures with durations of 1/10 sec. and shorter, or you can select the special emulsion Type L for longer exposures.

COLOR FILM BALANCE

Another criterion in the photographer's choice of color film has to do with color balance. I must again emphasize that the human eye is a great compensating instrument. For example, a white linen sheet, whether illuminated by the bluishness of daylight or by types of artificial light that have a reddish or greenish tone, will be perceived by the eye as white because we *know* it is white. But color film, manufactured and color-balanced for a certain type of illumination, will record the actual color present. In other words, natural-appearing color rendition can be expected only if the type of light matches the type for which the color film is balanced, as follows:

Daylight color film is balanced for daylight and electronic flash.
Type B color film is balanced for 3200 K professional studio equipment or photolamps.
Type A color film is balanced for 3400 K photofloods.

Color film should therefore be used only with illumination conditions for which it was manufactured. Only then will the color rendition approximate the color seen. Type B color film used outdoors without correction filters will give very bluish results. Type A color film (daylight-balanced) will give very reddish results when used under artificial light.

COLOR TEMPERATURE

Lord William Thomson Kelvin (1824–1907) introduced the Kelvin scale as a measure of respective light sources. It shows how much a black-body radiator (which reflects no light) would have to be heated to emit light of the same color as the light source with which it is to be compared. The Kelvin scale expresses color temperature as degree Centigrade +273. The lower a light source is rated on this scale, the warmer or more red its composition. A blue sky without direct sunlight is rated between 11,000 and 13,000 K, while an ordinary household light bulb might rate as low as 2000 K.

LATITUDE

The exposure latitude of color films is lower than that of black-and-white photographic material. Where black-and-white emulsions might still yield usable results when over- or underexposed by two full *f*/stops, color film can only tolerate errors of half an *f*/stop. Because of the dramatic changes in color rendition, it is accepted practice among pros to *bracket* exposures on assignments. To bracket exposures, a shot is first taken at the indicated meter reading and then two more exposures are made at half-a-stop over and half-a-stop under the indicated reading. We accept color shift under certain circumstances, and indeed dramatic results can be achieved with altered colors—colors that are not renditions of the actual object. As a color photographer, you should experiment. Color equipment has reached very high technical levels, which should very much encourage home processing.

FILTERS

A good investment is the skylight filter. It will prevent excess bluishness when pictures are taken in the open shade, under overcast conditions, or at high altitudes. No exposure compensation is needed for this filter. A polarizing filter will darken blue skies dramatically and give stronger overall color. A magenta filter will remove the greenish cast that fluorescent light produces. Cameras that do not make through-the-lens exposure measurements must be adjusted for increased exposure according to the filter factor inscribed on the filter rim.

Winter night. On a clear night, the moon was shot with the 400mm Nikkor using the upper right corner of the frame at 1/125 sec. and *f*/11. The film was rewound, and early the next morning, several more frames were shot using the 35mm Nikkor at 1/60 sec. and *f*/8 to create this multiple-exposure effect.

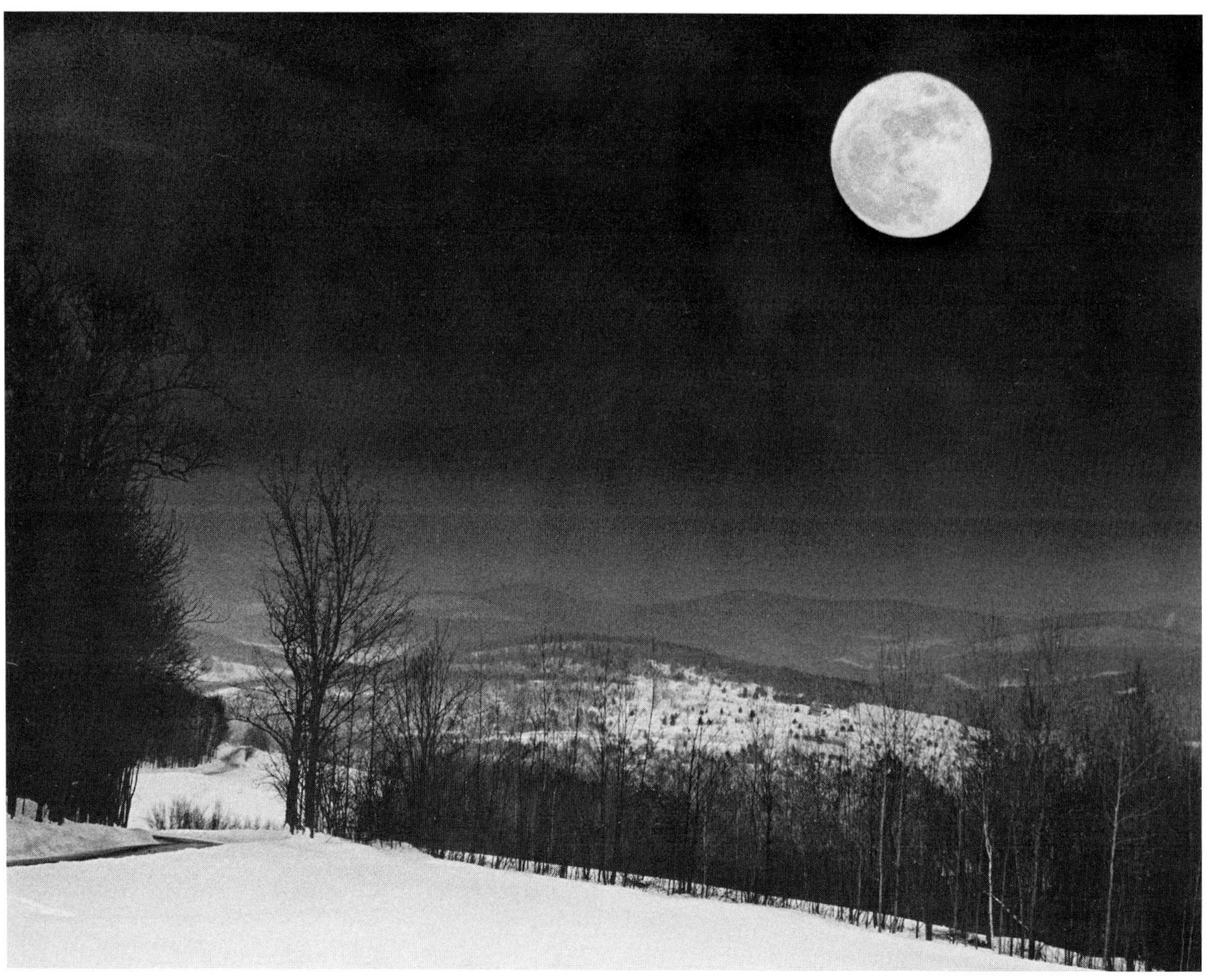

6

LENSES

Rather than speak of a lens as a single piece of glass, I shall discuss the compound lenses with which modern cameras are equipped. These lenses incorporate as many as 16 glass elements, usually both *positive* and *negative,* so that the negative elements correct unwanted lens defects, or *aberrations.* With cameras that allow us to change these lenses, you can increase the vocabulary of the photographic language.

A camera equipped with a 50mm (normal) lens will produce pictures that very much resemble the world as you and I see it. This is why we accept the resultant picture with its space and perspective as true and probably why we say: "The camera does not lie."

The human eye is more selective than the lens of a camera, which records every detail of the subject. Many students looking over their first attempts in photography will say: "I did not see it this way." That is because the eye was selective, extracting only a graphically important aspect of the scene, whereas the camera lens recorded everything within its field of view.

I have always maintained that photography is an art form and that the *creative* photographer can distort and produce a visual statement that does not conform to reality. Like the painter who interprets reality in his own fashion on his canvas, the creative photographer's final picture is not a mere copy of the world around him. So it is necessary to accept, from the beginning, the fact that a photograph always differs from the object depicted.

A vast array of lenses with varying focal lengths allows you to explore aspects of a subject otherwise not immediately communicable to others. They allow you to emphasize or de-emphasize, and you can distort for expressive gains. There are no set rules.

NORMAL LENSES

I mentioned the 50mm lens as the accepted normal lens. This is true only in 35mm photography as larger-format cameras have their own normal focal lengths.

In 35mm photography, there is a range of choices from 6mm to 2000mm. A slightly wide-angle lens, such as a 35mm focal length, and a slightly telephoto lens, such as an 85mm, will still produce pictures that are accepted as normal. Any lens shorter or longer in focal length will become truly wide-angle or truly telephoto and will render perspective in an unaccustomed way. The angle of coverage is what creates these different effects since the perspective is always the same regardless of the focal length of the lens. A 6mm fisheye lens has, for example, an angle of coverage as wide as 220° and will produce a circular picture. A telephoto lens with a focal length of 1200mm has an angle of coverage as narrow as 2°. These are extremes. That perspective is generally unchanged can be demonstrated by enlarging a negative taken with a short-focus lens. If this image is enlarged to the precise field of view produced by a telephoto lens, the pictures will be identical as far as perspective rendering is concerned.

TELEPHOTO LENSES

A telephoto lens compresses space and shortens distances in the direction in which it is pointed and there is a certain image flatness. Telephoto lenses also have a shallower depth of field, and an object is more easily isolated with precise focus. The inexperienced photographer should not try to shoot handheld pictures with lenses of 200mm or longer and shutter speeds below 1/250 sec., because with such a telephoto lens and slower speeds, camera movement is greatly exaggerated.

WIDE-ANGLE LENSES

The wide-angle lens is the opposite of the telephoto. Because its picture angle is great, the photographer can move in closer and cover cramped quarters. Focusing a wide-angle lens is not very critical because of its great depth of field. Image distortion grows as focal length diminishes.

Because of the apparent space exaggeration, such lenses are used in architectural work and in advertising campaigns. Some of these wide-angle lenses have perspective controls built into them. If a low viewpoint is chosen and camera and lens have to be tilted up, the resultant convergence of lines in the vertical is not easy to accept. By correcting perspectively, you actually falsify the laws of perspective. According to these laws, a low vantage point necessitates a third vanishing point and there should be convergence in pyramid fashion. The great Italian Renaissance painter Andrea Mantegna (1431–1506) left out the third vanishing point in his painting of "St. James led to Martyrdom." He chose a very low viewpoint and rendered all building lines vertical and parallel. A large foreground figure holding a flagstaff diagonally com-

Below: Early morning. Nikon FTN, a telephoto lens, the 200mm Nikkor, 1/125 sec. at *f*/16 on Tri-X. Bottom: Nikon F, a wide-angle lens, the 35mm Nikkor, 1/60 sec. at *f*/8 on Tri-X.

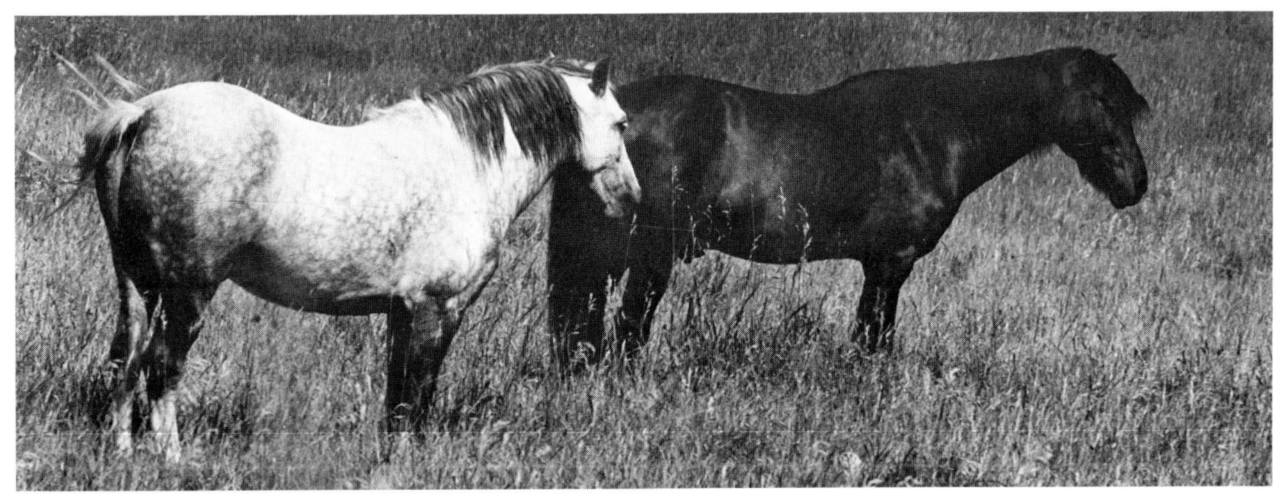

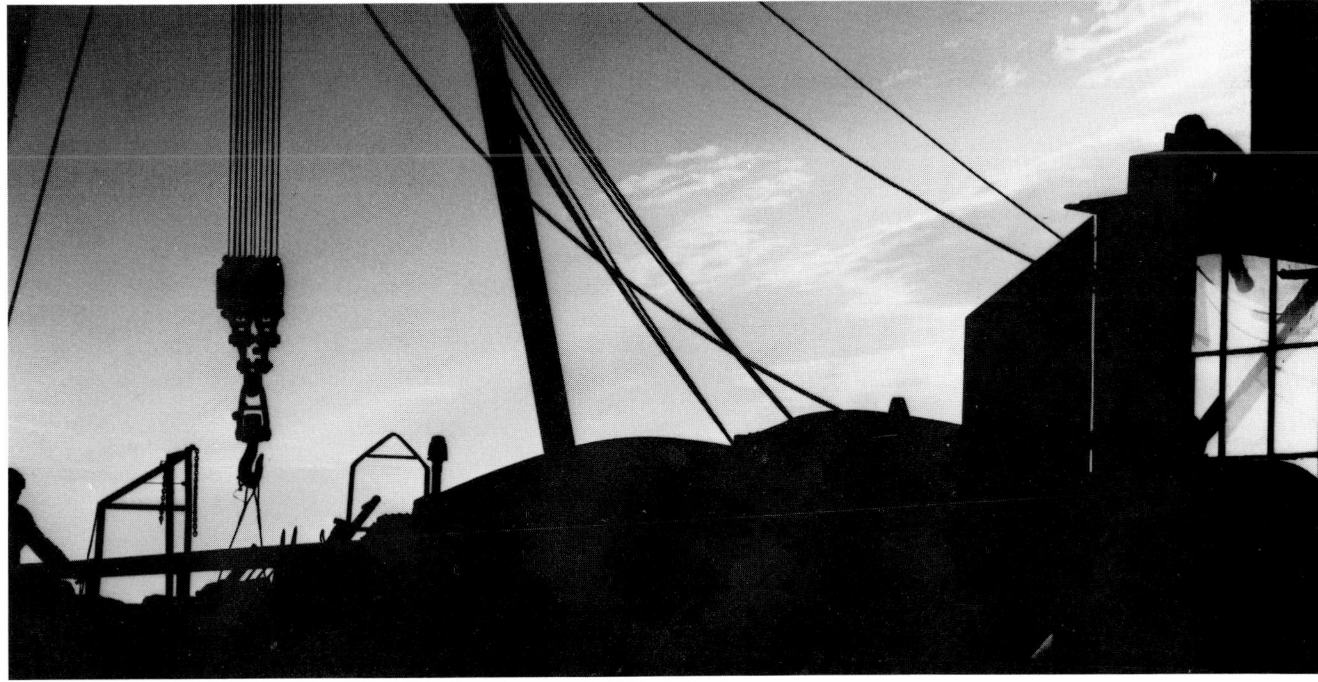

pensates the lack of perspective for the eye. His picture elements are thus unified and related to the picture's boundaries.

FISHEYE LENSES

It is somewhat harder to comprehend perspectives created by the so-called "fisheye" lens, because with such lenses, all the rules are broken and distortion runs rampant. Fisheye lenses are characterized by their extremely short focal length, extremely wide angle of view, great depth of field, and very short minimum focusing distance.

CHOOSING A LENS

I am constantly asked to give advice on the purchasing of lenses. A student will ask me which lens he should buy first and which should be his next lens or lenses. I always advise my students to start with a 35mm focal length. Such a lens, I feel, has many advantages. After some experimentation, it will give results that look very much like those produced with the 50mm normal lens. Its advantages include closeup focusing (slightly less than one foot), enabling you to work in cramped quarters where it is impossible to back up further. The next lens purchased should be a 135mm focal length. This telephoto lens brings sports action close enough and it also permits fine portrait photography.

I often recommend that a student go out with a lens of a certain focal length and try to shoot everything with that lens alone for a day or two. One day it might be a 300mm lens, and the next day a 20mm lens. The results might range from excellent to poor, but this technique will not only teach you to handle a lens, it will also show you how a familiar subject can be rendered in ways you have not seen before. You will learn to extract the visual importance, give objects a new perspective, and manipulate new relationships.

Most lenses today have their *f*/stops color coded and show on the distance scale exactly the depth of field for a certain distance setting in combination with the *f*/stop selected. Many photojournalists prefocus a camera. Reading their scales, they know in advance in which range sharp focus can be expected. In this way, they can rapid-fire shots without time-consuming focusing.

LENS ABERRATIONS

Once the decision is made to use a particular lens, there are a number of factors you should be aware of in order to get the optimum performance out of the selected lens.

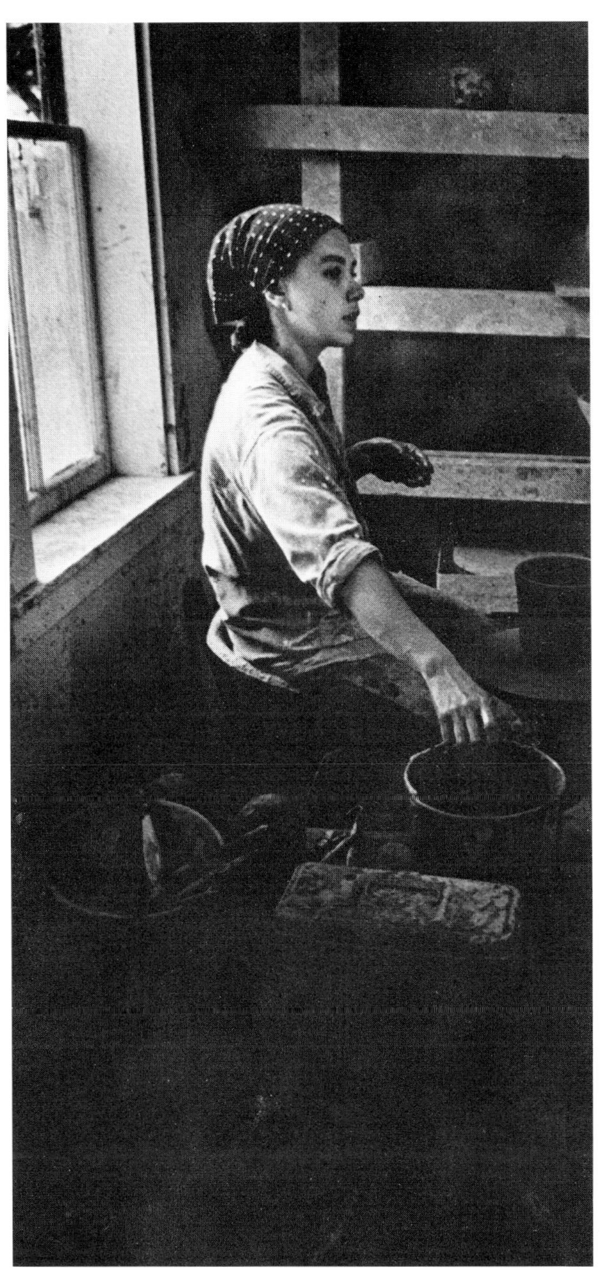

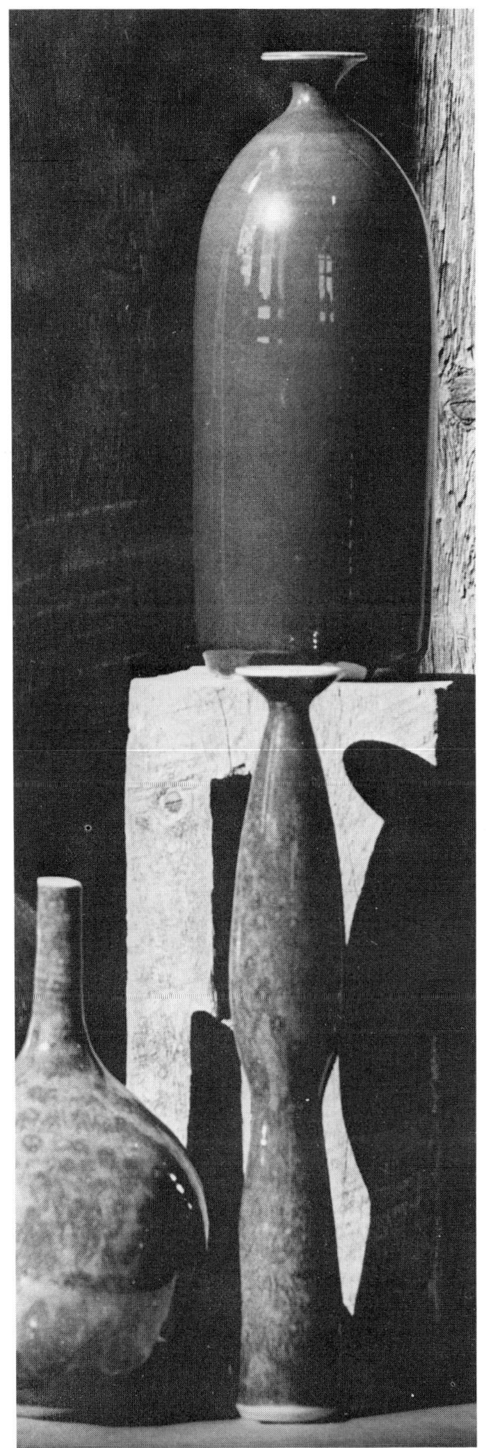

Above left: Nikon F2, 35mm Nikkor, 1/60 sec. at *f*/5.6 on Tri-X.

Above right: Nikon F2, 135mm Nikkor, 1/125 sec. at *f*/11 on Tri-X.

Nikon F, 135mm Nikkor, 1/1000 sec. at *f*/11 on Tri-X.

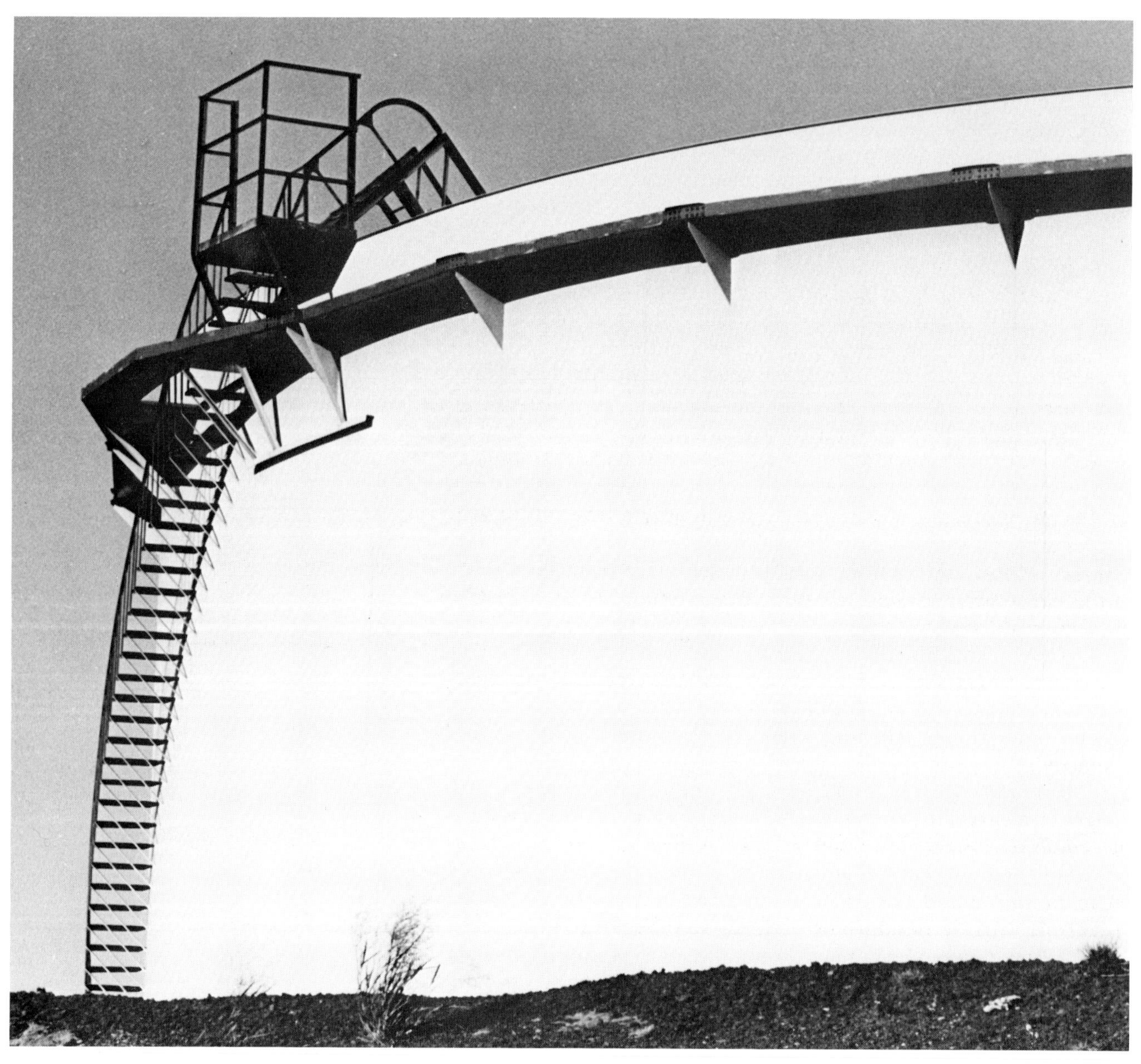

Axial Chromatic Aberration. This is the failure of the lens to bring light rays of different wavelengths to a common focus. Since white light is the product of the various colors of the spectrum, and since each color has its own wavelength, they form differing angles when they leave the lens to form an image on the sensitive film material. Violet will form the most acute angle and red will form an angle less acute. This is of no great importance when we use black-and-white film, but is a critical factor in color photography. Lenses must be highly corrected for chromatic aberration and this is usually accomplished by using various types of glass, including crown glass and flint glass.

Spherical Aberration. This refers to the way in which light rays entering the central portion of a lens fail to meet rays entering the outer portions of a lens in the same focal point. A haze of light that seems to overlay an image is the typical effect of spherical aberration.

Astigmatism. This is a by-product of spherical aberration. It means that a vertical and a horizontal line cannot be brought to focus at the same time on a flat surface. Lens designers overcome this fault by using rare-earth glass and spacing the elements in a lens group slightly apart.

Distortion. This is also a by-product of spherical aberration and simply refers to the inability of a lens to project a square figure with straight outside lines. The placement of a diaphragm is important in solving the problem of distortion. A diaphragm in front of the lens will render a barrel-shape figure (the sides of the square bulge out); a diaphragm behind the lens will render the square as a pincushion (the sides of the figure become concave). But a diaphragm placed in between lens elements reduces this problem.

Coma. This is a spherical aberration in which the image of a point source is a comet-shaped blur. In other words, all points of light that have to travel through the edges of a lens to form an image will not form a point but rather a teardrop shape of light because they travel very obliquely.

Curvature of Field. Since lenses are spherical in shape, they form images on a curved field. If a lens suffering from curvature is used with a flat emulsion, image definition will deteriorate steadily away from the center of the field. For example, a wheel rim in sharp focus would not mean the spokes and axle could be rendered sharp at the same time. For exact copy work, lenses must be designed to have a flat field.

Internal Flare. Light bounces around on the inside of the lens barrel, reflected from numerous lens elements. This causes ghosting or light areas on the finished print. Coated lenses and sunshades (lens hoods) on your lenses will eliminate this problem.

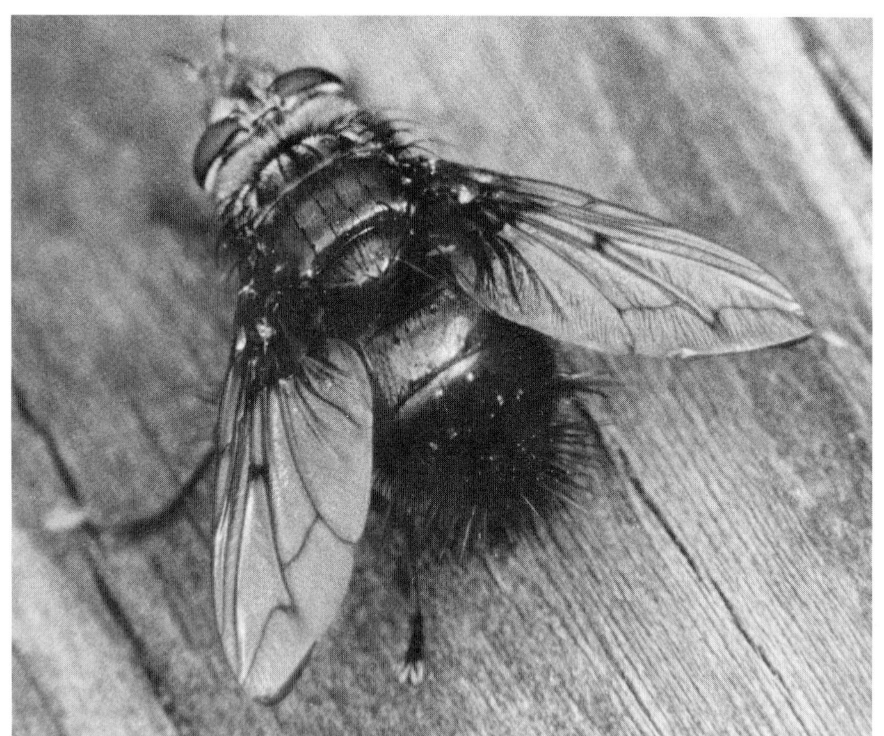

The author likes to shoot closeups in the following manner: A Nikon F2 is equipped with the Nikon bellows and the 200mm Nikkor is mounted. Metering is by the stop-down method. This setup allows a comfortable working distance from the object. The spider and fly in the two photographs are about three times magnified. 1/125 sec. at *f*/5.6 on Tri-X.

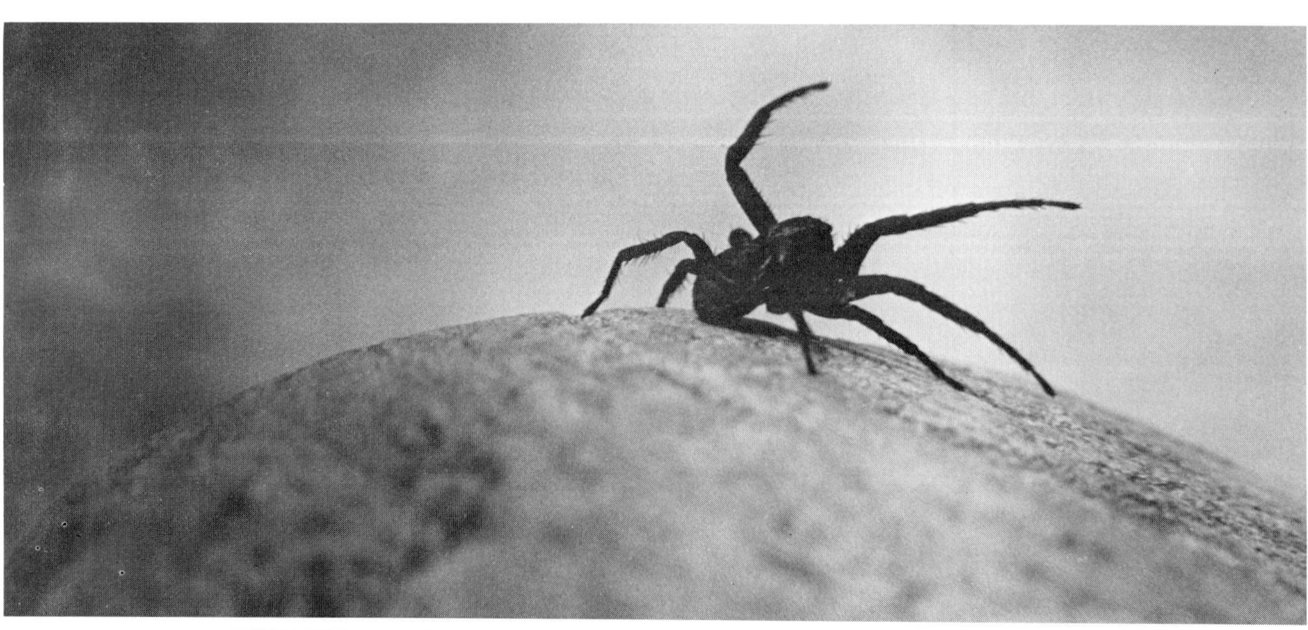

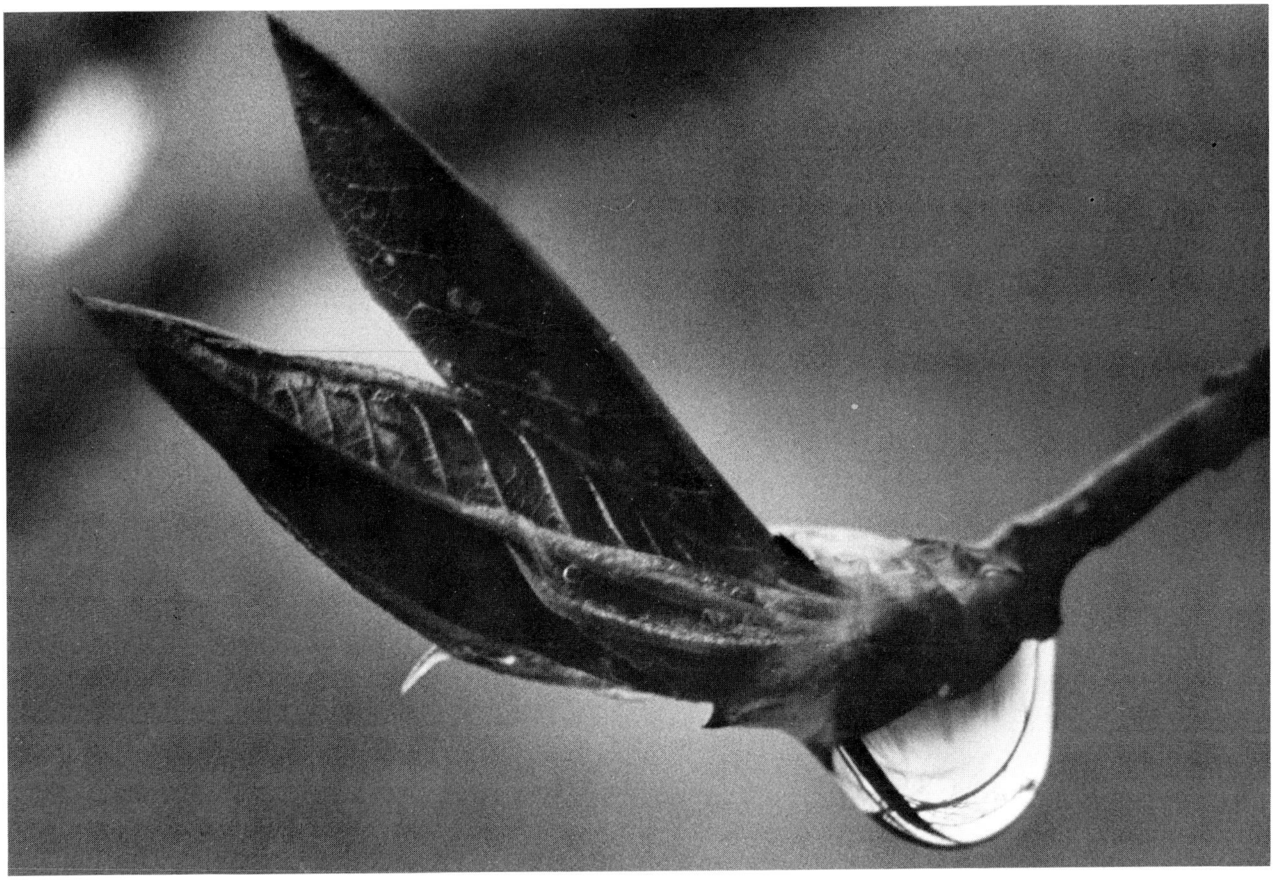

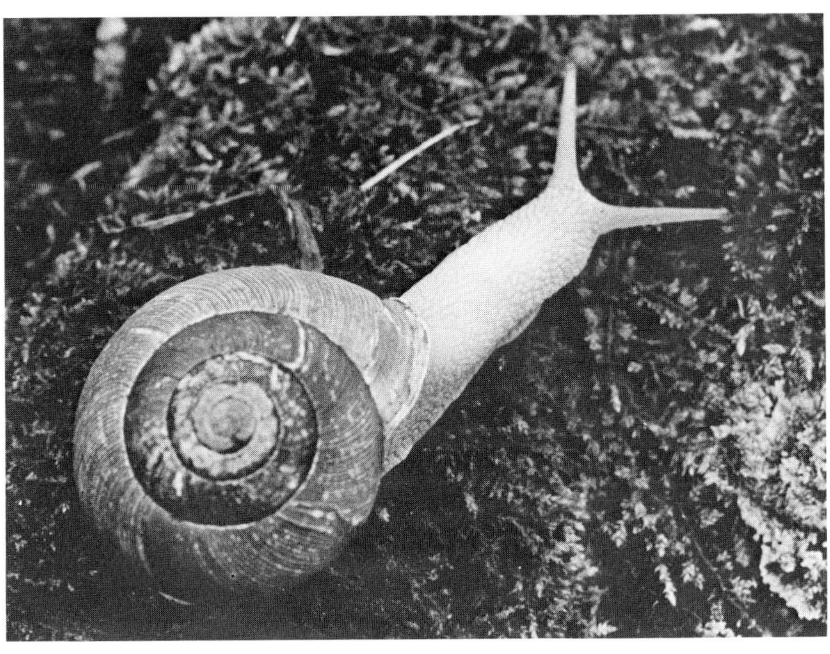

Above: During the rain. NikonF2, bellows focusing attachment PB-4 with 200mm Nikkor, 1/125 sec. at *f*/8 (stop-down metering) on Tri-X.

Left: Nikon F2, bellows focusing attachment PB-4 with 200mm Nikkor, 1/125 sec. at *f*/5.6 (stop-down metering) on Tri-X.

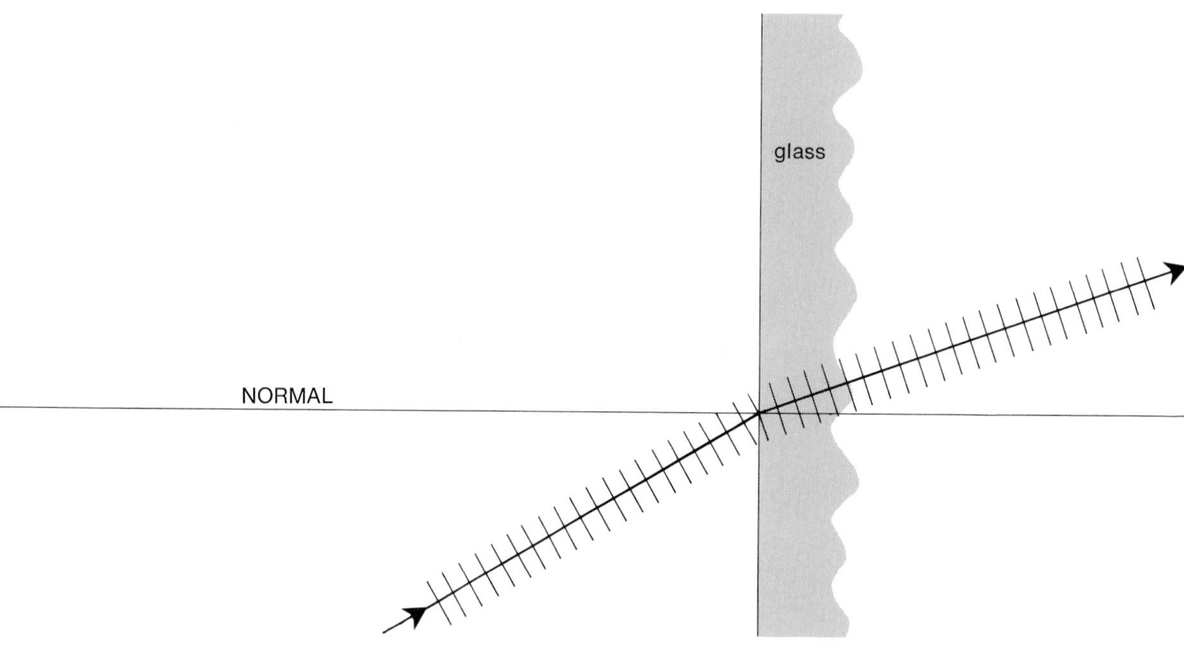

FIGURE 8A

LENS CARE

It is this delicate coating on a lens which dictates utmost care. Dust and fingerprints should only be removed with lens tissue and an approved lens cleaning fluid. It is good practice to buy a skylight filter for each lens you own and thus have the lens protected.

REFRACTION

The refraction of light is essential to photographic optics. Without it, lenses could not bend light rays to form images. Every child who has tried to ignite a piece of paper with a convex lens knows that such a lens converges the sun's rays. He also knows that he must move the paper to find the *focal point* of his lens.

If a light ray traveling through air enters a glass block at right angles, it is merely slowed down by a fraction; its direction is not changed. If this same light ray had entered the block of glass at another angle, something different would have happened: One side of the light wave would arrive at the glass first, and this side would be slowed down. The other side of the light wave would continue to travel through air at a higher speed for just a moment longer—just long enough for the wave front to heel over and the direction of the light wave would be changed (Figure 8A).

Light that passes into a less dense medium, for example, from a block of glass out into air again, accelerates with the part of the light wave that emerges first; the other part of the light wave travels slower for a fraction of a moment so that its direction now is bent away from the normal.

A light ray that passes through a parallel-sided block of glass is first bent toward the normal when it enters, and bent away from the normal when it emerges. The direction of travel is displaced, but it remains parallel to the original course.

The "normal" is an imaginary line through the glass at right angles to its surface. The angle formed by the incoming light ray and the normal is called the *angle of incidence.* The angle formed by the refracted ray inside the glass and the normal is called the *angle of refraction.* The bending inside the optically denser medium is always toward the normal.

REFRACTIVE INDEX

To find the *refractive index,* two points are marked off on the ray path. These points must be located even distances apart in free air and in the glass. These distances are marked a and a^1. The ratio of the two distances from these points to the nearest point on the normal (c and c^1) gives the refractive index. We can say that:

$$\text{refractive index} = \frac{\text{sine angle of incidence}}{\text{sine angle of refraction}}$$

and since $a = a^1$, the refractive index $= c/c^1$.

As we have seen, white light is composed of the various spectral colors. These colors represent different wavelengths and are refracted by slightly differing amounts. Blue is refracted most and bent most toward the normal, green somewhat less, and red the least. Therefore, refractive indexes are quoted in the middle of the visible spectrum. (If you photograph with infrared film, the focal point shift of infrared light is large enough to warrant refocusing to a red dot provided on many lenses.)

Today, it is possible to manufacture high refractive-index glass that yields lenses with shallow surface curvature. Such lenses have the same "light-bending power" as those manufactured with low refractive-index glass, except that the latter would be thicker and have steeper curvature of their sides.

LENS SHAPES

The behavior of a lens varies according to the number of curved surfaces and the direction of the curvature. When both surfaces are convex, or there is one convex and one flat face, the lens is a converging type. When both are concave, or there is one concave and one flat side, the lens is a diverging type. When there is one concave and one convex side, the lens may be converging or diverging, depending on the relative curvature. If both have the same radius of curvature, the lens is neither converging nor diverging. There are six basic lens shapes:

1. plano-convex 2. double-convex 3. converging-meniscus	All these lenses are *positive.* They are thicker at their centers, and they converge light rays.
4. plano-concave 5. double-concave 6. diverging-meniscus	All these lenses are *negative.* They are thinner at their centers, and they diverge light rays.

All negative lenses used must be weaker in their total power than the positive lenses, otherwise the lens could not refract light to a focal point.

FOCUSING

If the imaginary centers of the two spheres of a lens are joined, we speak of the axis of the lens that passes through its *optical center.* The optical center is defined as a point on the lens axis where a light ray passing through it suffers no deviation. It can be within, without, or on either surface of the lens. The *principal focus* of a converging lens is that point on the axis at which incident light rays parallel to each other and the axis, having passed the lens, converge in one point. Two focal points can be drawn on the lens axis: one in front, the other behind the lens. A photographic piece of film placed at the focal point will receive an image in sharp focus of a point from which this light ray has come. Other points on the object at an equal distance from the lens but above or below the lens axis will also be sharply focused in this *focal plane.* For a positive lens focused at or near infinity, a *real image* will be the result, and it is upside down and laterally reversed. The focal length of a negative lens is that point on the principal axis from which light rays, having passed through the lens, appear to diverge. This is a *virtual image,* and it is right side up.

Cameras have focusing screens through which you can always check the position of sharp focus. The groundglass reveals the image formed and is an aid on which your eyes can focus. If you remove the groundglass on an old large-format camera, you can form an aerial image by placing a finger in the exact spot where the groundglass was positioned. If you focus your eyes on the fingertip, part of the aerial image will be seen around it.

FOCAL LENGTH

The refractive index alone, however, is not a guide to the light-bending power of a lens. A new unit—*focal length*—results if you combine refrac-

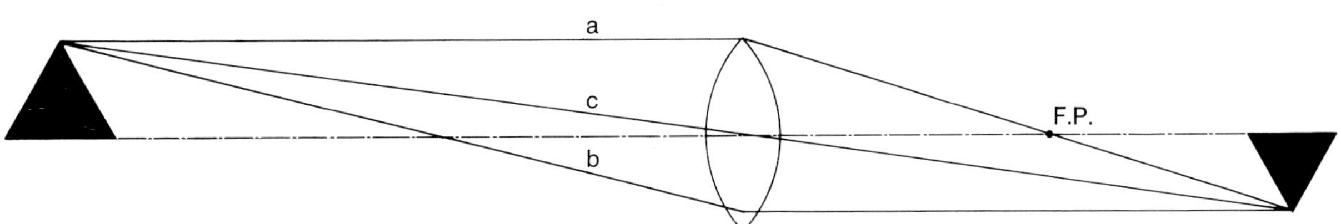

FIGURE 8B

tive index and shape. If a lens is focused at infinity so as to receive light rays virtually parallel to its axis and converges these rays in the principal focal point on this axis, then the focal length is given by the distance of the principal focal point to the center of the lens.

The image size produced by a lens is always in direct proportion to its focal length when an object is at or near infinity. Focal length decides the scale of the image, in other words, and the longer the focal length, the larger the image. When an object is closer to the lens, all light rays diverging from the object will reach the lens at increasingly steeper angles of incidence. However, since the light-bending power of the lens is fixed, the lens must produce a less converging beam of refracted light. Therefore, the image has to be farther away from the lens, and the image size becomes larger.

If you know the focal length of a positive lens, you can find the size and location of the image by drawing the path of three light rays. After you have marked the two principal focal points on either side of the lens axis, you only have to remember the following (Figure 8B):

1. A ray from the top of the object to be pictured, approaching the lens parallel to its axis, must be refracted through the principal focal point behind the lens (ray a).

2. Another ray from the top of the object, passing through the principal focal point in front of the lens, will be refracted parallel to the lens axis (ray b).

3. Still another ray from the top of the object, passing through the optical center, continues on its path unchanged. In effect, it meets two parallel surfaces (ray c).

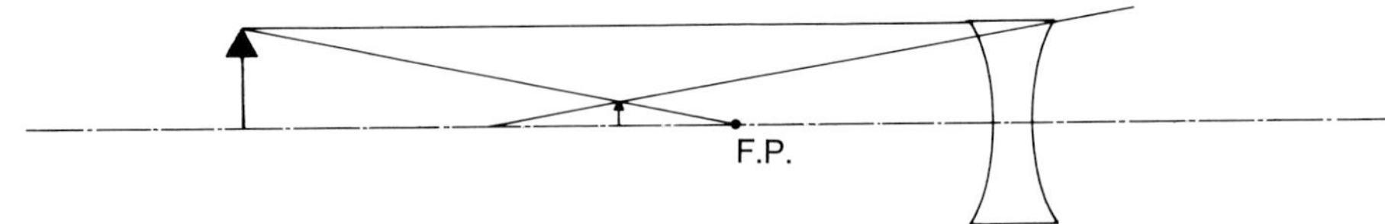

FIGURE 8C

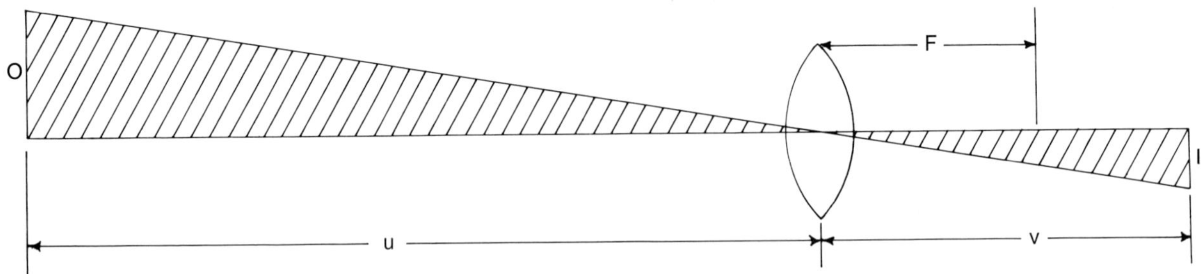

FIGURE 8D

If a ray from the top of an object approaches a negative lens parallel to its axis, it is refracted upward (Figure 8C). Instead of converging, the ray diverges and seems to come from the principal focal point in front of the lens. Another ray coming from the same object point going through the optical center is unchanged in its direction. If you look through such a lens, you assume that the top of the object lies where both rays cross each other. This is a virtual image and this image is always right side up. Remember, the image of a positive lens is upside down.

Generally speaking, the letter "F" is used for focal length, "I" for image height, "O" for object height, "v" for image distance, and "u" for object distance. Figure 8D shows the two similar triangles that form when a ray passes from the tip of an object, through the center of curvature, to the tip of the inverted image. We can therefore say:

$$\frac{I}{O} = \frac{v}{u}, \text{ and since } \frac{I}{O} = \text{magnification (M): } M = \frac{I}{O} = \frac{v}{u}$$

The practical applications of focal length and related phenomena in picture-taking will be discussed in Chapter 10: The Camera and the Human Eye."

LENSLESS PICTURES

It seems appropriate here to mention the pinhole camera, a still useful instrument that can produce pleasing pictures *without* a lens. It can easily be constructed from a cardboard box. With ASA 400 film, exposures of 10 seconds are sufficient. Since the diverging rays from an object to be pictured continue to diverge after passage through the hole, a sharp focus is not possible. Rather, large circles of confusion result on the film plane. This is discussed in greater detail in Chapter 11: "The Pinhole Camera."

7

PHOTOGRAPHIC HISTORY

Many complete books have been written on the history of photography; therefore, an attempt to condense the history of photography into a single chapter seems almost impossible. Only those persons directly responsible for great discoveries, important events, and processes advancing the "state of the art" are discussed here. Some discoveries, miles and countries apart, appear to have been made simultaneously; in order to list these events chronologically, credit must go to those who published their findings first.

Even chronology is not always useful. *Thomas Wedgwood* (1771–1805), a son of the English porcelain family, should be credited as the first man who tried to transfer pictures to his porcelain by the action of light alone. Around 1799, he made the first photographic experiments with the *camera obscura*. Going back much further, however, we must credit the work of various experimenters in the fields of mathematics, optics, chemistry (or alchemy), and the arts. Long before the eighteenth century, many scientific treatises and popular books of entertainment were already available with information of the necessary principles and formulas for photography. One wonders why photography was not invented centuries earlier.

THE IMAGE

Reports exist of early caravan travelers who were amused by scenes projected by the light coming through a hole on the opposite tent wall; camels and people walking outside of tents were seen upside down and in their natural color. What was observed, of course, was the same effect artists later obtained in their *camera obscura*, literally a "dark room." These instruments were widely used by artists of the Renaissance and may be seen as the direct forerunners of today's cameras. Rooms, tents, or boxlike instruments with tiny holes in their fronts projected the outside scene on opposite walls, white screens, or groundglass. A mirror, tilted 45°, like that in a modern single-lens reflex, was used in the portable versions, and tracings of the outlines of the projected image led to the discovery of the vanishing point perspective. Euclid, the father of geometry, used this principle to demonstrate to his students that light travels in a straight line.

Further back, in 350 B.C., while lecturing to a student sitting under a tree, *Aristotle* noticed the sun's image on the ground. This was caused by the arrangement of the leaves, which were acting like a diaphragm. Intercepting the rays with a sheet of papyrus, and moving it up and down, Aristotle demonstrated how the image size could be altered.

Some writers credit *Roger Bacon* with the actual invention of the camera obscura in 1267, and in fact, he described an instrument using a mirror to view pictures. However, a much earlier account can be found in the writings of *Ibn Al-Haitham,* also known as Alhazen of Basra, (965–1038) about such an instrument used to observe an eclipse in order to safeguard the eyes from direct rays of the sun. Since he does not claim to have invented the instrument, it can be assumed that other Arab scholars had known of its existence even earlier. It is also interesting to note that Ibn Al-Haitham was well aware of the relationship between the size of the aperture and the resulting sharpness of the image.

In 1558, *Giovanni Battista della Porta* (1538–1615), a young Neapolitan, published the book *Magiae Naturalis.* In it he gave the first really complete description of the camera obscura, and suggested, for the first time, its use as an aid to artists. He also described the combined use of a convex lens and a concave mirror in order to obtain right-side-up and enlarged images.

Most books credit the Venetian nobleman *Daniello Barbaro* with the introduction of a lens in the camera obscura. In his book *Practice of Perspective* (1568), he introduced the diaphragm as a spectacular novelty, demonstrating how an image sharpens when the diaphragm is closed down. Here, for the first time, we hear of a device so important in modern photography.

The first description of a convex lens in connection with the camera obscura appeared in 1550 in a scientific work by *Girolamo Cardano* (1501–1576), a professor of mathematics in Milan.

In 1601, *Thomas Hariot* formulated laws that govern the refraction of light. In a second book *Dioptrice*, published in 1611, the German astronomer *Johannes Kepler* (1571–1630) described the projected images of single and compound lenses. Doing land surveys in his capacity as imperial mathematician, he used a portable tent camera obscura fitted with a telescopic lens of the same basic construction as used in today's telephotography.

CONTAINING THE IMAGE

It was known for a long time that light forms images and that it has an effect on certain substances. Medieval alchemists, in their never-ending search to produce gold, also experimented with silver salts. They noted how the salts produced dark stains on the skin and also how these substances could be used for staining wood. It never occurred to them that this reaction was caused by light. The first to connect the darkening of these salts to the action of light was *Angelo Sala* in a booklet published in 1614. In it he stated that *lapis lunearis* (silver nitrate) turns black as ink when it is exposed to the sun.

In 1725, the first scientific investigation into the action of light on silver salts was performed by *Johann Heinrich Schulze* (1687–1744), a professor at the University of Altdorf, near Nuremberg. He conducted his experiments near a sun-filled window. Shaking a bottle containing a mixture of chalk, nitric acid, and traces of silver, he noticed that the part of the bottle facing the window darkened while the other side stayed white. Schulze then repeated the experiment, covering the bottle with paper from which he had cut words and entire sentences. Knowing that the effect was not due to heat, he was not surprised to find the writing clearly imprinted on the solution in his bottle. In later writings, Schulze stressed the importance of his discovery. Further investigation convinced him that the sun's rays, independent of heat, were responsible for darkening the silver nitrate. He also knew that the chalk in his bottle only served to provide a contrast carrier for his darkened writings.

The camera obscura used by artists had evolved into a small portable instrument, and photography could have been invented at this point. In 1777, *Carl Wilhelm Scheele* (1742–1786), experimenting with the action of light on silver chloride, pointed out, in his "chemical observations," the known fact that ammonia dissolves silver chloride, leaving metallic silver reduced by the action of light. Here, at last, was a fixing agent that could have provided Thomas Wedgwood with the substance to make his images on leather and glass permanent.

THE PRINCIPAL INVENTORS

Continuing with Wedgwood's lines of research, *Joseph Nicéphore Niépce* (1765–1833) exposed light-sensitive paper in his camera obscura, starting in April 1816. After sensitizing the paper with silver chloride, he partially fixed the image with nitric acid. His paper negatives could be viewed in sunlight but were eventually bleached out by the action of the acid. He did try to print through his paper negatives to reverse the tones but was unsuccessful. Niépce spent the following years experimenting with printing processes and was able to produce plates from existing engravings by the action of light.

After experimenting with a number of substances, Niépce took the world's first photograph on a pewter plate covered with bitumen of Judea. The exposure was eight hours, so the sun in the picture appears to shine on both sides of the courtyard.

Bitumen is hardened by the action of light, and the latent image was made visible by repeatedly washing the plate with mixed oil of lavender and white petroleum. The highlights were represented by the hardened bitumen and the shadow areas by the bare metal plate exposed by repeated washings. The resultant picture was a positive image and no additional copies could be made. The year for this first successful photograph taken from nature is 1826, nine years earlier than *William Henry Fox Talbot*'s paper negatives in 1835, and eleven years before Daguerre's first still life in 1837.

Louis Jacques Mandé Daguerre (1787–1851) is usually given credit for inventing the first practical means of photography, although much of his work was based on that of the older Niépce. Since both Niépce and Daguerre used Charles Louis Chevalier as their Paris lens maker, they were aware of each other's experiments. It was Chevalier who suggested that Daguerre write to Niépce. Both men were very secretive about their work, and each one feared that the other might have advanced further. Finally, a partnership agreement was worked out between the two men in 1829. It was a ten-year contract, but the partnership started on uneven terms. Niépce had to provide Daguerre with the most detailed account of his process while Daguerre contributed only his new camera obscura, talent, and drive.

Niépce died in 1833, four years after the partnership agreement had been signed. He died a poor man, having spent a fortune on his experiments without witnessing any real success.

Before his partnership with Niépce, Daguerre operated some of the then-fashionable "Dioramas"—theaters that provided spectators with fabulous illusions on painted screens that were 75 feet wide. These screens were of transparent material, such as gauze, and scenes were painted on both sides. By constantly changing the lighting from front to back, one scene dissolved into another. Daguerre was obsessed with the idea of using the images of the camera obscura for his realistic scenery. Working daily in a laboratory attached to his Paris Diorama, he accidentally stumbled on the possibility of developing the latent image.

Daguerre summoned Niépce's son Isidore to Paris and insisted that his own name now appear before that of Niépce in the partnership. Daguerre's process was definitely a major improvement; exposure times were still long, however, and moving objects in street scenes could not be pictured. It was also impossible to take portraits because of the long exposure times.

Daguerre was fortunate to have the support of François Arago, a member of the Chamber of Deputies and a well-known physicist and astronomer. Arago was instrumental in persuading the French government to acquire the daguerreotype process and to pay Daguerre and Isidore Niépce a lifelong pension.

Daguerre's process was demonstrated and published in numerous pamphlets: A silvered copper plate was cleaned and polished to a high luster. The plate was then sensitized in a box containing iodine vapor, which in turn formed a thin layer of silver iodide on its surface. After exposures of from 5 to 40 minutes duration as judged by the operator, and depending on the light conditions, the latent image was created. It was then developed by inserting the plate in still another box in which fumes of mercury were created by heating the metal over a spirit lamp. The mercury attached itself to those parts of the silver iodide which had been affected by the light. The picture was then fixed with hyposulfite of soda (earlier this was done with common table salt), and after washing, it was dried over a flame. This process was patented by Daguerre in England, Wales, and the colonies just a few days before the French Government donated it to mankind.

In 1841, *William Henry Fox Talbot* (1800–1877), an English chemist and mathematician, patented the "Calotype" process, which later became known as "Talbotype." This was a process that yielded a paper negative, which could be used to make a positive print. The pictures, because of the paper grain, were not as clearly defined as Daguerreotypes, but from the paper negative many more copies could be made. Just as Daguerre had stumbled on the possibility of bringing out the latent image, Talbot had a similar experience. When a number of his negatives of sensitized paper failed to produce an image, he tried to reuse them. For resensitization, he used a solution of silver nitrate, acetic acid, and gallic acid. To his astonishment, the image appeared immediately. Gallic acid, of course, is a developing agent.

At about this time, the Hungarian scientist *Josef Max Petzval* (1807–1891) designed special portrait and landscape lenses that transmitted 16 times more light than previous ones.

Frederich Scott Archer (1813 1857), an English photographer, introduced a new process, the wet Collodion process, in 1851. Collodion (derived from pyroxylin dissolved in alcohol and ether to produce an adhesive) was used to coat glass plates, which in turn were dipped in a solution of light-sensitive silver nitrate. These plates had to be used when wet and photographers had to carry along all equipment for processing. This type of photography produced a negative and became known as wet-plate photography.

By 1856, this method was in general use, although the glass plates were often replaced with metal ones to produce a positive image, called "Ferrotypes" or "Tintypes."

The most dramatic breakthrough occurred when the British physician *Richard Maddox* replaced collodion with dry gelatin in 1871. Gelatin has excellent adhesive qualities and is the perfect carrier for silver nitrate. With this, dry-plate photography really became mobile.

SOME LATER DEVELOPMENTS

The first war photographs for a London newspaper were shot by *Roger Fenton* (1819–1861) when he covered the Crimean War in the spring of 1855.

Mathew B. Brady (1823–1896), American photographer, organized the first picture service and the photographic documentation of the American Civil War by teams of photographers in his employ. Brady lost a personal fortune in these undertakings and had to sell his collection to the government in 1875.

Instead of just recording an event, photography at the turn of the century assumed a different role. Pictures were used to persuade and convince. *William Henry Jackson* (1843–1942) traveled through Yellowstone Park, and the pictures he brought back were used to persuade Congress to establish a National Park. At the same time, *Lewis W. Hine* (1874–1940) and *Jacob Riis* (1849–1914) began to take pictures of social evils in America. Riis became famous for his pictures of New York slums. New York's worst tenement section, "Mulberry Bend," was torn down as a result of his crusade. Hine, a working sociologist/photographer, exposed working conditions in factories and mines and pointed his camera at working children. His work led to the passage of child-labor laws.

COLOR PHOTOGRAPHY HISTORY

Ever since the beginning of practical photography, the earliest inventors and experimenters wondered how they could also capture the colors of nature. Many experiments were performed and there were some successes. However, none of these systems of early color photography was for amateur use; they were much too complicated. It was not until 1935 that Eastman Kodak was able to introduce its simple-to-use Kodachrome to the general public. Two amateur camera enthusiasts, *Leopold Godowsky, Jr.* and *Leopold Mannes*, had worked for years on the problem and were able to perfect their film material in the Kodak laboratories.

James Clerk Maxwell (1831–1879) was one of the early investigators of color photography. He took three black-and-white pictures of the same scene, exposing one through a blue, green, and red filter, respectively. Lantern slides were made from the three black-and-white negatives, producing positive transparencies. He then projected the slides into a single image through their corresponding filters. The projected color image was an additive method of color mixing.

Around 1925, the "Autochrome" process enabled magazines to print color. This process, invented by *Auguste* and *Louis Lumière*, two brothers, was also an additive process of color mixture, but instead of the three filters used by Maxwell, a photographic glass plate was covered with a thin layer of potato starch (0.01mm) that had been dyed blue, green, and red and over which the photographic emulsion was now poured. In order to let the tiny starch filters do their work, the plate had to be exposed through the glass from the back. Developed, such a plate records blue light behind a blue grain, green behind a green, and red behind a red starch grain. The blackened parts of the emulsion (where exposure had taken place) now had to be dissolved. This left the plate transparent in those parts which were opaque before. After another exposure to daylight, the plate had to be redeveloped. Now all parts not previously dissolved became blackened and opaque. The finished positive, when viewed with the starch grain layer toward the viewer's face, is a perfect transparency in natural colors. Only the transparent parts of the film are penetrated, and the transmitted light comes through the starch grains as blue, green, and red where these colors originated in the actual scene.

Since its invention, photography has been in a very fluid state. New processes are rapidly introduced. A survey of photographic history would not be complete without mentioning *Dr. Edwin H. Land* (b. 1909) and the invention of Polaroid cameras and films. He introduced a black-and-white film in 1947 and a color film in 1962. All these films—there are now many different types available, including Type 55 P/N, to yield a positive and negative in 20 seconds—provide instant pictures.

OTHER DEVELOPMENTS

Because of the enormous amounts of silver used in photographic applications every year, non-silver-base imaging becomes more important. Even before the practical invention of photography, the German physicist *Georg Lichtenberg* demonstrated how a permanent image of an electric discharge could be produced. A high-voltage discharge was sent over an insulator that had been covered with sulfur powder. This was the beginning of electrophotography.

Another new photographic process is the use of a transparent ceramic disk that stores a positive image. The device is an extremely thin ceramic ferroelectric plate with a photoconductive layer on one side and transparent electrodes on both sides. If an illumination level is applied, the photoconductive layer, which had acted as an insulator, now channels the voltage through the ceramic. This causes microscopic changes within the material. The affected areas appear darker since light is channeled away. Such a "Cerampic," as it is called, makes an image like a black-and-white slide.

Photography as an art and a science is still very young. Holography, a method of making three-dimensional pictures without a camera, may even take us beyond our wildest expectations.

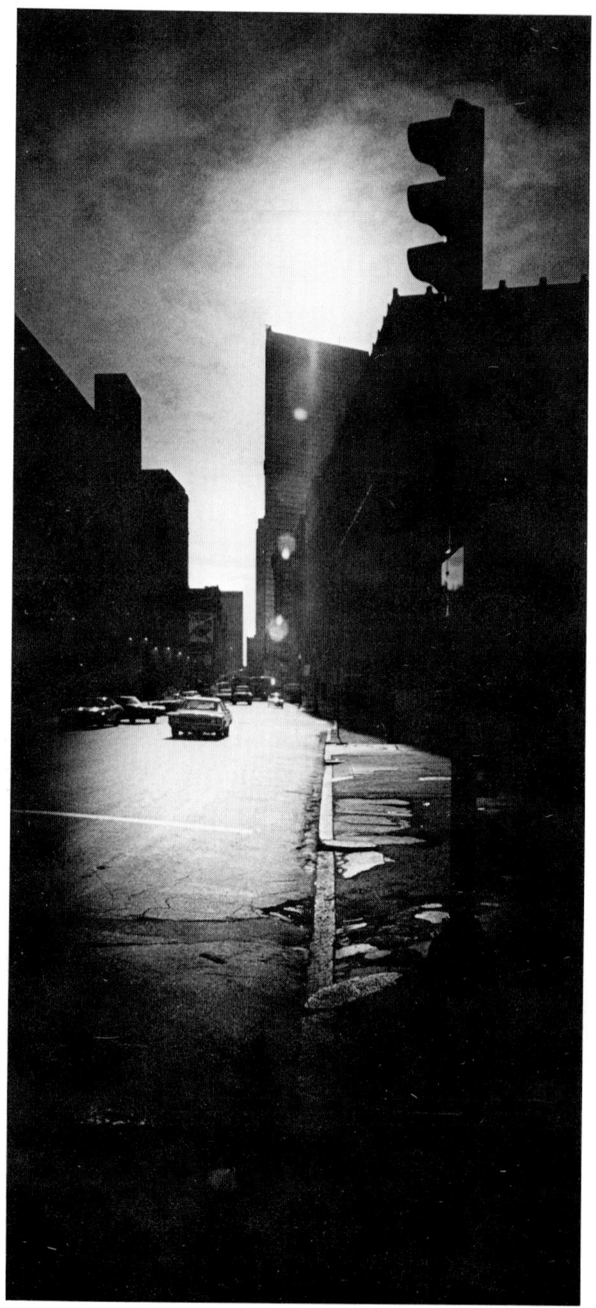

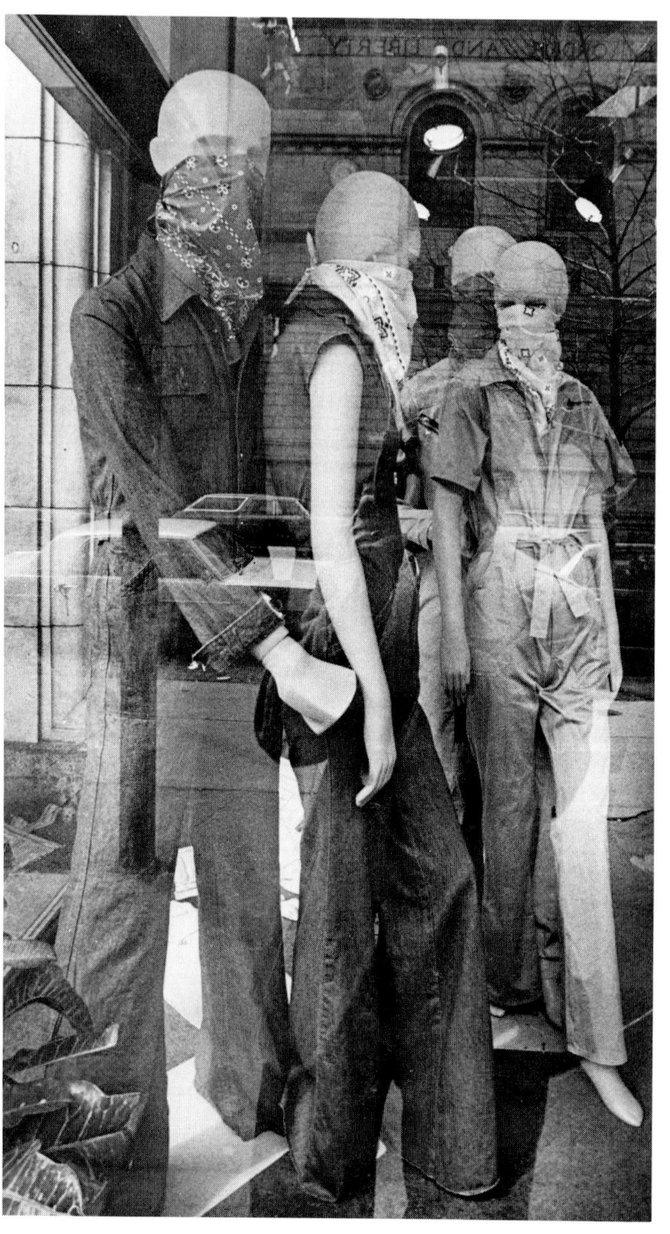

Above: Boston street. Nikon F2, 20mm Nikkor, 1/2000 sec. at *f*/11 on Tri-X.

Left: A window display becomes a group of faceless, robotlike strollers in a glass-reflected city. Nikon F2, 20mm Nikkor, 1/60 sec. at *f*/5.6 on Tri-X.

8

SENSITOMETRY

The serious photographer with his own darkroom, or one with access to a lab, has a very specific result in mind every time he makes an exposure. He has his exposure meter set to the recommended exposure index and expects predictable results. He knows that the old "trial and error" days of early photography are a thing of the past. He also knows that by following the exposure and development recommendations of a manufacturer, he will produce negatives or slides in which the full scale of the material is utilized and both his highlight and shadow areas will have some detail. But only if the student is willing to understand the mechanics of sensitometry is he in a position to take full advantage of film or paper.

Today's manufacturers offer a tremendous variety of film and paper for black-and-white and color processes. They also supply characteristic curves which, as the result of precision testing, show precise relationships of exposure and resultant density. These characteristic curves are usually supplemented by so-called "time-gamma curves," which show the resultant contrast in minutes elapsed in a certain developer.

I am often criticized for insisting on technical knowledge as a parallel path to a student's artistic goals. Each artistic medium has certain technical requirements, and even the great Michelangelo (1475–1564) had to learn them. When he started to paint the ceiling of the Sistine chapel in the Vatican in 1508, his first few months of work was ruined and had to be removed because his technical background in fresco painting was insufficient.

As you read on in this chapter, you will note that sensitometry has its own terminology. You will encounter such words as *exposure, density, opacity, speed,* and *latitude,* all of which are well explained as you read along.

For the moment, let's discuss speed. Film and paper speeds, in ASA (American Standards Association) or DIN (Deutsche Industrie Norm), are light sensitivity values assigned to photographic material with a great safety margin. They are not absolute values. The manufacturer makes sure that your exposures are slightly overexposed and that following his recommendations is safe, but you are not working the full speed potential of an emulsion. High ASA numbers indicate that this emulsion will record an image in low illumination. The higher the ASA number, the more pronounced will be the grain. Films with low ASA numbers have fine grain, but in order to render acceptable negatives (or color slides), higher illumination levels are needed.

The correct exposure of sensitive material is the key to successful prints. Although overexposed and underexposed negatives may be saved by various darkroom methods and printing techniques, these procedures are sometimes very time-consuming.

SENSITOMETRY AND EXPOSURE

In order to understand how correct exposure can be determined, you should acquire an understanding of the limits of tonal performance inherent in a given emulsion. To be able to do so, you need standards and precise terms; vague descriptions, such as "flat negative," "burnt-out highlights," or "no shadow detail," will not do.

A scientific approach is needed, a process for collecting data under strictly controlled circumstances. Such an approach must include a wide range of light dosages (to simulate object brightness in a given scene) developed under strict time and temperature control. The resultant varying tones of blackness in the light-sensitive material accurately measured can then be used as data for a *sensitometry curve.* The chief aim of sensitometry is to derive accurate numerical values for the exposure-density relationship of a material, to eliminate guesswork. The results, stated in units, can be universally applied and compared.

THE CHARACTERISTIC CURVE

The resultant curve could also be called a *performance,* or *characteristic, curve.* One variable is plotted against another, just as the engine performance of a car is plotted for fuel intake versus horsepower.

The characteristic curve of a photographic emulsion is a useful tool that provides the photographer with comparisons of speed, tonal response, limits of useful exposure, developer action, and the resultant negative-to-print quality.

Long before the turn of the century, when no such information was available, photography with gelatin-coated glass plates depended on trial and error. The first systematic emulsion evaluations were undertaken by Dr. Ferdinand Hurter and Vero C. Driffield in 1876. In 1890, the two published a paper entitled "Photographic Investigations and a New Method of Determination of the Sensitiveness of Photographic Plates." Today, the characteristic curve is often called the "H & D curve."

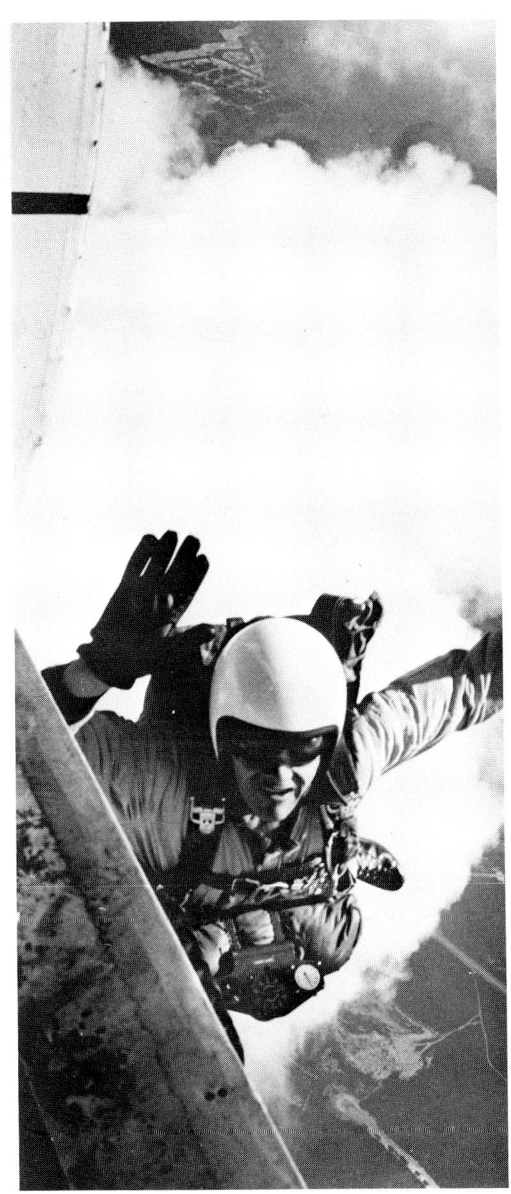

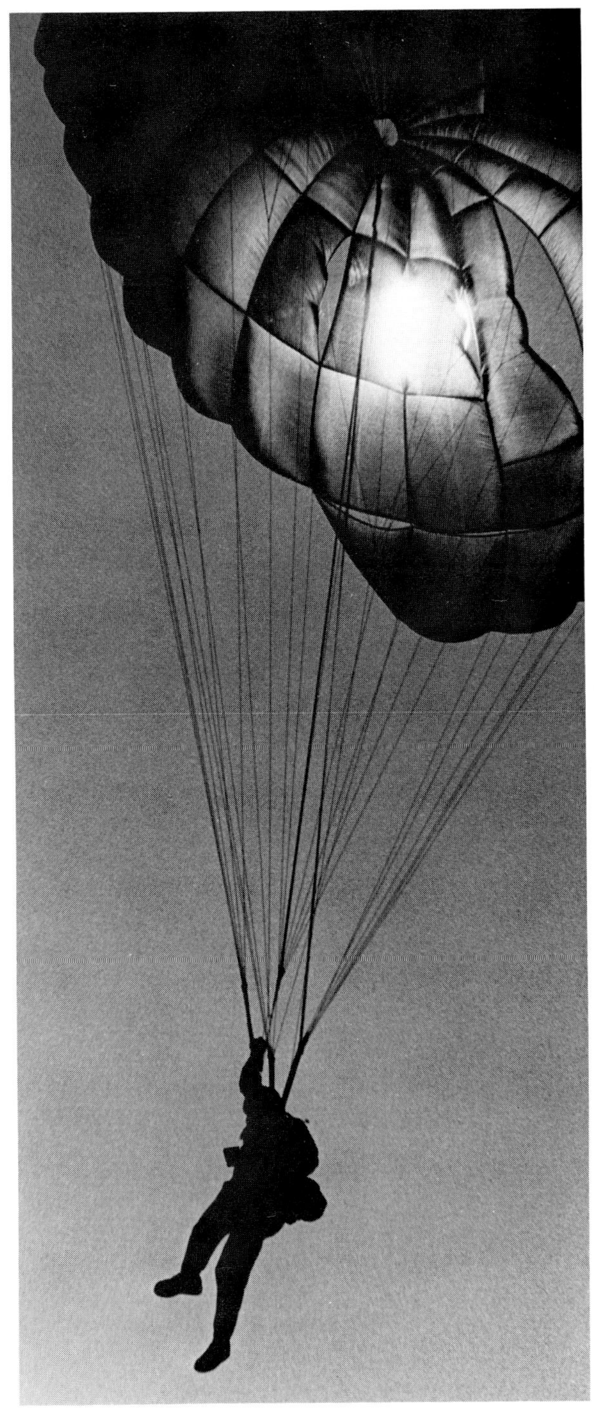

Above: Photographed at 12,000 feet using Nikon F, 35mm Nikkor, 1/500 sec. at *f*/16 on Tri-X.

Right: Nikon F2, 200mm Nikkor, 1/250 sec. at *f*/8 on Tri-X.

Late afternoon. Nikon F, 135mm Nikkor, 1/500 sec. at *f*/16 on Tri-X.

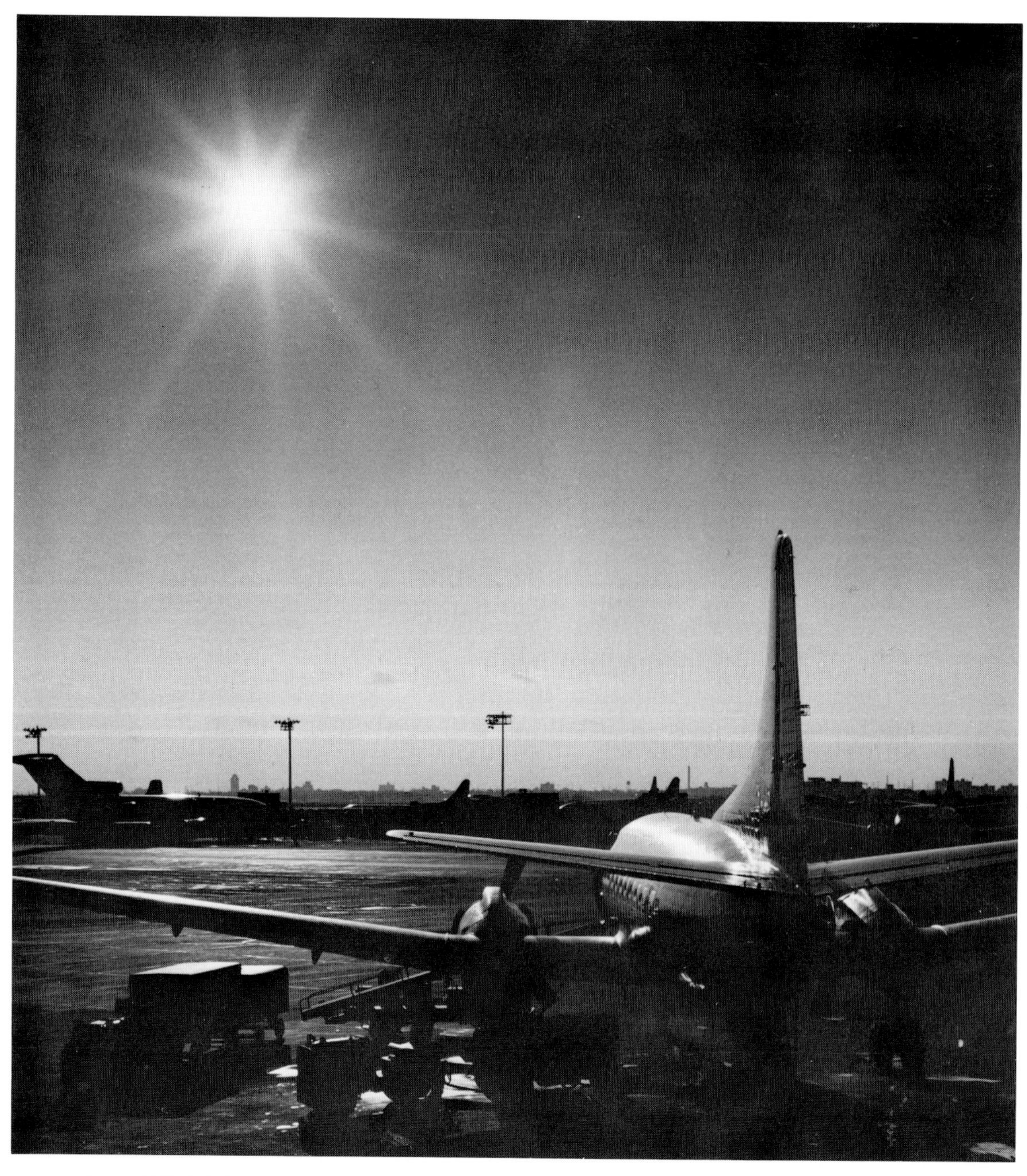

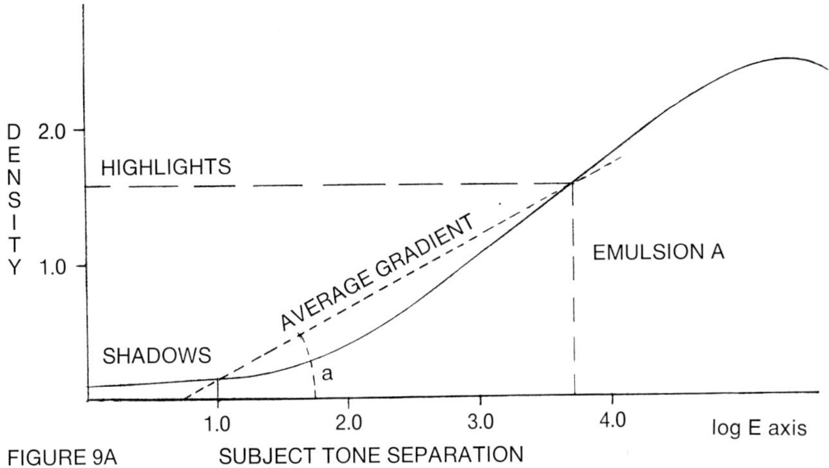

FIGURE 9A

The moment you take a picture, the emulsion is subjected to a wide range of light intensities. Darkest shadows to brightest highlights, with the corresponding scale of tones in between, project their values from any particular point in a scene. A silver deposit in the film emulsion forms on development. Every exposure (E), however, depends on two things: It is the product of the illumination (I) and the time (t) that light has acted on the film. The basic photographic equation thus becomes:

$$E = It$$

"I" and "t" are variables. If you adjust the lens aperture (*f*/stop), you of course vary the light intensities reaching the film. Too much light will result in overexposure and too little in underexposure. Shutter speed is the other variable with which you control time (t). Obviously, by changing your shutter speed from 1/250 sec. to 1/500 sec., you halve the exposure.

PLOTTING THE CURVE

To prepare a characteristic curve, the manufacturer of a negative material would be hard pressed to measure the relative brightness of every object in a scene. Therefore, the material is subjected to a wide range of doubling exposures in the laboratory. The film is exposed with a step wedge—a piece of glass divided into 15 equal sections; each of these sections progressively transmits half the light intensity of the previous one. The brightness range represented in 15 steps extends from 1 to 16,384—a range that would never be encountered in actual photography. (The brightness range of the average sunlit scene is 500 to 1, and for controlled studio lighting, 20 to 1.)

Since the intensity of illumination and time of exposure are known, and since development is controlled (as to developer dilution, temperature, agitation, and time), a two-axis graph can be prepared. Relative light dosage, or exposure, is plotted on the horizontal axis, and the resultant blackness, or density, on the vertical axis (Figure 9A).

Since the multiple progression of 1–2–4–8–16–32–64 and so on through 16,384 in 15 steps would render the horizontal axis impossibly long, it is graduated in a logarithmic progression, where 1, 2, 3, 4 represent 10, 100, 1,000, and 10,000. The horizontal axis is therefore referred to as "the log E axis." Similarly, the vertical axis on which you plot the resultant density would have to be extremely large to accommodate the opacity of all the different silver deposits (tonal representation in modern films might be spaced as wide as 500 to 1).

Opacity, in photographic terms, is the incident light divided by the transmitted light.

$$\frac{\text{Incident light}}{\text{Transmitted light}} = \text{Opacity}$$

In other words, if 100 units of light shine on a specific deposit of silver, but only 10 units of light are transmitted, we say that this particular tone in the negative has an opacity of 10.

Because the horizontal log E axis has been calibrated in $\log_{10}$, you also have to convert opacity into terms of logarithmic differences. (The eyes see tonal difference in logarithmic and not arithmetic proportions.) The logarithm of opacity is called *density.* In the above example, since density = $\log_{10}$ of the opacity, the density of this particular tone is 1.

The photographic researcher can obtain direct readings for the varying tones in density figures. For the measurement of transparent material (negatives and transparencies), he uses a transmission densitometer. The measurement of opaque material (prints) requires the use of a reflection densitometer. You can now look at the resultant characteristic curve where each relative light dosage received by the negative has been plotted against its resultant density.

THE "S" CURVE

Characteristic curves supplied by manufacturers generally are "S"-shaped. If the doubling or tripling of the log E exposure were followed by doubled or tripled density, an inclined straight line would be the result. However, film does not work this way.

There are four distinct parts in any characteristic curve (Figure 9B): the "toe" region; the "straight-line" portion; the "shoulder" portion; and the region of "solarization," where the curve starts to descend, and any further increase in exposure will not result in greater density. In fact, extreme overexposure will result in a sort of solarized positive image.

If you use shutter and aperture controls to give increasing amounts of exposure to a series of pictures, you arrange the object brightness range (illumination ratio from shadows to highlights) to the

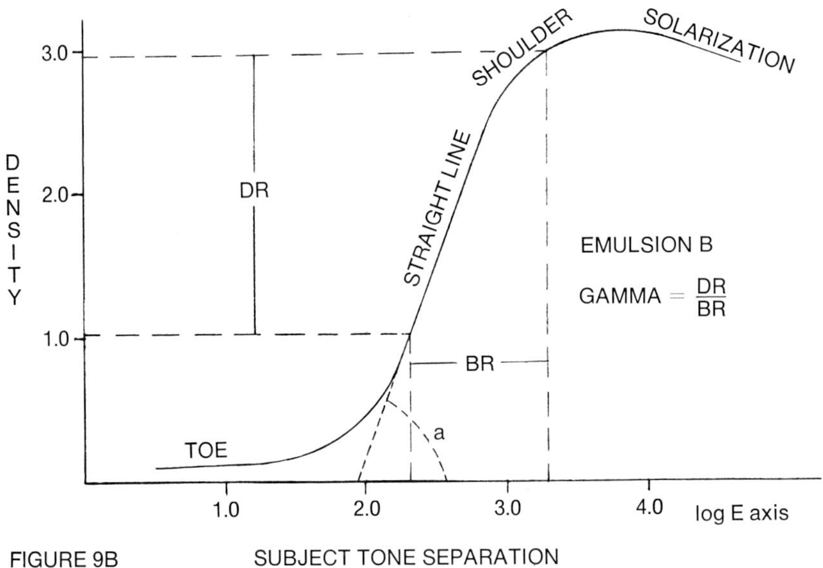

FIGURE 9B SUBJECT TONE SEPARATION

right or high side on the log E axis. With the same development, you must expect negatives with increasing densities and less tonal separation in the highlights. If you underexpose, the object brightnesses will be moved to the left side on the log E axis, and the overall effect will be that of less density and compression and loss in the shadow details. Since the characteristic curve is not a straight line, but rather a curve, the range in which you can alter the exposure must be limited. Exposure, with its resultant density, is the key to print quality.

In following exposure and development recommendations of the manufacturer, you place the principal object brightness on that part of the log E axis where the negative density will match the characteristic curve of the printing paper. Not only will you get a negative that is easy to print, but the finished print with its tonal separation will most nearly resemble the original scene.

GAMMA

Altering the recommended development time will, in effect, change the slope of the characteristic curve. Less development will result in lowered contrast, and more development will result in increased contrast. Referring to the slope of the straight-line section of the curve, we speak of *Gamma* (see Figure 9). Gamma is the ratio of the negative density range (DR) divided by the brightness range (BR). In the average recorded scene, Gamma should reach a value of 0.8. Emulsions for the sole purpose of recording line copy will have Gamma values as high as 3.0. These are high-contrast emulsions for this specific task.

$$\text{Gamma} = \frac{\text{DR}}{\text{BR}} = \text{the tangent angle of the straight line portion of the curve with the log E axis.}$$

Gamma is a variable factor: It depends on the film material used and also on the degree of development; it depends on object lighting;

and it depends on whether the exposure has been made on the toe, straight-line, or shoulder region of the characteristic curve. It also depends to some degree on the wavelength of the existing light. Color filters that exclude some portion of the visible spectrum will influence the final Gamma value of the processed negative. At high altitudes, where blue wavelengths are increased, you will usually observe a loss of contrast if you do not compensate for it.

Contrary to common belief that correct exposure is achieved when object brightnesses fall on the straight-line portion of the curve, it is much better to use part of the toe and the straight-line portion (commonly thought of as underexposure). This way, higher shutter speeds are possible, and you can use the maximum speed of the emulsion. The resultant negative, in this case, best matches the characteristic curve of modern printing papers; shadows will print with more contrast than the more heavily exposed highlights. Such an exposure, where shadow and highlight ratios do not fall on the straight-line portion of the curve alone, is quoted in "average gradient" figures. The two points touching the curve are connected with a line, and Gamma values are given in much the same way as they are quoted when the exposure falls on the straight-line portion.

APPLYING SENSITOMETRY

It is now easy to see that an understanding of sensitometry and the mechanics of the characteristic curve will give you an edge over the photographer who goes through his photographic life unaware of the manipulative possibilities of his medium. You can decide whether one specific emulsion will give you the results you anticipate under given circumstances, or if you would do better to make use of the characteristics of another emulsion.

Having a mental picture of a characteristic curve, you can judge how much exposure latitude a scene you are about to photograph will allow. If you photograph a scene in which all objects give off similar light reflections (a scene where shadow-to-highlight values are not spread very much), you know that this scene will occupy a small section on the log E axis. Such a scene will allow more exposure error than one where the highlight-to-shadow ratio may be 100 to 1, or more.

Tone compression is controlled by exposure, and density and contrast can be varied by development. So you can control and predict the physical qualities of your negatives and adjust these qualities to the printing paper you intend to use. If you cannot control the lighting in a scene, you can manipulate the exposure, the development, or both, to still get good negatives. A good negative is, of course, a prerequisite for good prints.

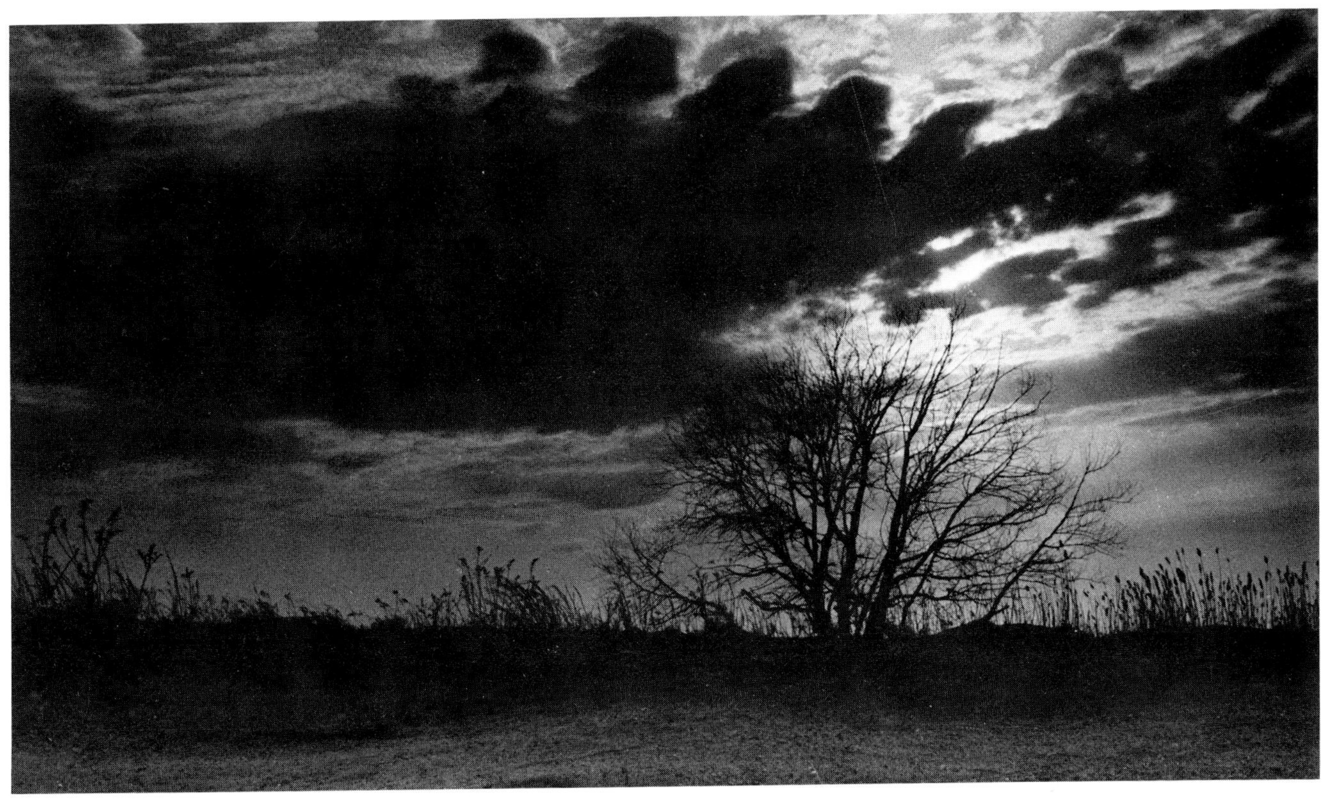

In this photograph, the emphasis is of horizontal movement in late afternoon. Nikon F, 35mm Nikkor with medium yellow filter, 1/125 sec. at *f*/11 on Tri-X.

Rather than constantly switching from one type of film to another, you should try to stay with your favorite emulsion and exhaust its possibilities through exposure and development changes. If you must photograph a scene that has a very wide range of brightnesses, normal exposure and normal development procedures will produce a negative with more than normal density. It will be too contrasty to yield a good print, and if the density is too great, it also will not produce a sharp print.

But there is something you can do. Rather than carry film in 36-exposure rolls only, always have some short 10-exposure rolls with you for the uncommon lighting situation. If you now encounter subject matter with highlight-to-shadow ratios of 100 to 1 (contrasty midday sun), you can shoot the entire short roll with increased exposure. If your exposure meter reads 1/125 sec. at a given *f*/stop, use 1/60 sec., but decrease development up to 25 per cent.

For flat lighting, weak lighting, or in hazy conditions, do the opposite. If your meter reading calls for an exposure of, let's say, 1/125 sec. at a given *f*/stop, decrease your exposure and use a shutter speed of 1/250 sec., but now increase your development time by 25 per cent.

Always remember that manipulating development will change the shape of the characteristic curve, and that changing exposure will affect the location of subject brightness to the right or left on the log E axis. If you learn to handle this phase of photography, your negatives will be far more "workable" than negatives produced by the snapshooter next to you.

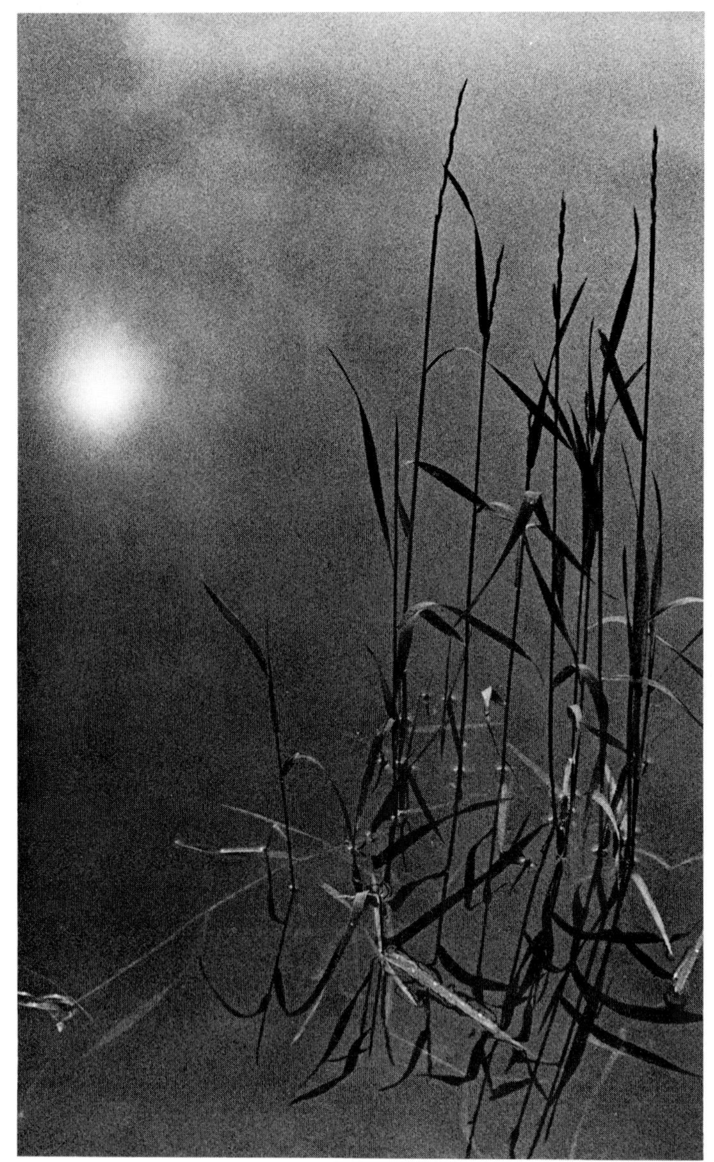

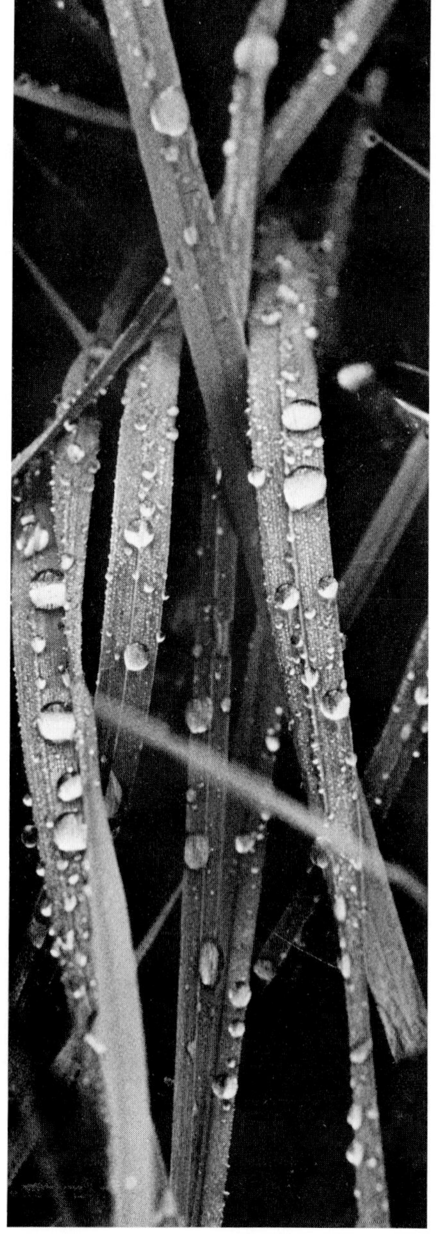

Above: Sun reflected in water. Nikon F2, 50mm Nikkor, 1/125 sec. at *f*/11 on Tri-X.

Right: Raindrops on leaves. Nikon FTN, bellows focusing attachment PB-4 with 200mm Nikkor, 1/60 sec. at *f*/8 on Tri-X.

9

THE LIGHT-SENSITIVE EMULSION

COMPONENTS

Regardless of the recent quest to replace silver and gelatin with other substances (see p. 75), none of these has been adapted for general use. Various synthetic polymers have been tried, just as other light-sensitive materials besides silver halides have been used.

At the very beginning of photography, it became clear that silver nitrate was too slow in its reaction to light. Photography, under such conditions, would not have evolved and become practical. Fortunately, it was soon noted that silver combined with a halogen* increased its sensitivity to light. Such compounds are known as *silver halides.*

GELATIN

A suitable support for the light-sensitive silver-halide crystals was found in gelatin. The gelatin has to fulfill some very specific requirements: It keeps the silver-halide grains in their positions, suspended so as to avoid clumping, which would result in graininess of the photographic image. It is a convenient medium for mixing and spreading the emulsion on a support such as film, paper, or glass. It is very transparent and grainless so that no undesirable characteristics are added. On immersion in chemicals, it allows penetration of the developer to the silver halides, and on washing and fixing, it allows the removal of soluble compounds and dissolved halides. It possesses a reasonable degree of permanence (against heat, abrasion, and the like) in the unprocessed and processed stages.

Gelatin provides another important benefit: It increases the speed of the silver halides because it is a "halogen acceptor." The formation of silver atoms during exposure releases minute quantities of halogen, which are absorbed by the gelatin. These amounts of halogen would otherwise tend to recombine with the silver atoms right after exposure, and the effect the light had produced on the emulsion would be canceled.

Photographic gelatin is prepared from calf hide, calf ears, pigskin, and animal bones. It is very pure. It must be free from bacteria; even the type of feed provided for the cattle and pigs determines the final outcome of the emulsion. Chemically, gelatin belongs to the protein

*Halogens are the nonmetallic elements fluorine, chlorine, bromine, and iodine.

group. Gelatin possesses both acidic and basic properties and is therefore amphoteric (capable of reacting chemically either as an acid or as a base).

EMULSION-MAKING

In the early days of photography, every worker had to prepare his own light-sensitive emulsion. In those days, glass plates were coated with collodion. This wet and sticky substance was the emulsion base on the plate, which in turn had to be dipped into a solution of light-sensitive silver salts. The collodion plate could not be allowed to dry and had to be processed right after an exposure was made. Photographers had to carry along a darkroom tent, bottles, trays, and all other equipment to their picture-taking locations. When, in 1871, the British physician *Richard L. Maddox* (1816–1902) replaced collodion with gelatin, photography was revolutionized.

Rigid manufacturing controls go hand in hand with extensive research programs before modern photographic materials reach the consumer. The actual process of commercial emulsion-making is surrounded by secrecy. The following description should, however, provide the reader with a basic understanding.

Depending on the emulsion required, one of the photographically important halogens (bromine, iodine, chlorine, or mixtures of these) is dissolved with pure gelatin in its halide form (potassium bromide, potassium iodide, potassium chloride). Assuming that the white soluble crystals of potassium bromide are used and dissolved with gelatin, this colorless first solution (KBr) is then poured into a kettle of chemically inert material.

Next, pure bar silver (Ag) is dissolved in nitric acid (HNO_3) to produce silver nitrate ($AgNO_3$). The silver-nitrate crystals form a colorless second solution in distilled water.

The lights must now be turned off. When the second solution is poured into the first one, something quite spectacular happens. The colorless solutions turn into a creamy-milky liquid, and the light-sensitive silver-halide crystals separate out. This is a simple double decomposition, which can be written as follows:

$$AgNO_3 + KBr \rightarrow AgBr + KNO_3$$

(silver nitrate + potassium bromide →
silver bromide + potassium nitrate)

At this stage, it is still a very crude emulsion, and many improvements must be made to decrease its contrast and improve its sensitivity to light. The speed with which silver nitrate is poured into the halide-gelatin solution and the amount of gelatin present determine the grain size and speed of the emulsion obtained.

The next stage in emulsion improvement is the so-called Ostwald ripening, a heating process of the emulsion to about 90 F. During this process, some of the silver halides dissolve and reform with others to yield larger grain size. Since the emulsion now contains a variety of grain sizes, the contrast is lowered and the speed is increased.

After the ripening stage, the emulsion is allowed to cool and to set and is then shredded in noodle fashion to be washed. During this washing period, all excess by-products are removed.

After the washing process is complete, the emulsion is prepared for "after-ripening" by simply reheating it. Sensitivity and contrast are further refined. This is brought about by chemical sensitizing, thought to be produced by impurities in the gelatin. Gelatin known to contain natural sensitizers may be added or sulfur sensitizers may be mixed in. The grain size itself is not altered during "after-ripening." Sulfur impurities create silver sulfide "sensitivity specks" on the crystal surfaces, which promote the formation of silver atoms when the emulsion is struck by light.

The final step in the process is dye-sensitizing. In this step, the spectral sensitivity is extended through the addition of optical sensitizers, which extend the emulsion response into the green and red portions of the spectrum. Other additions made at this point include preservatives and anti-foggants as well as emulsion hardeners in the form of chrome alum and formaldehyde. The emulsion is now ready to be spread onto coating surfaces—either glass, paper, or film.

THE LATENT IMAGE

In 1835, Louis Jacques Mandé Daguerre discovered the existence of the latent image quite accidentally. His silvered copper plates, which he had treated with iodine vapor, had again failed to produce an image. He then stored them in a cupboard, intending to repolish and use them in a few days.

Imagine his astonishment when he saw a perfect image on these plates which he had believed to be absolutely underexposed. Removing the chemicals present—one by one—and substituting more plates made with identical exposure times, he was finally able to demonstrate that the mercury vapor was responsible for making the latent image visible. The existence of the latent image had been proven by an after-process, development.

If you accidentally open a camera with exposed film and examine the emulsion, no visible proof of the latent image can be seen, but you know that later development would have been proof of its existence. The latent image is known to us by its activity, but we are unable to show it as a substance.

THEORETICAL NATURE

The many theories on the formation of the latent image can be divided into two categories: The first deals essentially with the characteristic curve and the relation between the developable density and amount of exposure. The second category deals with the theories of the actual latent image formation in the silver-halide grains.

In our discussion about the light-sensitive emulsion, we saw that optical sensitizers are needed for the emulsion to respond to spectrum regions beyond the blue, violet, and ultraviolet. Without these optical sensitizers, the silver-halide crystal itself must absorb light or radiation in the region of "inherent sensitivity" to be effective in latent-image formation.

ANALYTICAL APPROACH

Normal analytical methods are not refined enough to detect silver and halogen in grains that have been exposed to normal photographic levels; however, for many reasons, we must assume that the latent image is essentially silver. The chemical reaction of the latent image and silver are the same. Chromic acid, potassium persulfate, and free halogen oxidize silver, and these same agents will destroy the latent image. A heavy exposure produces detectable amounts of silver, and a direct proportion between the number of quanta absorbed and the silver liberated can be shown.

GRAIN FORMATION

When silver bromide or silver chloride is subjected to heavy exposures of photographically active light, free silver and halogen atoms are formed. A halogen receptor must be present to prevent recombination with the silver so that the effect of exposure is not lost. One silver atom can then be formed for every light quantum absorbed.

Under the electron microscope, discrete silver particles formed by heavy exposure can be seen very well. It is on these points that the development of exposed grains starts, after a sufficient number of silver atoms have been acquired. Some researchers maintain that this massing of silver atoms occurs only at "sensitivity centers," but it is not certain whether groups of molecules or atoms of a particular element or compound serve as these sensitivity centers.

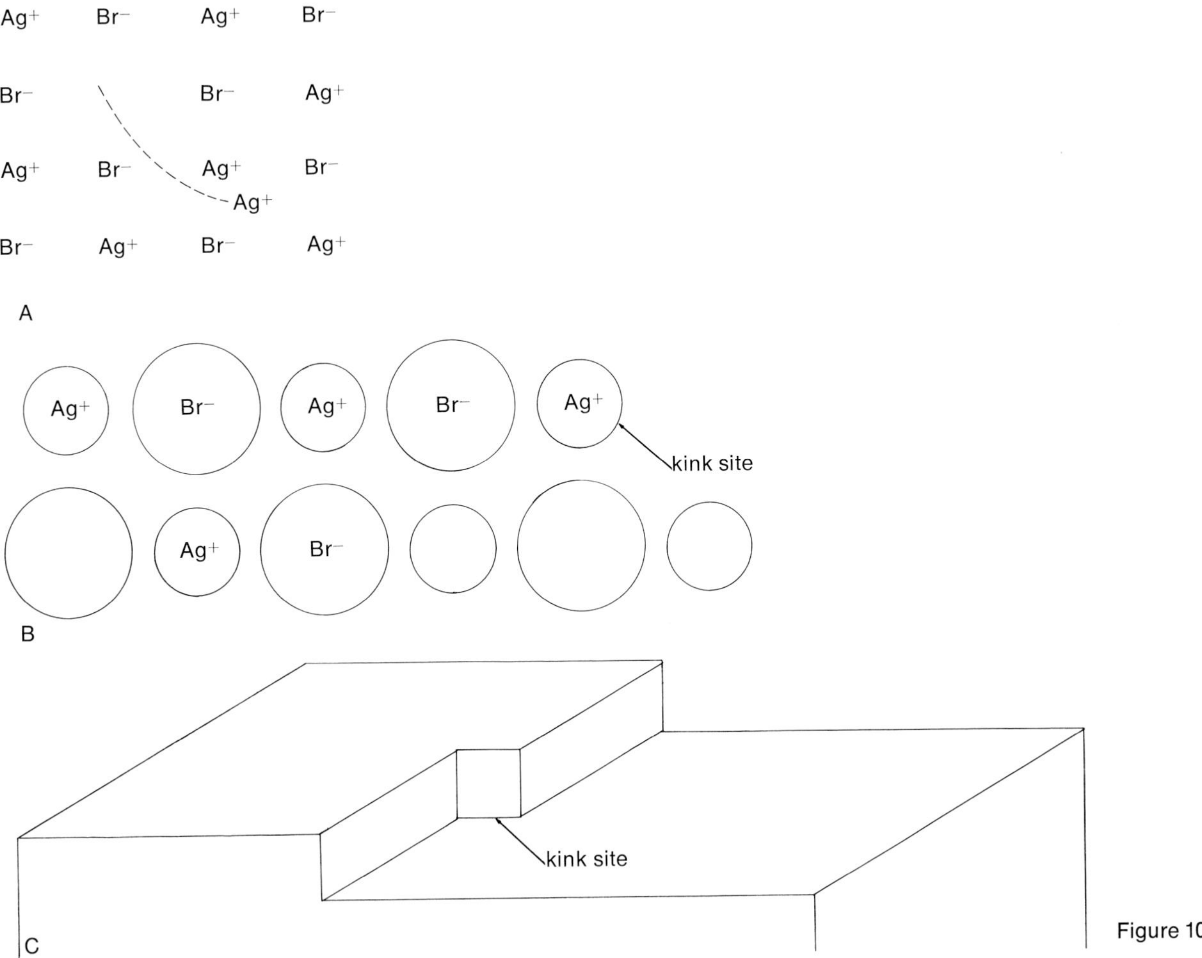

Figure 10

CRYSTAL DEFECTS

Recent theories point to actual imperfections in the structure of silver-halide crystals as the reason for photographic sensitivity and the forming of the latent image. These theories, supported by experimental evidence, suggest that the latent image cannot be formed in a structurally perfect crystal. A silver-halide crystal must possess defects, which play an important role in latent-image forming.

In the so-called Frenkel defect, an ion has moved out of its normal lattice position and occupies a position as illustrated in Figure 10A. Other crystal imperfections that play an important part in the surface latent-image formation are called "kink sites." This is an incomplete layer of ions on the crystal surface, and the last ion in this incomplete row is said to occupy a kink site (Figures 10B and 10C). If such an imperfection occurs inside the crystal, we speak of a "jog site." Both jog and kink sites can be occupied by a silver or a halide ion.

CONDUCTIVITY

A silver-halide crystal kept in the dark has a very low electrical conductivity, but exposed to light, this conductivity is suddenly increased. We speak of photoconductivity, and a parallel exists between photoconductivity, sensitivity, and the mechanics of latent-image forming.

The more light quanta absorbed in a given unit of time, the higher is the number of photoelectrons liberated and carrying the current. The light energy freeing electrons of halogen atoms in the silver-halide crystal lets these electrons move freely inside the crystal. The previously mentioned irregularities (a kink site, for example) in the crystal structure will stop this electron and trap it.

Existing silver ions in the crystal (thought of as atoms missing an electron) having a positive charge are drawn to the trapped electron with its negative charge. The silver ion and the electron together form an atom of metallic silver at the kink site. The trap is enlarged, and more electrons and more silver ions are caught as a result. This growing silver speck is the latent image; when it has grown sufficiently, it becomes a center where the development will later start.

DEVELOPMENT

Development is an amplification process multiplying the latent image by as much as a billion times. One silver atom formed at a structural irregularity in the silver-halide crystal is unstable and needs a second one to form a stable pair. If three silver atoms can be formed, then this speck can become a development center. There are many theories why the developer acts preferentially on exposed grains and will not act on unexposed ones. One theory maintains that a charge barrier around unexposed grains resists the active developer by electrostatic repulsion.

FIXING

The next important step in latent image formation is fixing. Hypo is an acidic solution of sodium thiosulfate. The process involved is also subject to speculation. We know that it leaves the metallic silver image but allows the dissolution of the silver halides out of the gelatin.

Latent-image formation is a two-fold process: a) an electronic stage connected with photoconductance; and b) an ionic stage that involves the attraction of positively charged silver ions.

Recent studies under the electron microscope seem to support such theories on the latent image. By subjecting grains to a brief development in order to enlarge the development centers, experimenters have shown these development centers clearly in random distribution on the crystal surface. Also, the application of an electric field has shown a shift of these centers in the direction opposite to that of the field. This is experimental evidence that trapping of photoelectrons is an essential part in the formation of the latent image.

10

THE CAMERA AND THE HUMAN EYE

The camera is often compared to the human eye. Both have a lens system to focus light rays and a diaphragm that controls the aperture, or the amount of light allowed to enter (the diaphragm of the camera is equivalent to the iris of the eye). When you look at a scene that is made up of extremely bright parts, but which also contains shadow areas, the eye contracts and expands its pupil as it scans across. The camera cannot do this. Its diaphragm must be adjusted for an average brightness range, and depending on the desired result, it may be adjusted for the highlights or shadow areas alone.

The human eye, with its flexible lens, is focused by muscles that change the curvature of the eye lens. In the camera, the lens must be moved back and forth to perform the same function.

Both the camera and the eye are lighttight chambers in which a picture is formed on material that is chemically sensitive to light—film in the camera, and the retina in the eye. The retina is a curved field, but in the camera light rays are collected on a flat piece of sensitive material. The eye can see only that part of the electromagnetic spectrum which we know as white light. The camera, loaded with special films, can record in the infrared, ultraviolet, and X-ray regions of the spectrum.

In the eye, a combination of nerves (rods and cones) transmit light stimulus via the optic nerve to the brain. This "cable" leaves the retina of the eye at a point known as the "blind spot"—a feature that would be highly undesirable in photography.

The human eye cannot store or amplify impressions. No matter how much you strain your eyes in dim light, you cannot see any better. However, sensitive emulsions in the camera react to increases in exposure up to a certain point and will amplify and store an image. Because images are easily stored in the camera, you can superimpose image upon image. The eye cannot do this.

The eye sees spatial differences in rectilinear perspective just as the camera. In picture form, we have learned to accept receding lines as converging toward the horizon even though we know that in reality these lines are parallel. But we generally reject convergence in the vertical since our eyes do not notice it. A camera with a short focal-length lens

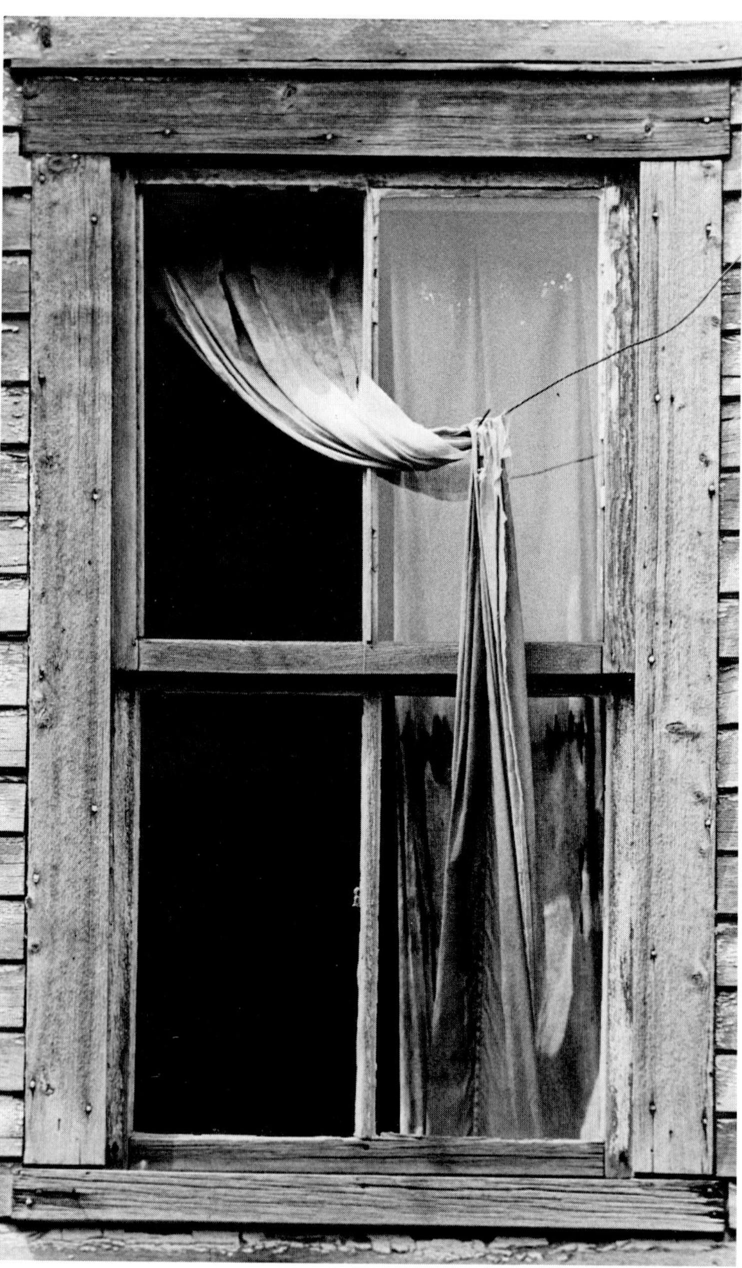

A deserted farm. During enlarging in the darkroom, the easel was tilted to compensate for the low shooting angle. Nikon F2, 135mm Nikkor, 1/250 sec. at *f*/11 on Tri-X.

will render vertical parallels as converging lines. To correct perspective, the photographer uses perspective-control lenses or a view camera, which permits tilting of the lens board. Tilting the enlarger easel in the darkroom will also help to correct perspective.

The focal length of the eye is fixed; but with interchangeable lenses, cameras have a wide choice of focal lengths, and the photographer can control the rendering of space and make it conform to visual requirements in graphic layouts. With wide-angle lenses, he can create illusions of greater depth; and with telephoto lenses, he can compress or even eliminate the feeling of space.

With the exception of special cameras which, like the human eye, produce stereoscopic vision, ordinary camera vision is monocular, and depth in pictures must be presented in symbolic form (by such cues of depth perception as decrease in size, sharpness, texture, overlapping, and the like).

To the eye, most things appear sharp. When you look at a scene, your eyes shift focus as you look at distant or near objects in rapid succession. The camera will only produce sharp zones for its predetermined depth of field. This constant shift of focus in human vision is the downfall of most photographers.

Human vision, which is dependent upon psychological interpretation by the brain, is very subjective; subconscious memories work hand in hand with what you see and influence your acceptance or rejection of it. The camera, alternatively, objectively records everything present in a scene. Human vision is also selective; that is, you usually see what you like to see and what interests you most. Most beginners' photographs are crowded with needless subject matter because the camera—a mechanical recording device—impartially records what is present.

A photograph renders what you have seen in isolated form. A three-dimensional world is translated into symbols on a two-dimensional surface. The various objects of a scene are seen in relationships to each other only, and they form a design on which you focus your attention. The eye, however, sees all subject matter in a scene not as an overall design, but as successive pieces of a large whole.

The eye sees everything in color, but unless a camera is loaded with color film, it will translate all color into varying gray tones. The eye accepts these shades of gray but subconsciously assigns color to them upon viewing a black-and-white print. Color film very often renders color differently than the way the eye sees it. (See Chapter 5: "Color.")

PHOTOGRAPHIC VISION

The most complicated process for the beginning photographer is to learn to **see** in photographic terms—to make the decisions for the camera. You must learn to exclude elements, including other senses, that influence your vision. Only in this way can you isolate and heighten your sense of sight.

It might be helpful to carry a 35mm cardboard mount in your pocket or, if you shoot 2¼″ × 2¼″, a slide mount appropriate to this format. Once in a while, look at the world through it. Hold the mount just far enough in front of your eyes so you can see the cutout sharply. The cutout seems to isolate your subject matter, but by removing or isolating part of a scene, you will be surprised how easy it is to see it as a projection on a flat surface. This exercise will force you to previsualize a scene in terms of design, pattern, light areas and shadows, color, and perspective.

Try this for one day: Carry your camera all the time, no matter where you walk, drive, fly, or sit in a room. Try to shoot a picture about every half hour. Look as often as possible through the viewfinder of your

The handheld camera can travel anywhere to capture an exciting new visual experience. In some aerobatic maneuvers, the camera will be too heavy to lift to the eye, but coming over the top of a loop presents no problem. Nikon F2, 20mm Nikkor, 1/1000 sec. at *f*/8 on Tri-X.

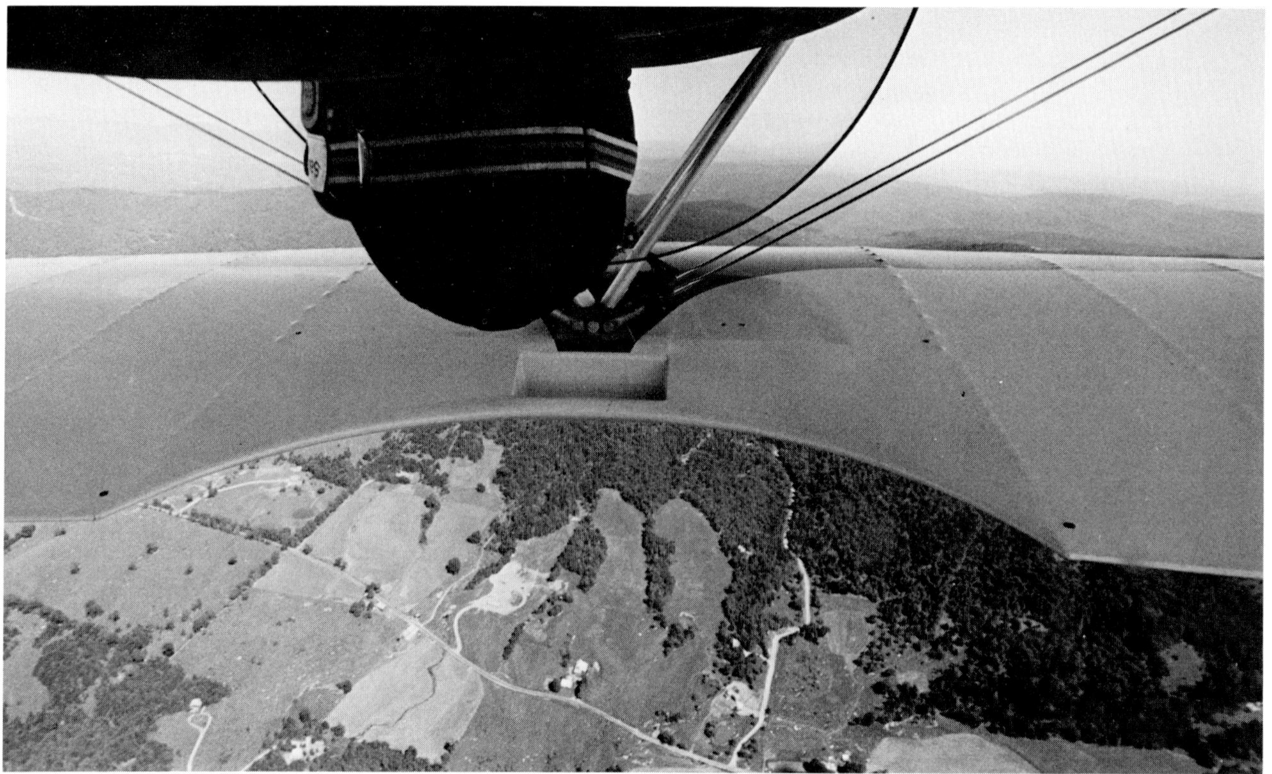

camera and use lenses of different focal lengths. Try to see the world around you in terms of graphic posters. Try to recognize a possible picture. Is not the moment of recognition the moment that precedes the pressing of the shutter release? Try to compose as carefully as possible. Cropping in the darkroom should be kept to a minimum. If you must enlarge a tiny speck to show your picture, you waste much of the negative area, and you have not learned to see yet. When you have done all this, make a proof sheet of your effort and analyze the results.

Once you learn to see in photographic terms, once the camera becomes an extension of your mind, guided by your sense of sight, creative freedom will come. You can now approach what you like to photograph with discipline, and you can make demands on the attention you give to your subject. You must evaluate and re-evaluate what you see not only in terms of design and color, but also in terms of your own involvement. This personal involvement is the difference between the snapshooter and the photographer who ultimately will be able to communicate emotion and whose images will show subjective content.

The camera is only a recording device; it cannot make decisions. It does not get involved, and subject matter is unimportant to it. As a good photographer, you must become its director, engineer, prop man, and much more. Photography is the art of arranging shape, light, color, or its tonal representation in a gray scale into a design in which their relationships and adjustments in space visibly form a dynamic rhythm. If you, the photographer, want to be an artist, you must concern yourself with the interrelationships of these constructive elements which constitute your composition.

These techniques can be learned, and the student of photography must enlarge his knowledge of all the visual arts. Study not only the works of known masters of photography, but also art history as well, and visit museums as often as possible. Some people argue that this might lead to imitation. However, I believe that the good student of photography will continue with his medium. Serious photography demands sensitive students, and the degree of sensitivity will determine the amount of objective or subjective interpretation of the world around them. It does not take long before the student's pictures become clear extensions of his mind. Looking through an assortment of pictures in my classes, I can, with a high degree of accuracy, assign each one to its originator.

CAMERA CONTROLS

More than a quarter century ago, when box cameras were predominant, photography was very simple. In bright sunlight, the camera was aimed at the subject and the shutter release was pressed. It was not necessary to focus the lens; the aperture was fixed, and shutter speeds were always the same. ASA ratings of film did not vary much, and exposure problems were not as critical as today.

The demand for pictures under practically all lighting conditions brought improved films of high speeds. With these films came cameras fitted with lenses controllable over a wide *f*/stop range and shutters that permitted the selection of many speeds.

CAMERA TYPES

Cameras on today's market can be grouped into three main categories: (1) nonautomatic, (2) semi-automatic, and (3) fully automatic.

Cameras in the first group should be used with a handheld exposure meter. Either shutter speed or *f*/stop is selected, depending on subject matter. If you want to control subject speed, you must select a

SLR CAMERA CONTROLS

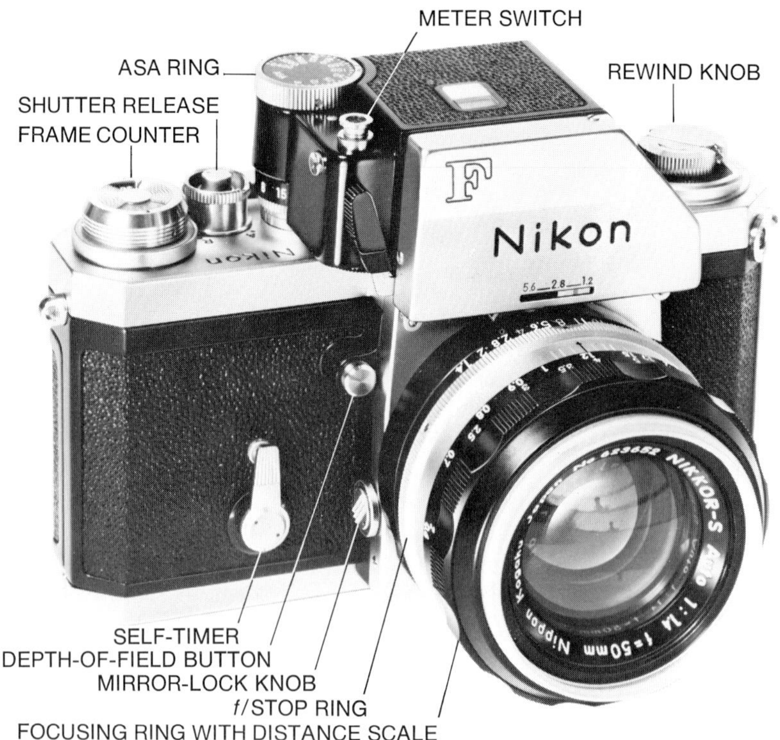

FIGURE 11

shutter speed and take the corresponding *f*/stop from the meter reading. If you want to control depth of field, you must select an *f*/stop and find the corresponding shutter speed for the meter reading.

Semi-automatic cameras are cross-coupled and could be called "preselect automatics." With this system, either shutter speed or *f*/stop is preselected, and the needle of the built-in exposure meter is centered on a mark to adjust to existing light conditions. Cameras in this category allow full creative control. Several of the newer "fully automatic" 35mm reflexes are really semi-automatic, except that after you set either the shutter speed or *f*/stop, the camera meter automatically sets the other.

True fully automatic cameras have both aperture and shutter speeds coupled to an exposure meter. Exposure determination follows a predetermined program. In this type of camera, the fastest shutter speed is used down to a point where light conditions permit one particular aperture, say *f*/5.6. If light conditions become too dim for the combination of fastest shutter speed and *f*/5.6, the automatic mechanism selects an increase in exposure time. Since it is often impossible to override these programs, it is obvious that this type of camera is less suited for creative work.

METER SETTINGS

Let us look at a modern camera and its various controls. The camera controls must give you full control over the image brightness. The exposure meter, either built-in or handheld, will provide the first information. It must be set for the appropriate ASA rating for the film in use. The ASA system sets standards of film-emulsion sensitivity to light. You set the meter to the ASA rating by turning a ring or dial on the camera to line up a red mark with the desired number, usually found on the film package. Settings on cameras might read from ASA 6 to ASA 6000 and on handheld meters, from ASA 0.8 to ASA 25,000.

It is good advice to start with published ASA ratings. As you gain confidence in shooting and experience in darkroom work, you can vary exposure ratings to suit your equipment and technique. Kodak Tri-X Pan film is normally rated at ASA 400. However, many workers prefer to rate this film at ASA 800, thereby gaining an extra *f*/stop in low-light situations. Rated at ASA 1200 and developed in Acufine, this film still produces full negatives with no noticeable grain in enlargements up to 8″ × 10″.

Films with low ASA ratings are not as sensitive as those with high ratings, but they have finer grain. Which film to use is up to the photographer, depending, of course, on the desired result and the lighting conditions at the location.

The exposure latitude of black-and-white film is greater than that of color film. An exposure error of two stops might be tolerated with black-and-white film, whereas color transparency film will permit only half an *f*/stop error in over- or underexposure. With color film, you have to be precise and find the "correct" exposure.

Every exposure actually depends on three factors: first, the "speed" (sensitivity) of the film in use; second, the amount and quality of the light; and third, the shutter speed.

DIAPHRAGM

The diaphragm of a lens allows the aperture to become smaller or larger. If the aperture is large, the amount of light that enters the camera at a given moment is also large. The diaphragm inside the lens consists of metal leaves that overlap more and more as the *f*/stop ring is turned. Small *f*/numbers (such as *f*/1.4) indicate that the diaphragm leaves are retracted, the aperture is large, and the lens is open. High *f*/numbers (such as *f*/16) indicate the diaphragm leaves are overlapped, the aperture is small, and the lens is almost closed.

The diaphragm, with its variable aperture openings, gives you the means to control the depth of field. All points nearest and farthest from the camera that appear in sharp focus embrace this depth of field. The distance between sharpest points increases as the lens is stopped down (closed).

Early lenses were constructed in such a way that metal plates with different size holes ("stops") were inserted into a slot to change the effective aperture of the lens. They were called "Waterhouse stops," after John Waterhouse, who invented them in 1858. This system was very cumbersome, and only fixed *f*/numbers could be used. The invention of the iris diaphragm around 1900 has made possible the use of an infinitely variable number of *f*/settings between the marked stops.

The f/stop. But what is an *f*/stop, really, and how have we arrived at such a system?

If you insert a stop in any lens, the incident-light beam entering it is narrowed down to the size of the opening. We speak of the *effective aperture*—the diameter of the incident-light beam now filling the real aperture. If this circle is, for example, half the diameter of a previous stop, its area is reduced to one quarter. The resultant image brightness would also be reduced to one quarter of the previous stop.

If you had to photograph with two lenses of different focal lengths, one a five-inch lens, the other a ten-inch lens, something else would become apparent. The light passing through the lens with the ten-inch focal length would travel twice as far and would form an image two times larger (four times the area) than that passing through the shorter lens. If you wanted negatives of the same density from both lenses, you would have to expose four times as long with the longer lens. The image brightness would again be reduced to one quarter as the image-to-lens distance is doubled.

A constant ratio between these two variables had to be found so that modern lenses, regardless of their focal lengths, would produce images of the same brightness when stopped down to the same *f*/stop. If the five-inch lens were used with an effective aperture of one inch, and the ten-inch lens were used with an effective aperture of two inches, then both lenses would use an effective aperture of one fifth of their focal length, and both would produce images of the same brightness.

Relative Aperture. Expressing the effective aperture in terms of the focal length of the lens gives us its *relative aperture.* Both sample lenses would be *f*/5 lenses. The formula is:

$$\frac{\text{Focal length of the lens}}{\text{Diameter of effective aperture}} = f/\text{number}$$

Introducing an *f*/number series like *f*/1, 2, 4, 8, 16, and so on would have created complications. It would have meant halving the *diameter* of the *aperture,* with the resultant illumination dropping to one quarter. Photographically, it is more desirable to have a scale whereby each successive *f*/stop admits half the *illumination* of the previous one. More intermediate stops had to be added. So if you multiply the *f*/numbers each time by the square root of two ($\sqrt{2}=1.4$), you halve the *area* of the aperture, and such a scale becomes: *f*/1.4, 2, 2.8, 4, 5.6, 8, 11, 16, 22, and so on. *Each f/number in this universally accepted scale progressively halves the illumination.*

Aperture control. Modern lenses for 35mm cameras are constructed in such a way that the moment they are inserted into the camera body, two things happen: A protrusion on the *f*/stop ring engages with a pin of the exposure meter and couples the lens to the meter. At the same time, a protrusion in the back of the lens (a pin or lever) engages with an arm inside the camera. This arrangement holds the spring-loaded diaphragm in the wide-open position. This is of great advantage if you must focus the lens under dim light, since it admits the greatest amount of light. The instant the shutter is released, the lens diaphragm stops down to the selected *f*/stop.

SHUTTER

Another important camera control is its shutter. With the shutter, you control the amount of time light is allowed to act on the sensitive emulsion. You also account for the movement of objects to be photographed. A rapidly moving object photographed with a slow shutter speed will exhibit blur. The same object photographed with a faster shutter speed will be "frozen" on the film. (If you use a medium shutter speed on a fast-moving object and swing the camera—"pan"—in the direction the object is moving before releasing the shutter, the object will be sharp and the background will be blurred, conveying the sensation of speed.)

The early cameras did not need shutters. Plates were so slow that the exposure could be made by merely removing the lens cap and replacing it after some time had elapsed. Such shutters were very crude. Some resembled window roller blinds; others were rubber domes that opened up like a mouth if the photographer pressed a rubber bulb.

Shutter Types. Today, we distinguish between two main types: the bladed between-the-lens shutter, and the focal-plane shutter. The blade shutter usually allows speeds up to 1/500 sec. Its blades start to open from the lens center, going outward in a growing star shape, so that each section of the film receives an even amount of exposure. Such shutters can synchronize with flash at any shutter speed. In the case of interchangeable lenses, this type of shutter is expensive since each lens must have its own shutter built-in.

Most modern 35mm cameras have a focal-plane shutter. It is built into the back of the camera at the film plane; therefore, all lenses with this system can be unshuttered. The shutter itself is a moving curtain with a slit in it. Most shutters on small-format cameras work with a fixed curtain speed; the shutter-speed-control knob varies only the width of the slit. Since the curtain moves just in front of the film, only a part of the frame is exposed at any one time. The *effective* shutter speed is the time the slit uncovers any part of the film. Some of these shutters are calibrated in the following manner: T, B, 1, 1/2, 1/4, 1/8, 1/15, 1/30, 1/60, 1/125, 1/250, 1/500, 1/1000, and even 1/2000 sec. The T (Time) setting leaves the shutter open until the release is pressed again. The B (Bulb) setting also leaves the shutter open, but the release button must be kept pressed during the length of the exposure. Focal-plane shutters can only be flash synchronized up to moderate speeds (usually 1/60 sec.).

Shutter Speed Selection. Shutter speed progression is set up in such a way that each higher speed again halves the time of the previous one. Obviously, with various shutter speed and *f*/stop combinations, the same amount of exposure can be obtained. This is best illustrated with the following table for the same total exposure:

	Shutter Speed	*f*/Stop
High object-stopping power, shallow depth of field.	1/1000 sec.	*f*/4
(Do not use very long lenses with slower speed.)	1/500 sec.	*f*/5.6
Good overall speed, good depth of field.	1/250 sec. 1/125 sec.	*f*/8 *f*/11
No object-stopping power, large depth of field. (Do not handhold telephoto lenses. Use a tripod.)	1/60 sec. 1/30 sec.	*f*/16 *f*/22
Most people will introduce camera shake.	1/15 sec.	*f*/32

From this table, you can see that the selection of shutter speed and *f*/stop calls for evaluating the picture requirements under a particular set of circumstances. If you want to stop movement, a high shutter speed is more important, and you can choose an *f*/stop to match the illumination and shutter speed. If the required depth of field is very shallow (a single object, a portrait, or the like) the highest shutter speed with a wide-open lens is the likely combination. If depth of field is the important feature, you must close down the lens and select a slower shutter speed. In this case, it is important to know how slow a shutter speed you can tolerate without introducing blur because of camera shake. Many people cannot take a sharp picture with shutter speeds under 1/30 sec. using a 50mm normal lens. Longer lenses require faster shutter speeds.

VIEWING AND FOCUSING CONTROLS

Further camera controls include the focusing mechanism—usually a ring on the lens barrel for extending or retracting the lens—aided by some optical guide—either a rangefinder or a reflex viewing system.

Looking into the viewfinder of a rangefinder camera, your eye sees two separate images. Focusing the lens turns a prism that aligns the two images into one. But since focusing is not achieved by viewing

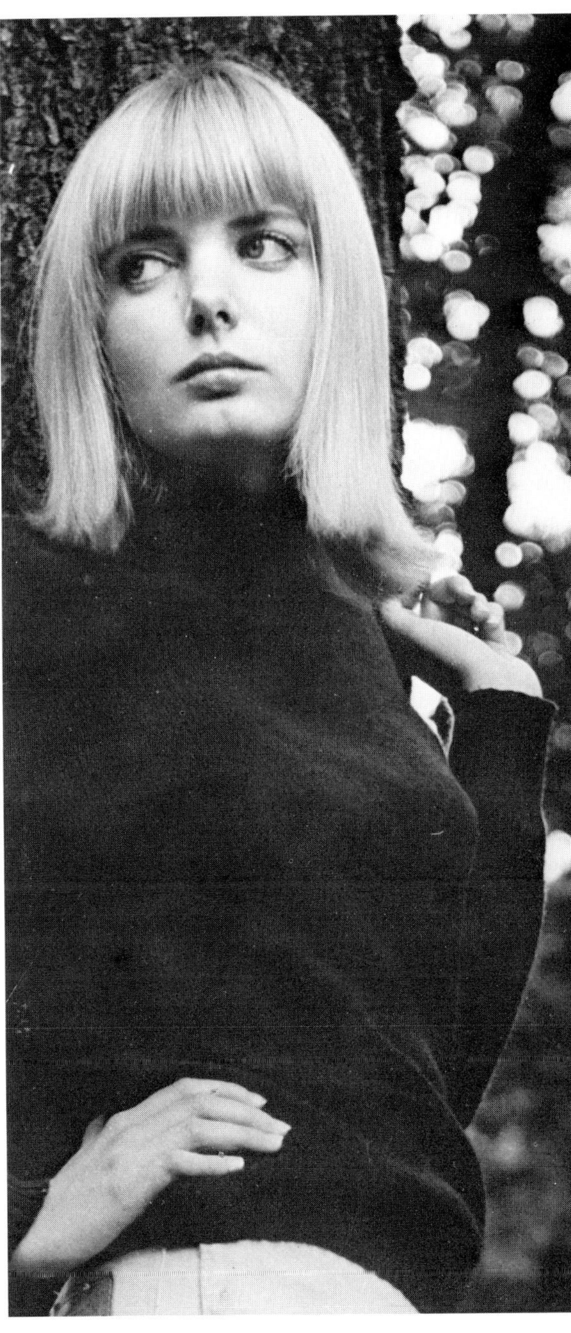

Left: In the park. Nikon FTN, 200mm Nikkor, 1/500 sec. at *f*/4 on Tri-X.

Below: In the Bowery. Nikon FTN, 50mm Nikkor, 1/250 sec. at *f*/8 on Tri-X.

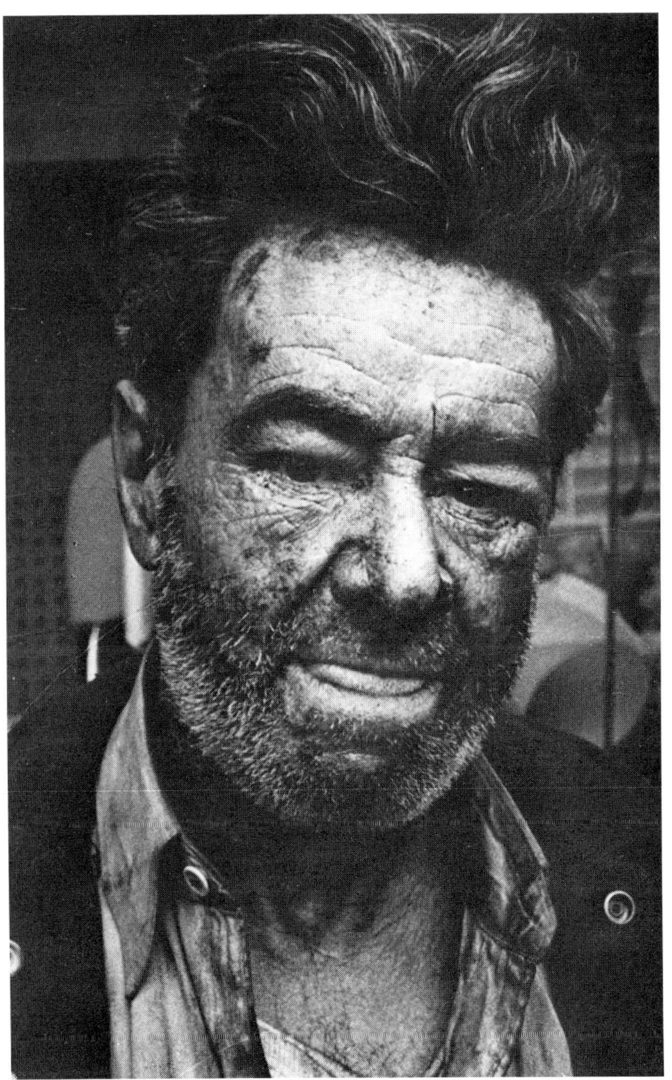

through the lens, the image of the viewfinder does not represent the picture area on the negative. If you use lenses of different focal lengths, frame outlines appear in the viewfinder to indicate the approximate picture area for the particular focal length. In closeup photography, the viewfinder will not "see" what the lens will see. This problem is called parallax.

Larger-format cameras use the groundglass viewing system. Light reflected from objects enters the taking lens and is directly projected onto a groundglass that is precisely in the same plane as the film will be when the film holder is inserted. The lens usually moves, set in a lens board, on a geared track that contracts or extends the camera bellows. You can control distortions of the image by tilting the lens board horizontally or vertically or by raising or lowering it.

The groundglass focusing and viewing system is also employed in twin-lens reflex cameras. Such cameras employ a taking and a viewing, or focusing, lens. In closeup photography, each lens again sees a different field and parallax corrections must be made. When the focusing knob is turned, both viewing and taking lenses move in tandem. An object focused in the viewfinder is also focused for the taking lens.

Focusing a modern single-lens reflex camera is accomplished by turning the lens and aligning a split image in the center of the viewfinder or sharpening the image on a variety of interchangeable screens. Since the viewing system produces an image that corresponds to what the lens sees, there are no parallax problems and the area outlined in the viewfinder corresponds to what the lens sees, regardless of focal length. At the moment of exposure, a mirror is moved up, making this type of camera a bit noisier than a rangefinder type.

FILM TRANSPORT CONTROLS

Other controls include the advance and reverse mechanism to transport and rewind film. Some cameras are fitted with release buttons to make double exposures intentionally. This can be accomplished on some cameras by setting the film advance to rewind. It is then possible to rewind one frame by lining a dot up with its former position and shooting again on this previously exposed frame. On others, it is merely necessary to press the rewind button and advance the film-advance lever, which now will not transport film but only wind the shutter.

DEPTH OF FIELD, DEPTH OF FOCUS, AND HYPERFOCAL DISTANCE

Let us differentiate between *depth of field, depth of focus,* and the *hyperfocal distance.* Some photographers confuse the first two and have the greatest difficulty explaining all three.

1. *Depth of focus* is the small permissible movement of the film plane along the lens axis before sharply focused points become circles of confusion.
2. *Depth of field* is the zone of sharpness in a scene. The distance between the nearest and farthest points of a scene that are in sharp focus on the film is said to be the depth of field.
3. *Hyperfocal distance* is the distance from the lens to the nearest point of acceptable sharpness when the lens is focused on infinity. Focusing on this distance yields the greatest depth of field for any lens.

DEPTH OF FOCUS

Depth of focus is related *only* to the permissible movement of the film plane. Large-format cameras are usually constructed in such a way to allow movement of their fronts and backs along a geared track. Such a camera back, holding the focusing screen or film plane, can be moved toward the lens, away from the sharpest point of focus. It can also be moved back beyond the point of sharpest focus. In both instances, the movement is restricted by the widening of the cone of refracted light to a circular patch of light that can still be accepted as sharp. The distance between these two points is the depth of focus.

Circle of Confusion. The diameter of the intersected light cone is called a *circle of confusion.* (Unprecise focusing of the lens will also produce circles of confusion.) If these circles are larger than an acceptable standard, the best camera and lens combination will produce unsharp negatives, and the best enlarger will produce unsharp prints. Fortunately, the human eye has a limited resolving power, much less than the resolving power of today's lenses. Visual sharpness depends on an individual's eyesight, lighting conditions, and the distance from which a finished print is viewed. A circle of 1/100-inch diameter, if viewed from a distance of one foot, will still be seen as a point by most adults. Naturally, there is a relationship between negative size, circle of confusion, and anticipated enlargement.

An 8″ × 10″ enlargement from a 35mm negative is an 8× magnification. (Magnification is linear in photography.) Since the permissible circle of confusion for the finished 8″ × 10″ print (to be seen sharp) is 1/100 inch, the permissible circle of confusion in the negative can only be 1/800 inch. These critical values decrease with an increase in negative size.

DEPTH OF FIELD

To understand depth of field, assume that you have to photograph three trees, A, B, and C, and that these trees grow at distances of 100 yards, 200 yards, and 300 yards from the camera position (see Figure 12).

The lens is focused on tree B. All light rays coming from this tree have been refracted and are fully converged on the film plane. The lens is set at full aperture (wide open) but now each point on tree B is recorded as a needle-sharp point.

However, light rays coming from the nearest tree, A, have not fully converged when they reach the film plane. Their focal point lies behind the film plane, and the sensitive material actually intersects a small cone of light, and patches of light are produced. With the lens wide open, these patches usually are larger than the permissible circles of confusion. The resultant image is unsharp and out of focus.

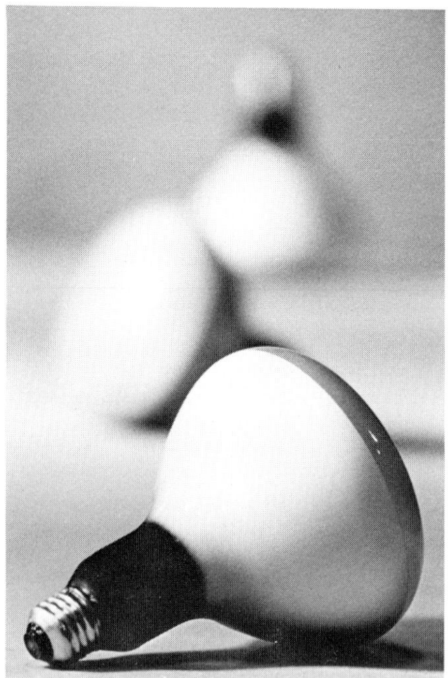

A

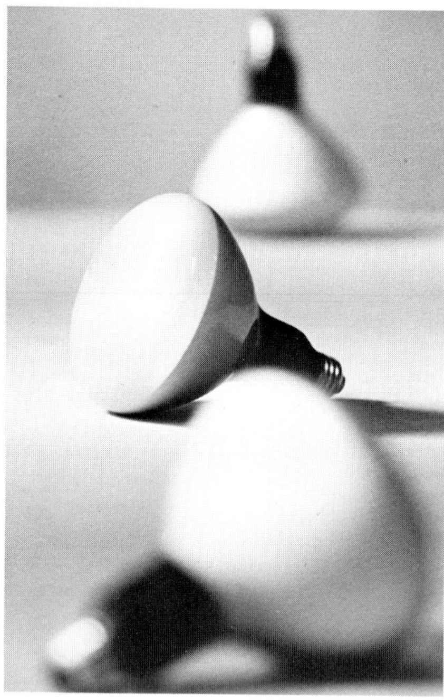

B

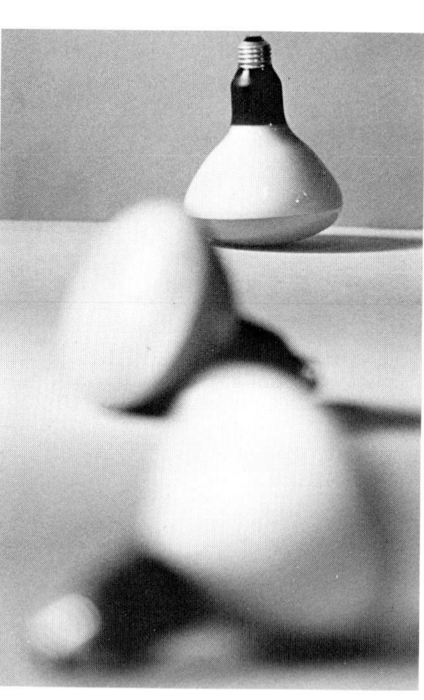

C

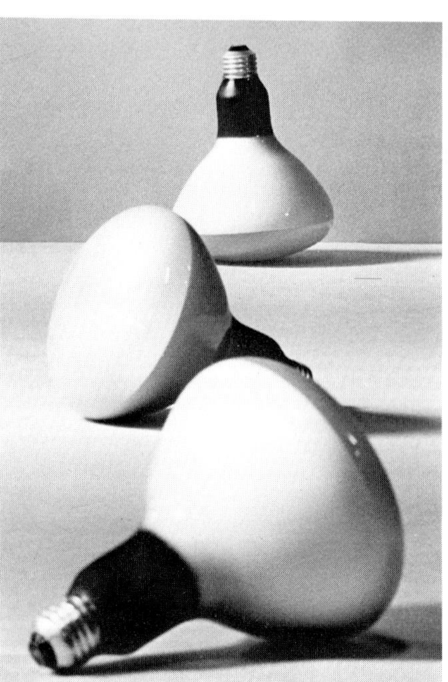

D

FIGURE 12

The principle of depth of field, described in the text, is illustrated here using light bulbs instead of trees. Figures A, B, and C are focused on the front, center, and back objects, respectively. In Figure D, all objects in fore-, middle-, and background are rendered in sharp focus with the aperture stopped down to *f*/22.

Similarly, rays arriving from the farthest tree, C, will be focused in front of the film plane and have begun to diverge again before reaching the film plane. They will also be recorded as circular patches of light. The image will be unsharp if these circles of confusion are larger in diameter than acceptable standards.

Therefore, when the lens aperture is large, the angle between the converging rays is large, and the resultant circles of confusion have large diameters in front of and behind the actual focal plane. The resultant pictures are described as having a shallow depth of field.

When you close down the lens, setting the diaphragm at a smaller opening, only the center portion of the lens is now used, and the converging light cones will be slender. Objects that are quite a distance from the one focused on, either in front or beyond, form *small* circles of confusion. If these remain sufficiently small, the enlargement from such a negative will be seen as sharp. The resultant pictures will have a great depth of field.

For practical applications, a few things should be remembered. Depth of field decreases rapidly as an object gets closer to the lens. Lenses of long focal length (telephoto lenses) have very shallow depth of field, and short focal lenses (wide-angle lenses) have enormous depth of field. Depth of field always extends a greater distance beyond than in front of the object focused on, at a ratio of two to one; thus the rule of thumb: "Focus one third in." This means that you will get sharp pictures as long as you are focused one third inside the required depth of field. This technique is very important when shooting live action. Stopping action at its peak moment does not leave time to focus precisely. A lens preset in this way can be of great help.

Depth of field, then, depends on four factors. Each one will vary the amount of depth of field when the others are held constant. *The f/number.* When you increase the *f*/number (smaller lens opening) the depth of field will increase. *The circle of confusion* (itself dependent on *f*/number). If you accept a larger circle of confusion before you consider the resultant picture unsharp, then the distance covered by the depth of field is large. *The distance focused upon.* As an object to be photographed moves farther and farther from the lens, the distance in front of and behind the object covered by the depth of field also increases. *The focal length.* All lenses with shorter focal lengths have greater depth of field. Lenses of long focal lengths have shallower depth of field.

Most modern lenses have depth-of-field scales inscribed on them, which are specific for their focal length. The allowable circle of confusion is calculated for an average-size enlargement from the negative size of the camera on which the lens is used. Therefore, only two variables are present: object distance and *f*/number. The specific *f*/number is simply read against the distance focused upon, and the resultant depth of field can be read on the scale without visually checking by means of the "preview button."

HYPERFOCAL DISTANCE

The lenses of simple cameras are prefocused on the *hyperfocal point* rather than on infinity. You have already seen that various factors will influence depth of field. If you recall that the depth of field extends farther beyond the point focused on and is more limited toward the camera, you can then see that by focusing on infinity, you in fact waste depth of field. The zone beyond infinity cannot be realized if your lens is focused on infinity already. It would be wiser to focus on some point nearer to the camera, which would still allow the depth of field to extend back to infinity.

This can be done by refocusing the lens on the nearest point of sharpness when the lens is focused on infinity. This point is the *hyperfocal point,* and the distance from this point to the lens is called the *hyperfocal distance.* With the lens focused on this point, depth of field will extend back to infinity and forward to a point half the hyperfocal distance from the lens—the maximum depth for that *f*/stop.

Again, the hyperfocal distance varies with the focal length of the lens, with the selected *f*/stop, and with the acceptable diameter of the circle of confusion. However, with modern cameras, it is easy to find this point visually by depressing the preview button and refocusing on the nearest point that is sharp for the *f*/stop selected.

The formula for calculating the hyperfocal distance is:

$$\frac{\text{Focal length}^2}{f/\text{number} \times \text{diameter of circle of confusion}} = \text{Hyperfocal distance}$$

FIGURE 13

IMAGE TAKEN WITH A PINHOLE CAMERA
f/300, 15 seconds

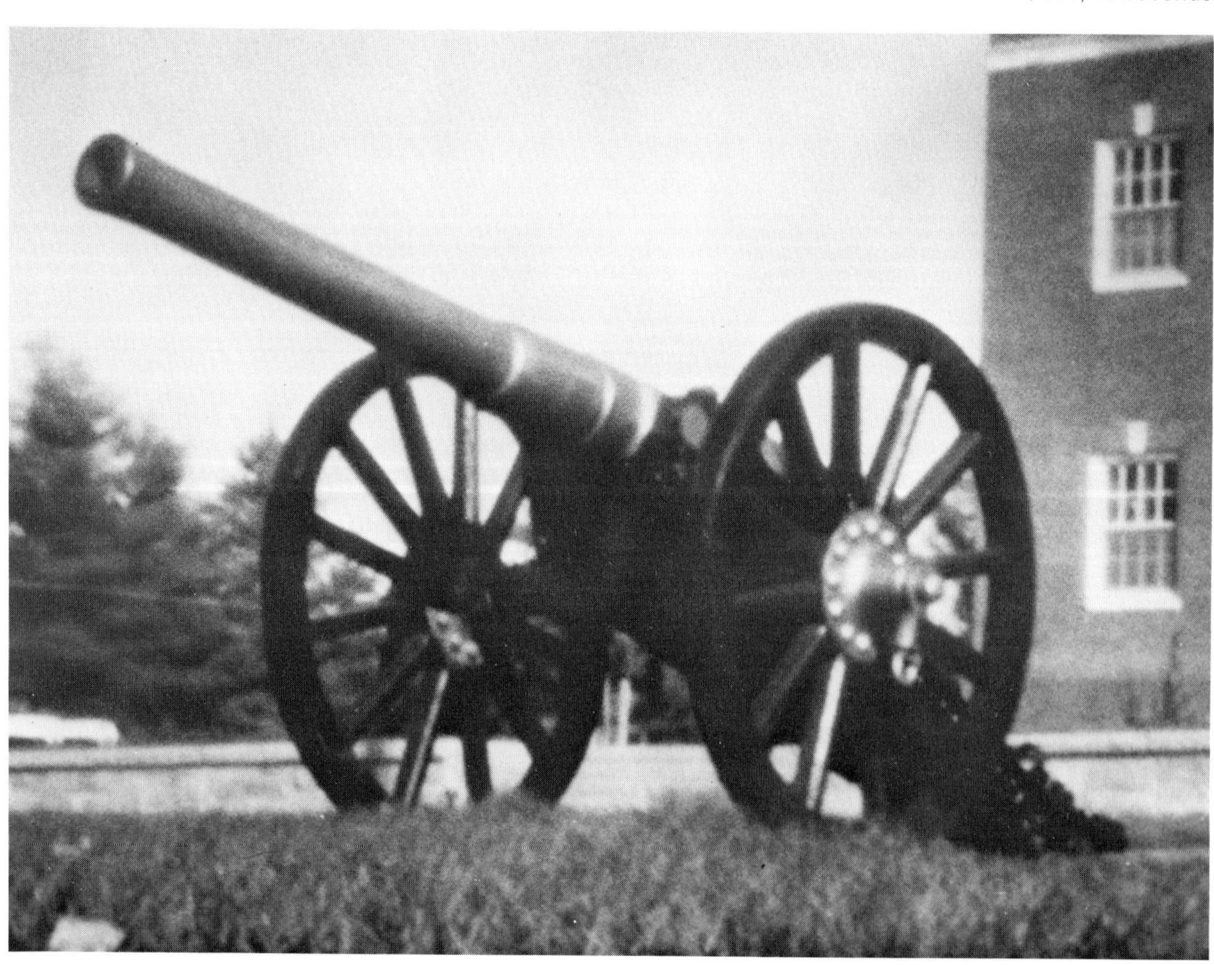

11

THE PINHOLE CAMERA

It is always interesting to construct a simple pinhole camera. This experiment is suggested for several reasons: First of all, it provides the student with an opportunity to handle 4″ × 5″ sheet film; second, the student is always surprised with the pleasing results. Since only one picture can be taken with a pinhole camera before the photographer must return to the darkroom, more thought must be spent on subject matter, composition, and lighting. (See Figure 13 opposite.)

Because you substitute a small hole for a lens, all rays from every point on the subject continue to diverge after they have passed through the opening. When these light rays finally arrive at the film plane, they will not be focused to a point; rather, they will be small circles of confusion. The film emulsion intersects a cone of light, and a multitude of very small light circles makes up the image, which always exhibits a very soft quality. A landscape photograph taken with a pinhole camera might actually be enhanced by its technical inferiority, as it takes on a very pictorial quality.

CONSTRUCTING A PINHOLE CAMERA

The actual construction of the pinhole camera is a simple affair. A cardboard or wooden box six inches long, five inches wide, and four inches high will do. You will have to make a tight-fitting lid, and both the box and the lid should be painted matte-black on the inside. Next, cut a half-inch hole in one of the 4″ × 5″ sides. Cut and pierce a square piece of black paper (the kind found in photographic paper boxes) in the center with a sharp needle. For good results, this hole should be about 1/50 inch. Make some provision for covering and uncovering the pinhole with black tape; this will be the shutter. You can use an empty 5″ × 7″ photographic paper box if you insert another piece of cardboard to make its length six inches.

EXPOSURE

In the darkroom, tape a 4″ × 5″ piece of film (Kodak Royal Pan, or similar) on one end of the camera so that the emulsion side faces the hole. Most 4″ × 5″ film materials have code notches. If you hold these notches to the upper left, the emulsion side will face you.

A simple calculation will give you the *f*/stop for the pinhole camera. The length of the box, which is six inches, determines the *focal length*. The *aperture* is 1/50 inch. The calculation becomes: 6 inches divided by 1/50 inch.

$$\frac{6}{1/50} = 6\left(\frac{50}{1}\right) = 300$$

The camera operates with an *f*/stop of 300. If you know the speed of the film material, exposure calculations should be easy. In full sunlight with Kodak Royal Pan film, exposure of five to ten seconds should give good results.

Selecting an even smaller opening than 1/50 inch would not improve the definition of the image. If the diameter of the hole becomes very small, *diffraction* will set in and the image will become really blurred. Diffraction is a phenomenon that occurs when a light ray passing close to an obstacle does not follow the law of straight line propagation; rather, light rays are modified to produce fringes of parallel light and dark colored bands. The light rays in the center will continue through the hole with their original speed while the rays at the edge will be somewhat slowed down. In order to get good definition, the center rays should not differ in their path length from the opening to the film by more than half a wavelength from those rays at the edge of the opening. This is why manufacturers limit the smallest *f*/stop opening on their lenses and why optimum photographic definition is usually not obtained with the smallest *f*/stop.

VARIATIONS IN PINHOLE CAMERA DESIGN

The construction directions given in this chapter for a simple pinhole camera will give excellent results. Since the construction of the camera is a fairly simple affair, more experimentation should be encouraged. Why not try to think of other design possibilities?

You could use two boxes slightly angled and spaced to produce stereo pairs of images; or you could design a double-hole or multiple-hole camera to produce side-by-side or overlapping image rendering. Instead of using a box, a container will provide still other possibilities. The negative or paper will have convex or concave shape, and the resultant pictures will surprise you with space and shape variations hardly possible with normal cameras and lenses. A camera made from a soup or coffee can also serves as a developing tank.

When the camera works and you have established your exposures, it should not be difficult to arrive at exposure calculations for other film materials. This might be the time to give color film or color paper a serious try.

12

THE CREATIVE DARKROOM

This book assumes that you are familiar with darkroom techniques. You should be proficient enough to make a large exhibition-type print and be able to handle without effort procedures like paper-surface determination, variable-contrast printing, and dodging and burning-in. Your knowledge of these techniques must be subordinate to your creative processes.

The question of whether the creative photographer should have his own darkroom must be answered with a resounding "yes." A darkroom can be very simple and inexpensive—a kitchen or bathroom space or a self-contained cabinet that can be rolled out when needed. Or it can be a complex setup with color enlarger, color analyzer, drum processor, and temperature controls.

There is nothing more satisfying than to step back and contemplate a large print—a work of art that you have just created. Many test strips and full-size attempts might have preceded it, each one approaching the preconceived ideal, but there it is finally, glowing with full tonality from velvety blacks to sparkling highlights. It is the end in the long chain that started with recognition, composition, and a negative, and has now been condensed into a print that communicates idea, content, and emotion after image manipulation. Something unique and probably unrepeatable has been created, a new reality removed from the reality of the physical world. The darkroom encourages discipline and experimentation alike. It gives creative freedom.

A darkroom opens new dimensions and possibilities, and you can explore a wide range of unusual effects. Many books on creative darkroom technique have been written. Unfortunately, many photographers with limited imagination easily succumb to printing gimmicks that remove and destroy the original purpose of the image. There are, however, some advanced and standard techniques frequently employed by advertising agencies for special visual effects. These are: posterization; bas-relief; tone-line effect; and the Sabattier Effect, also called solarization, where thin contours appear around boundaries of great tone difference.

Two separate light beams were refracted through glass objects, creating an intricate light pattern on the photographic paper. This was photographed on high-contrast film and the paper was flashed during development. A positive and a negative were used to obtain this graphic black-and-white image.

A symbol of life and death? Does one form renew itself? Do you feel the presence of an unknown force? How do you react to this surrealistic image?

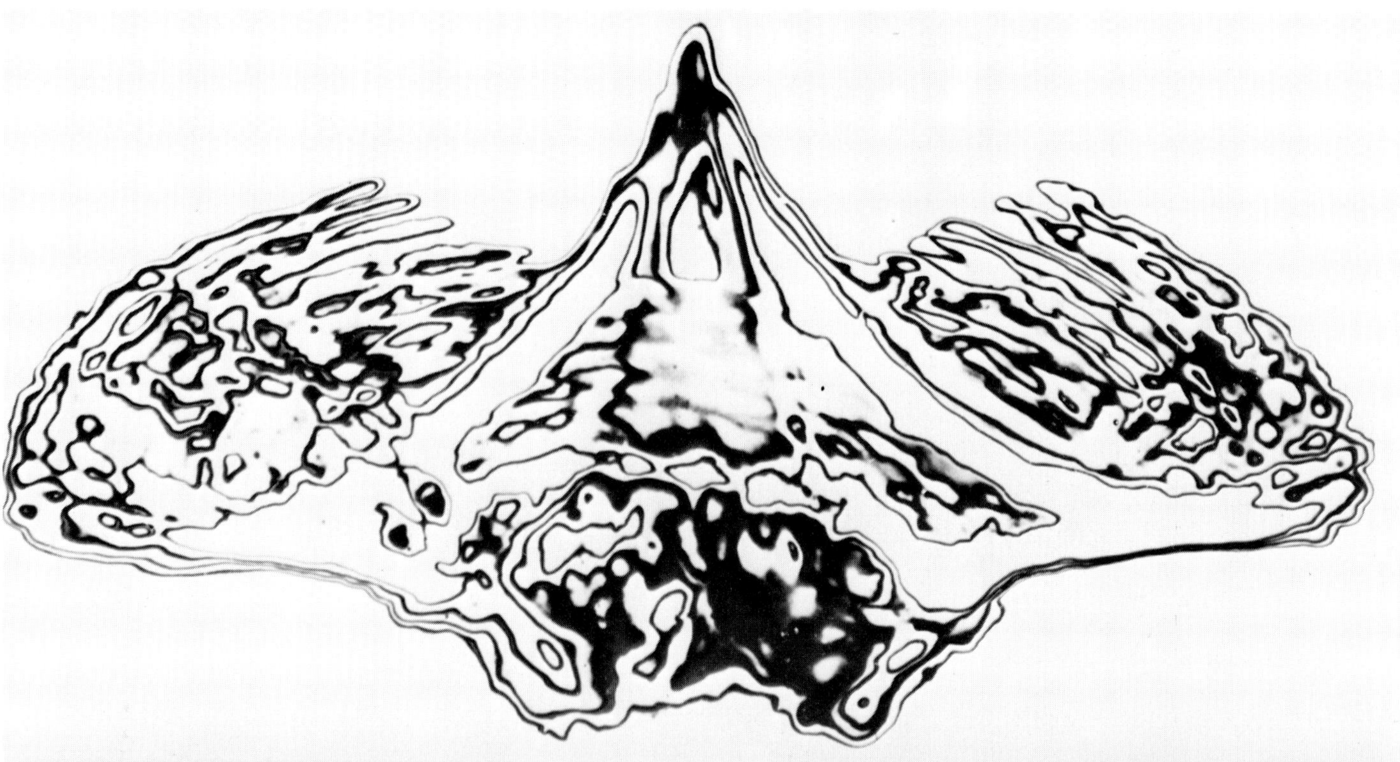

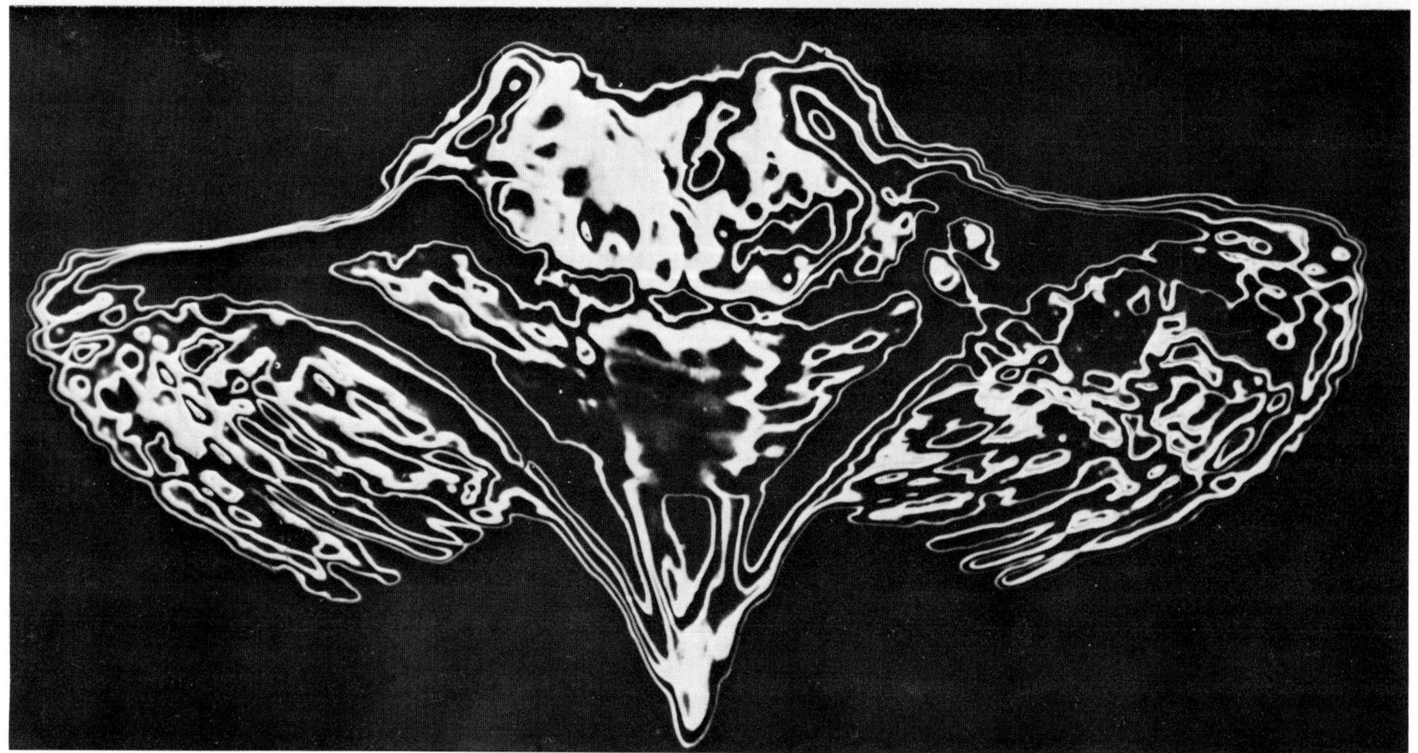

POSTERIZATION

Posterization refers to a technique in which the extended graduated tones of a negative are broken down into high-contrast separations. These separations, printed in register one after another or as a new master negative from the separations on continuous-tone material, will yield prints with flat, nongraduated tones of white, gray, and black. The entire range of gray tones in the original scene is eliminated to achieve a strong, posterlike graphic effect.

The technique requires the making of interpositives on high-contrast material such as Kodak Kodalith film, which can be purchased as 4″ × 5″ sheets. Interpositives can be made by contact-printing or by enlarging 35mm negatives directly onto the material. Three exposures should be made, the first one underexposed to register only the shadows of the original negative. Since you copy or enlarge on high-contrast material, shadow areas record as dense blacks; all other negative tones appear as clear film. The second exposure must be long enough to record dark middletones of the original. The third positive must be overexposed enough to record shadows as well as dark and light middletones, but not enough to register the highlights; these should remain as clear areas on the film. This set of three positives must now be printed in exact register onto continuous-tone film. They have to be printed with the same exposure time for each. The result is a master negative with contoured areas of three tones. From this negative, prints can now be made and they should be printed on paper of high-contrast grade. The final result is an image of clearly separated tones—one black, two gray, and one of pure white.

NOTE: In posterization, two separations will produce a print with one black, one gray, and one white area. Three separations will give final prints with one black, two gray, and one white tone. Five separations result in one black, four gray, and one white tone. This technique allows further, intriguing mutations. Separations on color material lend themselves to manipulation in color balance or to the assignment of a specific color to each posterized separation.

BAS-RELIEF

The technique of bas-relief yields prints that have a sculpted, three-dimensional appearance. From a negative, a positive transparency is made by direct contact-printing on continuous-tone black-and-white material. From the negative and the positive, a sandwich is made in such a way as to show slight lateral displacement. The direction and the amount of displacement determine and influence a variety of effects.

The final print from such a sandwich can show predominantly positive or negative features, depending on the densities of the negative or positive. Experience proves that flat-lit subjects or overcast scenes give

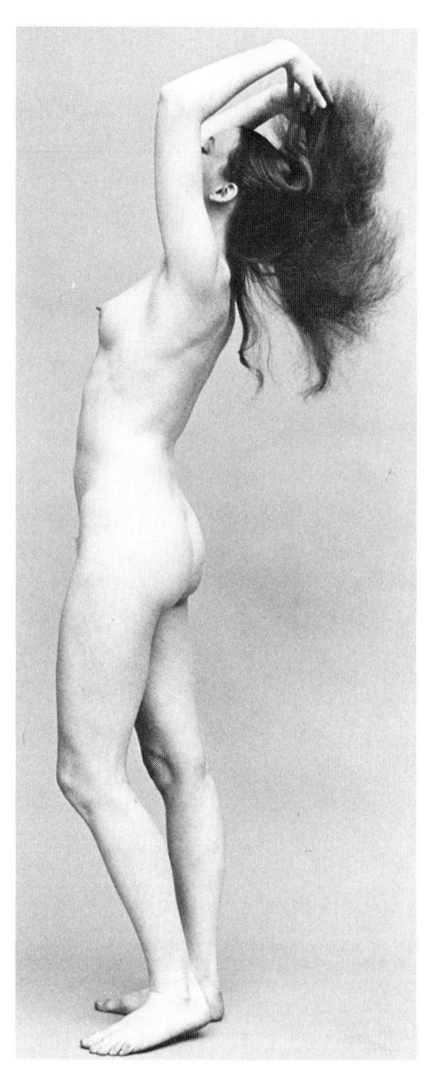

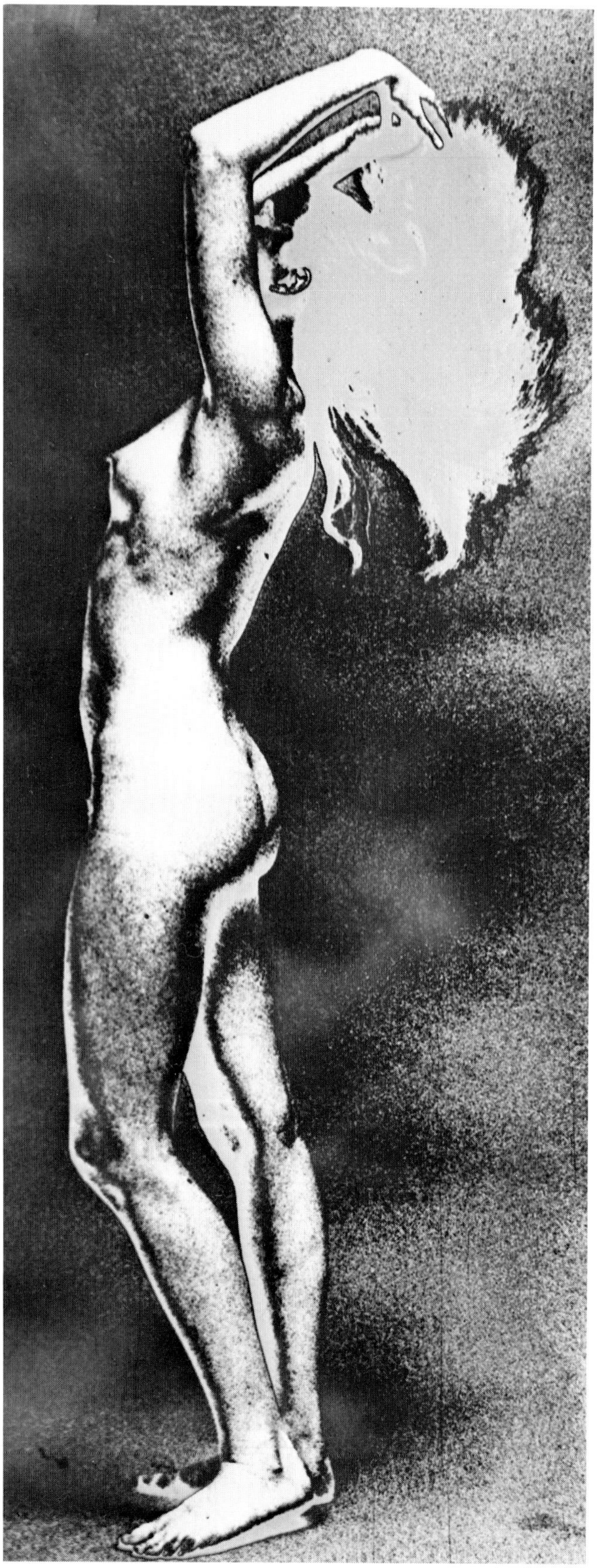

In the picture above, flash was bounced from the ceiling at *f*/8. Nikon F2, 105mm Nikkor, Tri-X. The same negative was enlarged onto a 4″ × 5″ sheet of high-contrast Kodalith film and developed in Kodak Ektaflo. After 20 seconds development time, the sheet was flashed with a 60-watt light bulb at four feet and at an angle of 45° for 1/3 sec. Development was then continued for a full minute. This technique is referred to as solarization, or the Sabattier Effect.

best results. It is, of course, easier to maintain the desired degree of negative-to-positive displacement by taping the sandwich together. If the positive and the negative are of the same density and contrast, you can try the following different technique.

TONE-LINE EFFECT

Tone-line effect converts continuous tone into line so that a print will resemble an artist's drawing in pencil or ink. The negative and the positive of the sandwich must now be taped together in exact register. If held up to a light source, they should cancel each other totally. The sandwich should look like a dense piece of film; no image should be seen. It is advisable to enlarge a 35mm negative onto 4″ × 5″ continuous-tone material to get a positive from which a negative can be contact-printed on another piece of the same film. It is necessary to form the sandwich in such a way that the emulsions do not touch each other. The emulsions should be separated by the thickness of the film material, and it is this separation which determines the final thickness of the line in the finished print.

If a heavier line is desired, this can be accomplished by inserting another piece of clear film as a spacer. The sandwich is now placed on high-contrast copy film and a light source, held above at an angle of 45°, is used for the exposure. The sandwich must be rotated 360° during the exposure. Some form of turntable works fine for this. It is also possible to construct a cross-arm arrangement with four light bulbs at the end of each arm. Considerable experimentation might be necessary. A 60-watt bulb at a distance of two to three feet will work. The resultant negative, in this case, is a piece of clear film with all outlines of the original scene rendered as line. The resultant print will be a white line on black. If a black line on white ground is preferred, the negative has to be contact-printed again.

SABATTIER EFFECT

Often referred to as *solarization*, the Sabattier Effect usually works best with negatives of considerable contrast or objects clearly delineated against the sky. For example, a lone tree on the ridge of a hill is a good subject. The negative is shot in the normal manner, normal development is begun, then the negative is given a short exposure to light before development is resumed.

Since the Sabattier Effect is very difficult to control, and since the results of the technique are a constant source of surprise, the following might be the preferred way of experimentation. Enlarge a negative onto high-contrast Kodalith film. Exposures from a normal 35mm negative range between one and two seconds with the enlarger lens set at *f*/5.6 or *f*/8. Develop the positive on high-contrast film in paper developer under normal safelight conditions. About 20 seconds into the development, expose the positive to light. Hold a 60-watt light bulb at an angle of 45° over the developer tray and give between one-half to one-second exposure at a distance of two feet. Continue development for one minute. The positive will become very dense and black in appearance. Considerable experimentation might be required before the right effect is achieved.

If this technique works properly, previously unexposed shadow areas attain greater densities than middletones and even highlights. At the same time, fine, lighter lines appear along tone boundaries. In addition, the positive will have areas of negative tones. The positive is then contact-printed to yield a negative from which prints can be made in the normal manner. The steps described above can be continued to achieve an image more and more removed from the original. For example, the contact-printed negative can be exposed to light during its development. Each successive step will drop out more middletones since you are working with high-contrast material.

HIGH-GRAIN EFFECTS

Depending on subject matter, it might actually be desirable to enhance a grain effect rather than suppress it. Kodak Recording Film 2475 with its very high speed is an inherently grainy film material. If such a negative is enlarged onto orthochromatic film and developed in paper developer, the effect is further exaggerated. That negative, again projected on orthochromatic film and developed in paper developer, enhances the grain effect still further. Similar effects might be achieved by inviting *reticulation* of a negative. The method involves the actual destruction or partial destruction of the gelatin emulsion during processing. Extreme changes in temperature during the washing process will actually shrivel parts of the emulsion and produce surreal effects.

THE PHOTOGRAM

William Henry Fox Talbot (1800–1877) used a strong solution of salt water as a fixing agent and made permanent records of leaves and lace on his sensitized paper. A new world removed from everyday reality came into being. Ever since, students and artists alike have been fascinated by the creative possibilities of a process which, without a camera, allows the creation and control of an image.

With your newly gained knowledge of balance, shape, form, and space, you should try this technique and see how these pictorial elements

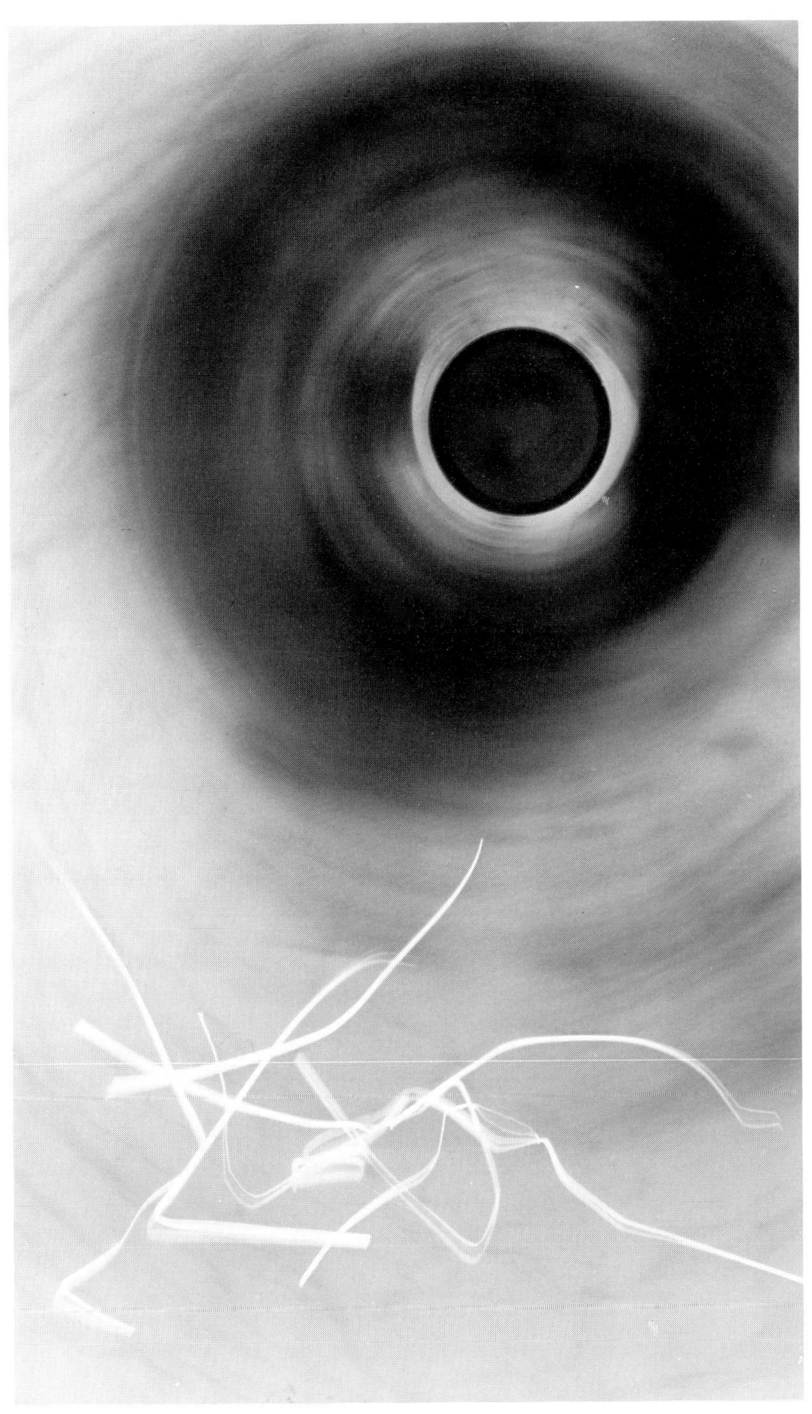

A ring and parts of a wineglass create a whirlpool in space. Some paper shavings add more dimension in this photogram.

function and interact. Opaque objects to form contour, and translucent and transparent ones to reveal texture and tonal gradation can be placed directly on photographic paper. Exposures are made with a stationary or movable light source from above. Images obtained in this way (by placing an object on a sensitized surface and turning on a light) are called photograms, shadowgraphs, or rayographs. Artists like Lászlò Moholy-Nagy (1895–1946), Alvin Langdon Coburn (1882–1965), Man Ray (b. 1890), and Francis Bruguière (1880–1945) worked seriously in this medium and produced pictures of abstract beauty.

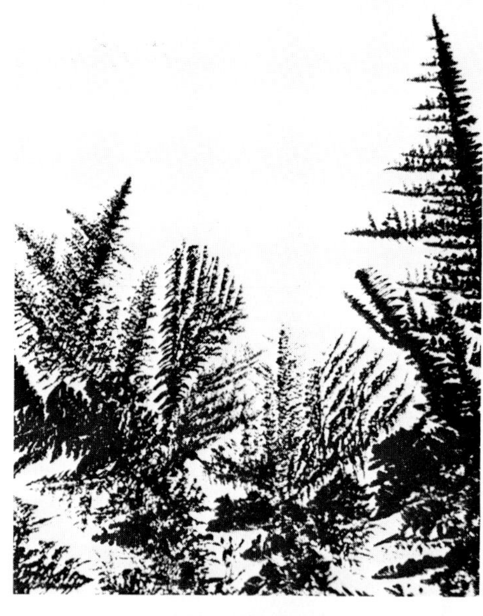

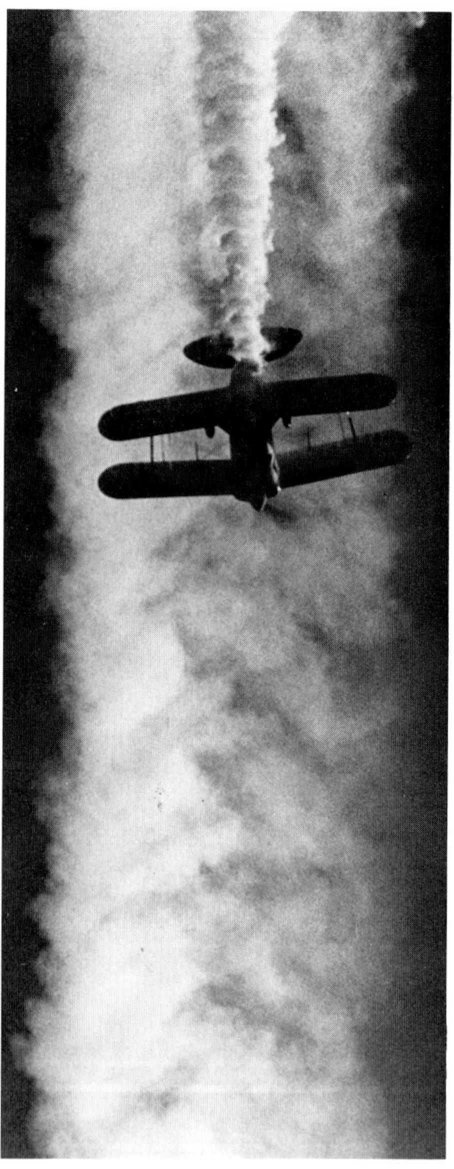

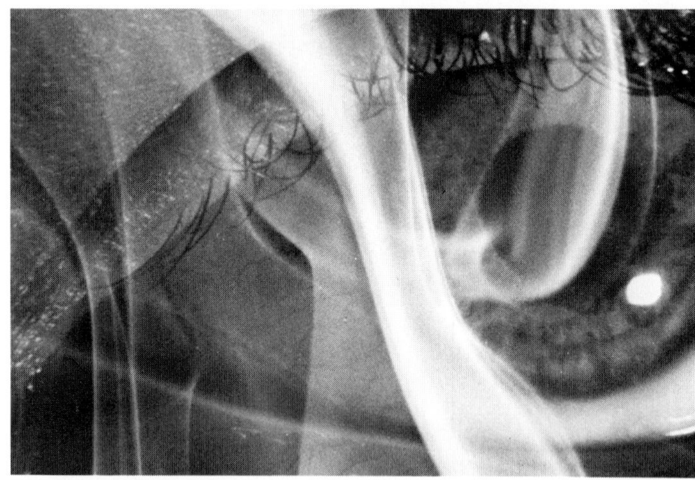

A layout exercise in creativity.

CREATIVE TECHNIQUES

An unlimited range of experimental techniques will introduce you to later image manipulation in the darkroom. You can try multiple images and printing with a positive and a negative sandwiched and slightly out of register to produce a line effect. You can try tone reversal with an additional flash exposure of a partially developed image. Or you can vary the light intensity during exposure and can, after initially placing objects on photographic paper, try to capture patterns of light refracted through glass from a distance. There are no limits to the imagination.

13

IMAGINATION AND SELF-EXPRESSION

The painter may elect to use charcoal or pencil, he might use tempera or oil paints, and he might execute a fresco painting on walls or ceilings. He uses technique as a way of offering a solution in his search for artistic expression. In mastering technique, he gains freedom. Mastering technique is just as important for the photographer. Familiarity with darkroom procedures—making good negatives and prints—has to come first. It is this turning point in his photographic life which will enable him to walk in any desired direction. Technique should catapult the imagination and free the mind from the brake shoe of doubt.

Photography is a visual language not aided by the senses of sound, smell, and touch. If you walk toward a beach, long before you see the ocean, you hear its sound, you smell its air, and you may feel the sand and grass under your feet. If you make a photograph that says "ocean," you cannot rely on ears, nose, or feet to communicate that image. The picture must be strong enough to overcome the absence of all other senses. The picture of the ocean must emphasize how you feel about your subject, and you must find the most fluid way to compress it into a timeless answer. How far you take this abstraction of reality as an individual photographer depends on how intelligent, educated, or artistic an audience you try to reach. If your work is to be successful, it must go beyond the casual appearance of what is to be presented.

IMAGINATIVE ASSIGNMENTS

If you carry abstraction to levels where the viewer is unable to extract its meaning, the picture might become so subjective that it ceases to communicate on an ordinary level. As an assignment, you could make a picture of an abstract pattern the wind had created in the sand, changing from a wide-angle lens to a 500mm mirror lens to double expose ring-shaped highlights of light on the water over the previous scene. You could print from two different negatives sandwiched together and change these scenes to totally abstract patterns of graphic black-and-white. This would be but one approach. Your imagination can move on a ladder with an infinite number of rungs. Of course, you cannot "learn"

Following are five illustrations that might illuminate what I have said.

1. This picture might be called "summer wind". To only photograph a branch of a tree would have been very dull indeed. So a shot was taken first with a Nikon F2 and 135mm Nikkor on Tri-X. The exposure was 1/500 sec. at *f*/4. The camera was mounted on a tripod, allowing for slow shutter speeds on the next exposure when a gust came along. All further exposures were made at 1/15 sec. at *f*/22. Many exposures were made, and after careful study of the proof sheet, two negatives were printed together.

2. Strong morning light created a dramatic sculptured effect of the doll on the white bedsheet. By exposing for the strong highlight, shadows were made to go black. It was clear that nothing would be recorded beyond the white sheets. This simplified matching a cloudy sky in later printing. Nikon FTN, 50mm Nikkor, 1/1000 sec. at *f*/1.2.

imagination, but with mental exercises, latent imagination can be stimulated and put on the alert.

With a self-assigned project like "ocean," try to think of new ways to illustrate the theme and see if you can find new points of view. The very obvious would be the snapshot view of an entire beach crowded with people. But how about an extreme closeup of a sunoil-drenched face and the reflection of the beach scene in the lens of a sunglass. Or footprints parallel with the water's edge, leading to a tiny figure far away? Maybe you could symbolize the ocean's force or its timeless, life-giving quality. At dawn or sunset, you could focus your camera on some rocks and, by closing your lens down, arrive at a time exposure. This would render the rocks with extreme sharpness, and the surf, moving in and out, rising and falling, would be rendered in a dreamlike fashion with an emphasis on movement. You could even try to show the fear-creating aspects of an ocean—the force of a hurricane or a very high tide. You could create a surreal image and imprint a just visible image of a large fish on the surface of the water. Stop for a moment and try to think of still other ways to make a statement that will shout "ocean."

Don't be afraid to give yourself assignments. Many times a student will come back to me, totally convinced that he cannot approach anything with imagination. He might say: "I have walked around the town square for half an hour and not shot a single picture." Things usually start to happen when I send him out again, this time with an abstract assignment. I might tell him to shoot an entire roll of film under such headings as sound, calm, rain, wind, sorrow, or excitement. When the student returns to the town square, this time he will notice the old man on the bench who resembles the bronze statue behind him; the little children holding hands in the fountain under a spray of water mist; the priest chatting with an old woman on the steps of his church. He is now learning to **see**, and his imagination is working. Visual stimulation lets you store more and more impressions and memories, and it is this subconscious knowledge or intuition which becomes a self-generating stock for further self-expression.

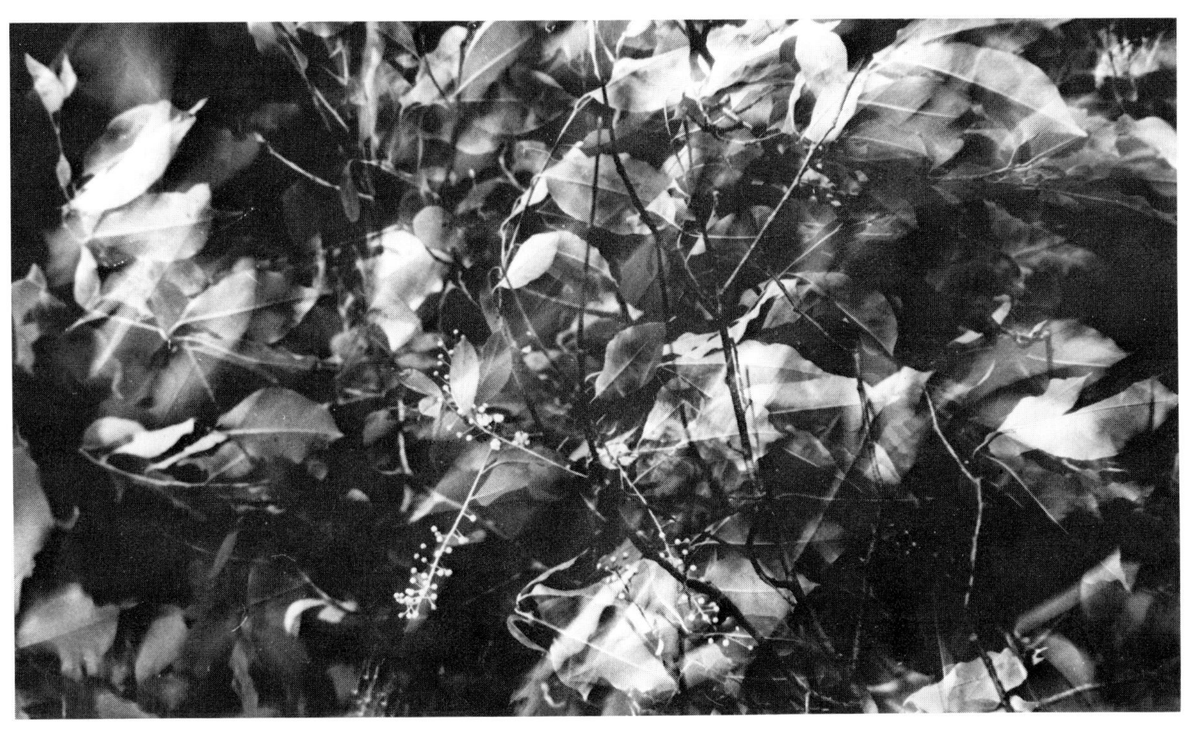

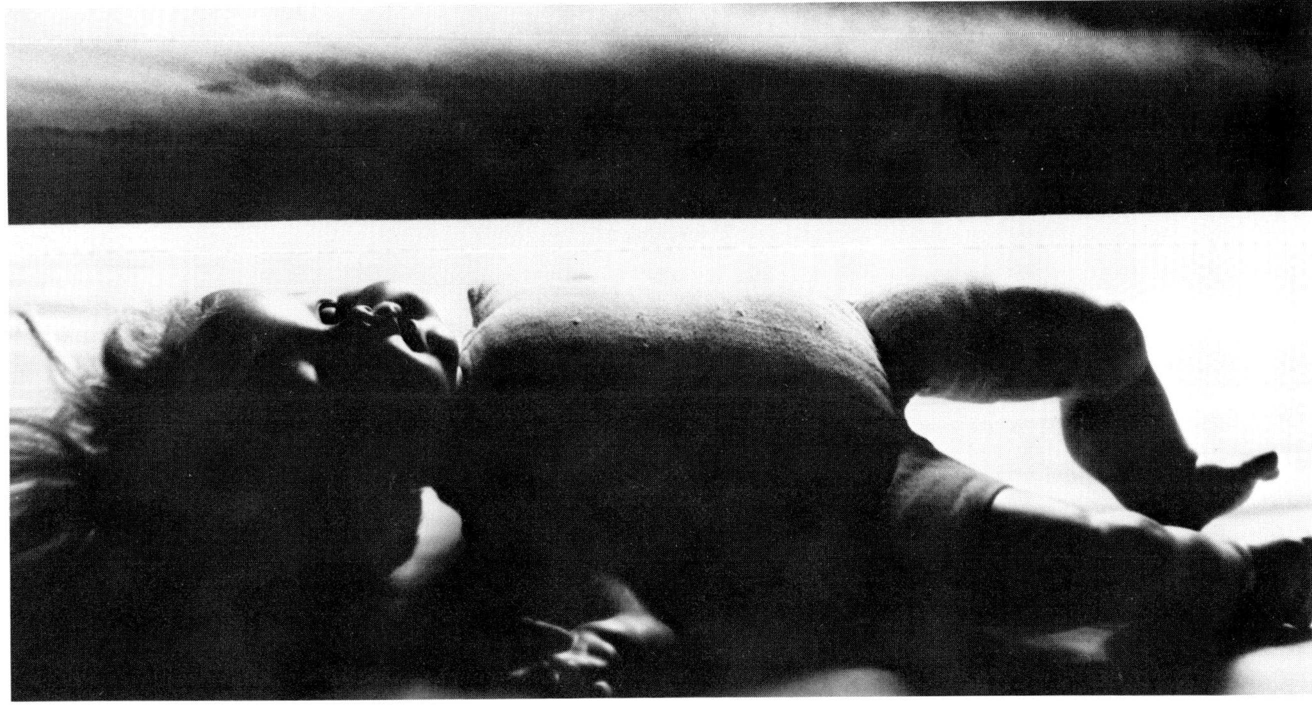

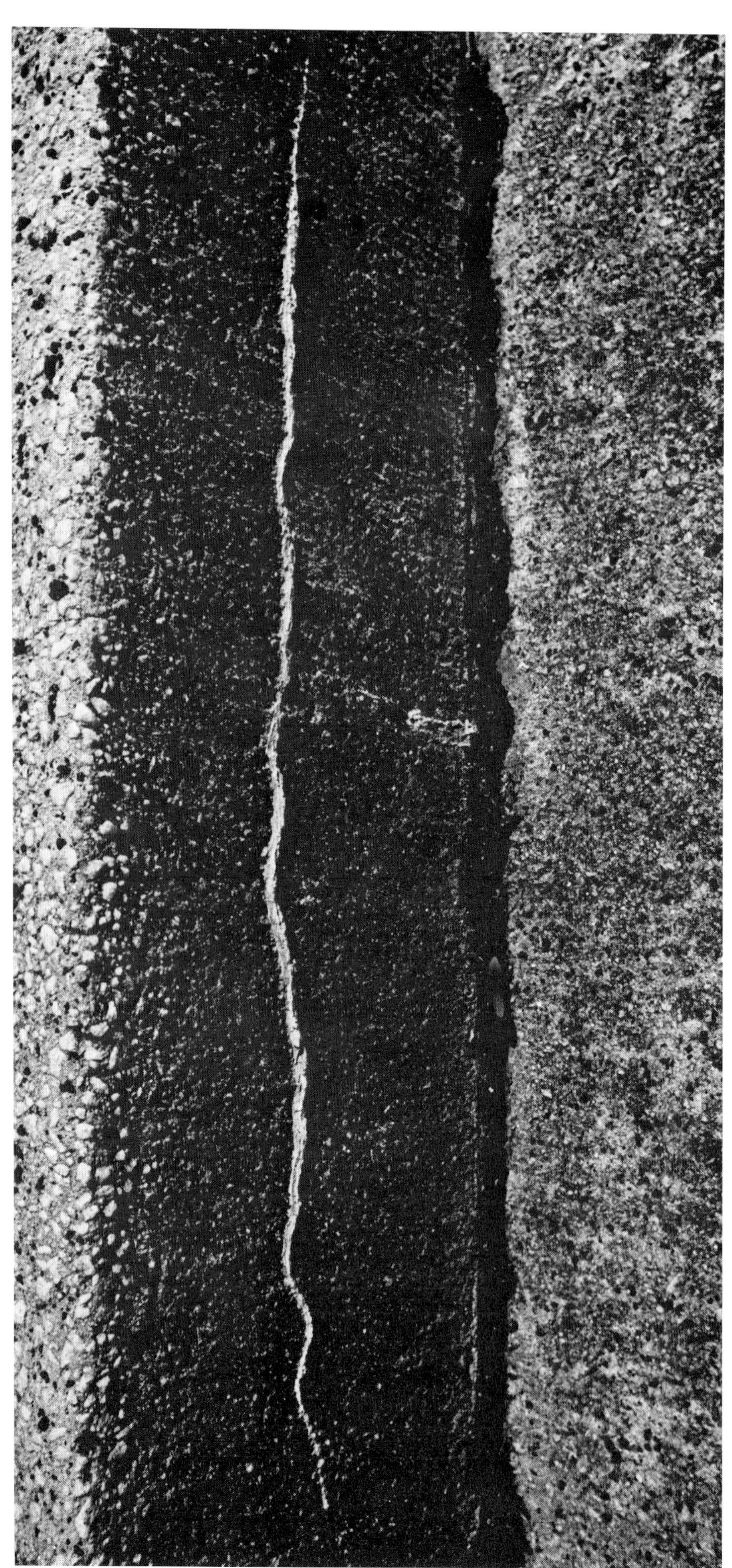

3. Some lines in cement work create their own patterns of light and dark. In printing, great care was taken to adjust light and dark areas into certain relationships. By turning the picture vertically, the horizontal cement step was further abstracted. Nikon F2, 24mm Nikkor, 1/250 sec. at *f*/8 on Tri-X.

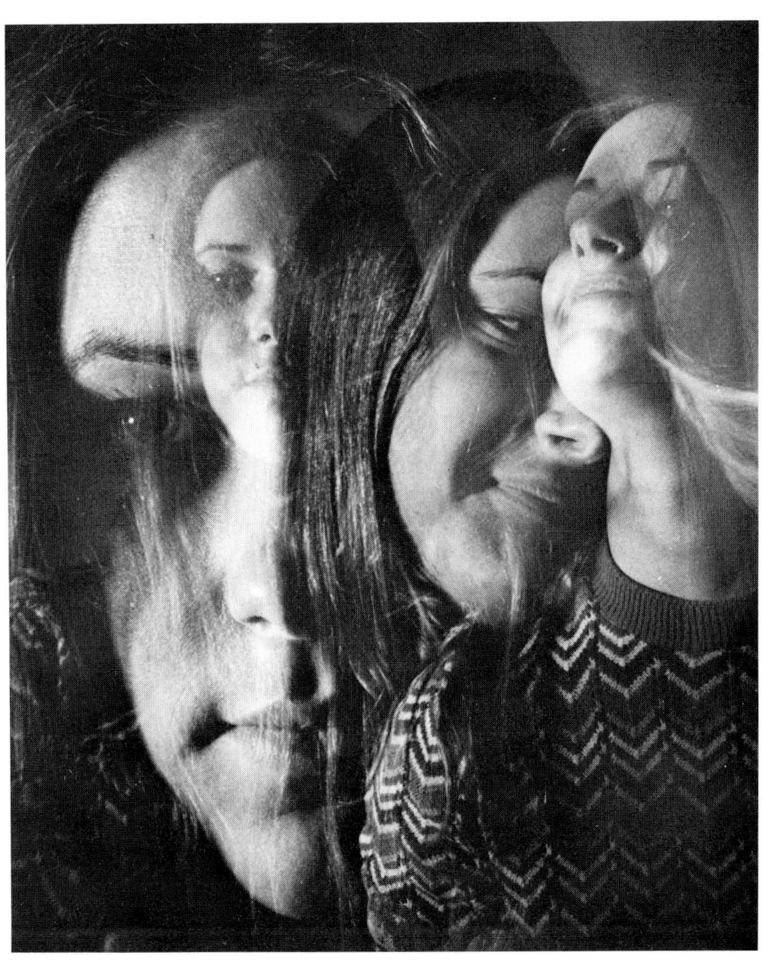

4. A multi-image portrait of a young girl can express various moods. It is necessary for the photographer to remember where in his viewfinder a previous image was placed. Such a technique allows use of different focal-length lenses or even a zoom lens. Double images are easy with the Nikon F2, simply by pressing the rewind button and advancing the film lever, which now winds only the shutter, leaving the film stationary. The two faces on the left side of the picture divide the picture plane with a strong vertical that divides the picture in a ϕ relationship. The other two faces set up a strong diagonal force. The picture surface can be seen in terms of ovals, squares, and triangles. Nikon F2, various focal-length lenses, and electronic flash shot into an unlit room.

5. This picture is also a composite, and it could be seen as a surreal landscape. A closeup of an eye and smoke was taken with a 200mm Nikkor on a bellows unit, electronic flash at *f*/22. Another shot was taken with the same setup, this time of the edge of window ice. The tiny 1mm ice crystals were recopied on high-contrast film and a negative sandwich was finally printed. Nikon F2, 1/250 sec. at *f*/11 (stop-down metering).

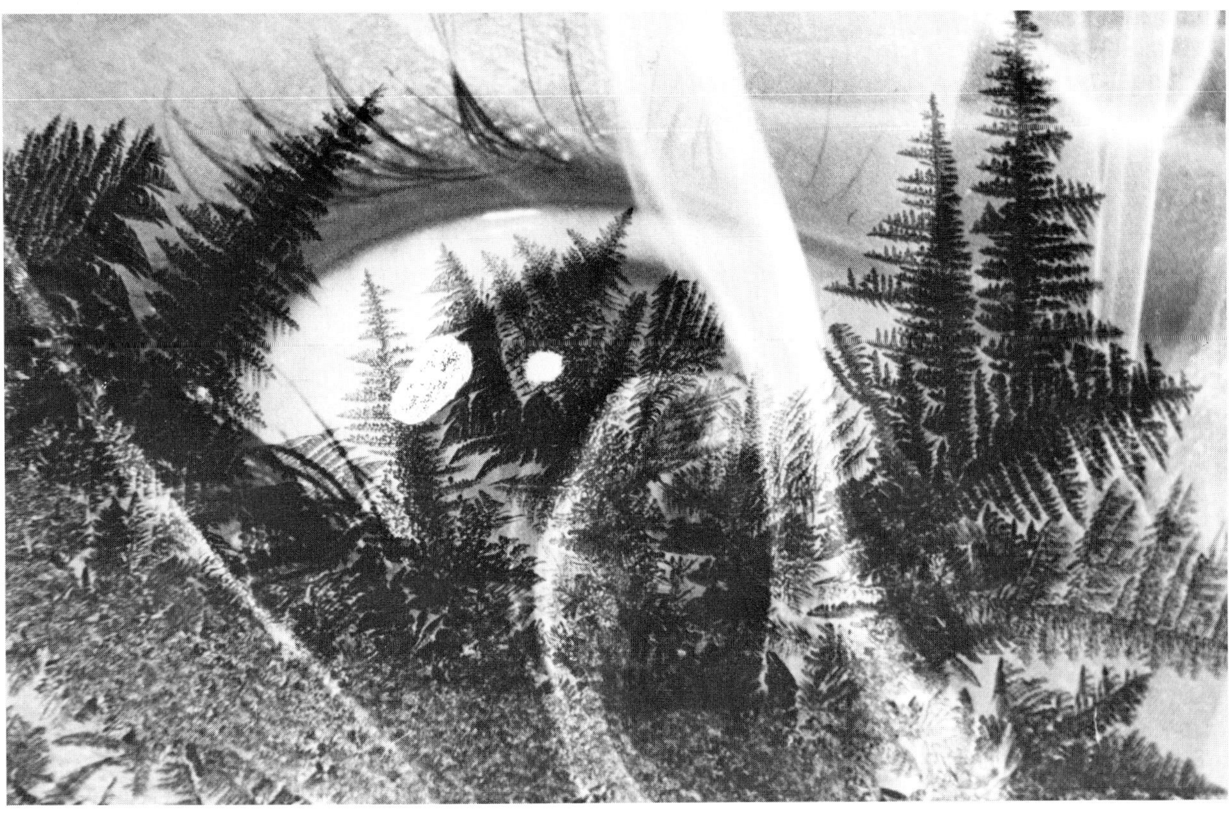

Right: Mud was flowing on the surface of ice and a drop in temperature fixed this lyrical pattern. Has Kandinski been here? Nikon F2, 135mm Nikkor, 1/125 sec. at *f*/11 on Tri-X.

Below: A pond awakens from winter. Nikon F2, 200mm Nikkor, 1/250 sec. at *f*/8 on Tri-X.

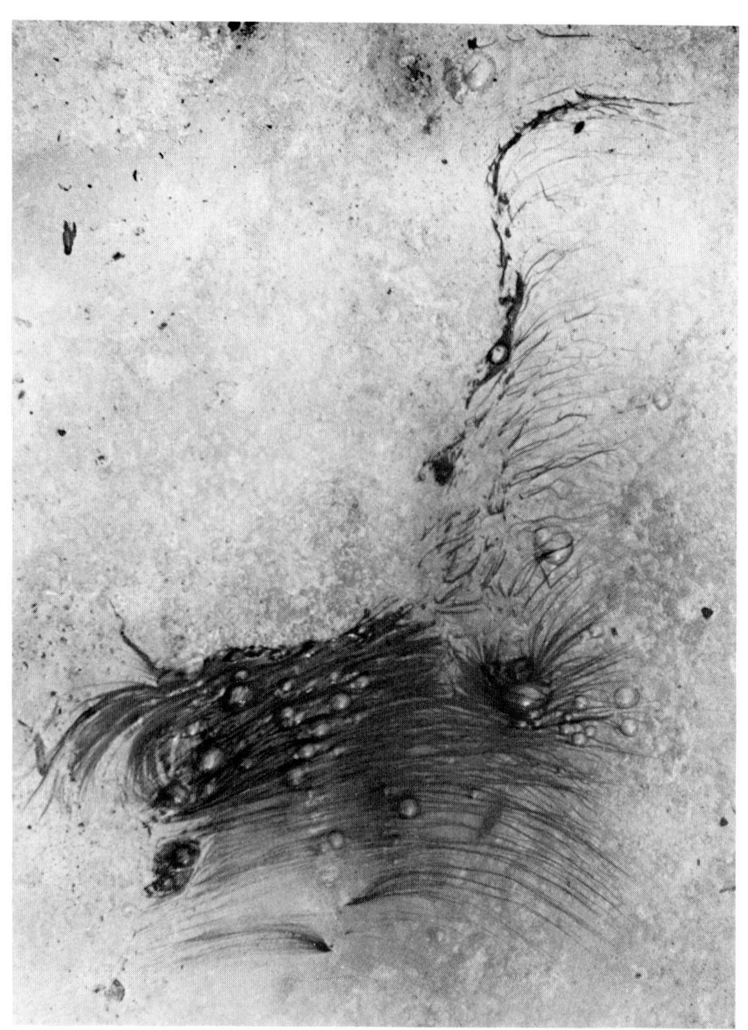

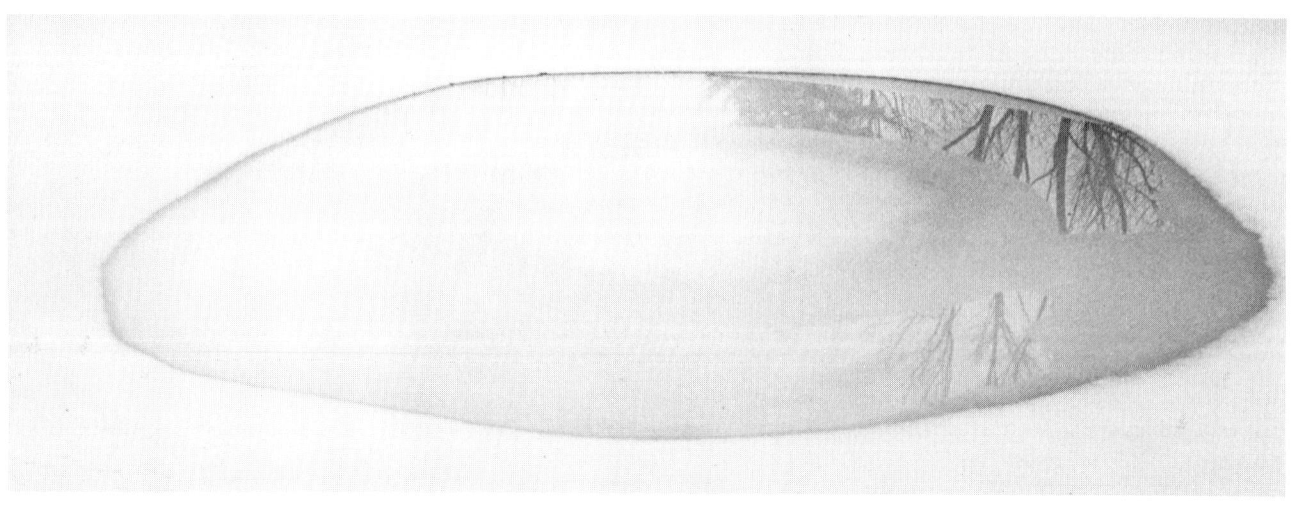

14

PHOTOGRAPHY AND THE ARTS

When the French painter Paul Delaroche (1797–1856) saw a Daguerreotype for the first time in his life in the 1840's, he was stunned. He exclaimed: "From today painting is dead." Interestingly enough, photography was officially declared an art in 1862 as a result of a lawsuit in Paris. When the case was decided in favor of photography, the French painter Jean Auguste Dominique Ingres (1780–1867) tried hard to appeal the verdict. But in spite of his action, Ingres remarked to his colleagues: "Photography does everything so much better than I have been able to do all my life."

The invention of photography in the first half of the nineteenth century forced artists to reassess their notion of reality. Man's faith in the trustworthiness of his visual perception was shaken. Was it not now possible to minimize artistic communication between painter and portrait sitter by simply releasing the shutter of a mechanical device? Portrait painting declined and was more and more replaced by portrait photography. Painters and sculptors began searching for a new reality, one removed from the accidental appearance of objects in the physical world.

Students of photography, the studio arts, and art history ask many penetrating questions. Examples: Does our modern age still have reasons for the creation of art, and do not latest trends point to the end of all the visual arts? Will artists not be replaced by machines, and cannot the computer generate random numbers of art?

John Baldessari gathered his accumulated stock of paintings, burned them, and installed the ashes behind a wall. "Great reductive piece of art," hailed the critics; "negative and anti-art," said the public.

Is the literary description of an event replacing the visual art object? This raises many questions. The American artist Christo wrapped one million square feet of the Australian coastline in cloth and rope. This abstraction of nature was temporary, but associations with Egyptian mummification again point to the question: "Are the visual arts dying?" Or does the photographic record of this event become a priceless piece of art? A visual record then seems necessary, whether it exists on a plane surface or as a volume. We just are not able to communicate art by telepathy alone.

Many artists of the last decades became convinced that traditional aesthetics were nothing but historical ballast. The visual vocabulary, the system of symbols, has been exhausted, they wrote. This sort of thinking led to their decision to stop involvement in the arts altogether. But can human creativity, imagination, and man's questioning stance toward the physical world around him be stopped by throwing a switch?

It is true that today's fast change of theories and ideas in the arts reflects the temporary quality of life itself. Art is characterized by feuding movements, each trying to establish supremacy over the other. But civilization tends to become more and more world oriented. Modern art in an age of science has become very international, and new symbols and images are invented, which will rise from the ashes with new meanings not restricted by societies and borders.

Good art is built on unshakable foundations and continuously reinforces and renews itself through armies of artists marching in the footsteps of those who broke trails from the caves at Lascaux to the art of today. Art is an evolutionary process; there is much trial and error. The history of art continually shows that not everything old is necessarily good, and I am convinced that later centuries will prove much of today's art a mere curiosity among a valid stock.

Let us point to some fundamentals again, something that should be rethought by painters and photographers, by architects and sculptors alike. Everyone will agree that different cultures have produced specific and particular forms, or symbols. But what is often overlooked is that they all have something in common. Their unifying appeal arises from the dynamic rhythm of relationships inherent in their form. This is not only true in painting styles of different regions and times, but can be shown in architecture and sculpture as well. Dynamic rhythm, the constructive element in the visual arts and its execution in limitless variations, is what arouses us visually. Proportional relationships are everywhere; we must, however, learn to see them. ϕ proportions (1:1.6) exist in the way veins grow in a leaf, and they can be shown in the relationship of St. Peter's dome to the rest of its architectural mass. They can be found in the human figure, in Le Corbusier's architecture, and in Piet Mondrian's paintings. ϕ proportions are the building blocks of all the arts.

Movements and their styles come and go. We have learned to live with rapid change. Cubism, Expressionism, Fauvism, Futurism, Orphism, Vorticism and Suprematism, De Stijl, Dadaism, and Surrealism had to be accepted by a former generation. After World War II, more movements came into being that left the uninformed—unable to trace principal or secondary influences—somewhat confused. From Abstract Formalism, Abstract Expressionism (Action Painting), Op, Pop, Minimal, Kinetic, Happenings, and Psychedelic Art, from Conceptual and

Process to the New Realism, we have witnessed a great circle drawn that has been closed again. The New Realism in photography and painting in the twentieth century only reexamines the question of the essence of reality, a question that also occupied the minds of artists at the beginning of the nineteenth century.

The problem of reality can be traced through many periods in the fine arts. To understand the two different approaches to reality, it becomes necessary to look back into the past a bit. As soon as the Dutch Masters of the fifteenth century lost the patronage of the courts and the church, they were forced to look at the world in a new way. The old themes demanded by altar painting, the illustrative painting of heroic deeds, and the themes from mythology had to be shifted to genre, still life, and landscape painting to open a market among the general populace. This was the start which led to today's New Realism. Today's realists, products of a changing society, are more concerned with concepts of discontinuity and hyperdimensionality. Space is no longer dimensionally bound, and fragments of visual perception take on new significance. Parts of a larger whole become important subjects for artistic expression, and the state of the human condition is expressed through peripheral segments.

All this has been made possible through modern photography, which has taught us to see beyond traditional modes of perception. Today, it is not unusual to find large photographs physically incorporated into modern works of art (as collages in paintings or silk-screened onto sculpture), and, of course, large photographs are accepted as works of art.

The rebirth of today's Realism is strongly influenced by the superior ability of the camera to render realistic images. Many painters and sculptors have taken up photography. In their hands, the camera becomes an extension of the mind to help organize the creative process. Photography helps the artist to see in new ways, again leading to new visual interpretations of our age. Although painting and photography appear to have gone their separate ways, their paths have crossed frequently. Today, we can see photographers looking for abstract patterns in nature, inspired by the work of abstract painters. And we frequently see paintings that make use of photographic techniques.

At the beginning of our historical epoch stood the two French painters Jean Auguste Dominique Ingres and Eugène Delacroix who pioneered different approaches to the problem of reality. This was also the time when photography was invented. Ingres's approach was intellectual, and he probed reality with his personal style that favored emphasis on probing, biting line. Delacroix opposed this style and, in his paintings, exploded emotions not known in the arts before. Ingres probed reality and its outward appearance. Delacroix confronted us with

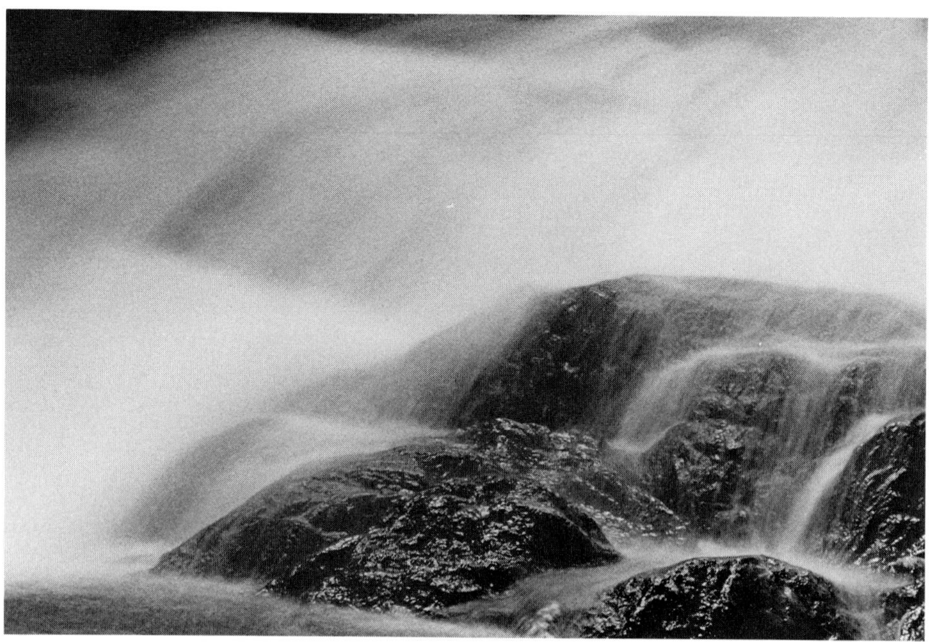

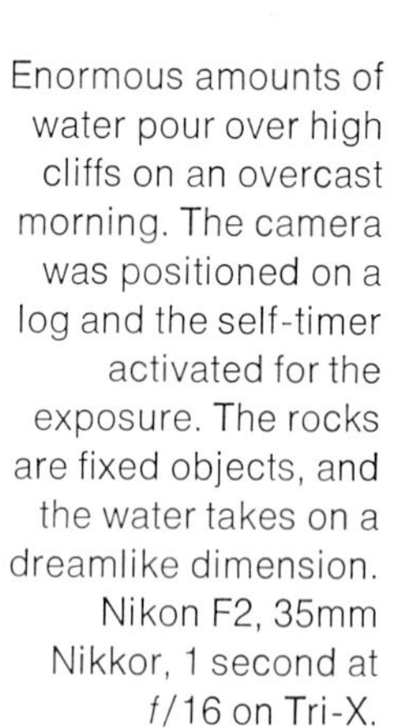

Enormous amounts of water pour over high cliffs on an overcast morning. The camera was positioned on a log and the self-timer activated for the exposure. The rocks are fixed objects, and the water takes on a dreamlike dimension. Nikon F2, 35mm Nikkor, 1 second at *f*/16 on Tri-X.

the inner substance, a new reality that was not dependent on the outward appearances of the world. The polarity between these two painters can be shown again and again in the works of other contrasting artists, for example, Cézanne against Van Gogh, Mondrian against Kandinski—experiences of this outer or inner reality, one directed by the intellect, the other by emotions alone.

Years and years of experimentation helped the painter and the photographer to realize that their mediums are not really alien. Rather, they complement each other, and a creative painter and a creative photographer are both artists in their own right. Both had to realize that the painter's duty is to produce paintings and that it is the photographer's duty to produce photographs. Unfortunately, even today one can still find people who call photography a nonartistic medium, leftover comparisons from the early imitative beginnings of photography. These people lack the understanding to see the grand undercurrents that have fertilized the arts, always inspired and stimulated by discoveries of artists, scientists, philosophers, and psychologists.

If we fail to recognize the real function of photography, its possibilities and its limitations, the good that all arts have derived from interaction will be lost. Photography cannot be an attempt to imitate the other arts. It is here that many of the early photographers were not on solid ground, and many who came from painting could not see the potential of photography. Their attempts to illustrate scenes from literature were doomed to failure. William Lake Price, a watercolor painter turned photographer, introduced just such types of pictures in the photographic salon of 1855. His elaborate compositions were made up of many negatives and carried such titles as "The Baron's Feast," or "Don Quixote in His Study." Price failed to use photography as an artistic medium. He was, however, prophetic when he wrote: "If photography is to take a stand as an art, those who practice it must qualify to study for artistic requirements."